Practical Data
Administration

BCS Practitioner Series

Series editor: Ray Welland

Practical Data Administration

Brian Horrocks
Judy Moss

Prentice Hall
New York London Toronto Sydney Tokyo Singapore

First published 1993 by
Prentice Hall International (UK) Ltd
Campus 400, Maylands Avenue
Hemel Hempstead
Hertfordshire, HP2 7EZ
A division of
Simon & Schuster International Group

Typeset in 10/12 pt Times
by MHL Typesetting Ltd, Coventry

Printed and bound in Great Britain by
Dotesios Limited, Trowbridge, Wiltshire

Library of Congress Cataloging-in-Publication Data

Horrocks, Brian.
    Practical data administration/Brian Horrocks, Judy Moss.
        p.   cm. — (BCS practitioner series)
    Includes index.
    ISBN 0-13-689696-0 (pbk.)
    1. Electronic data processing — Management.   I. Moss, Judy.
II. Title. III. Series.
QA76.9, M3H67 1993
005.7 — dc20   92-38512
                                         CIP

British Library Cataloguing in Publication Data

A catalogue record for this book is available
from the British Library

ISBN 0-13-689696-0 (pbk)

1 2 3 4 5   97 96 95 94 93

Contents

Figures

Tables

Editorial preface

The aim of the BCS Practitioner Series is to produce books which are relevant for practising computer professionals across the whole spectrum of Information Technology activities. We want to encourage practitioners to share their practical experience of methods and applications with fellow professionals. We also seek to disseminate information in a form which is suitable for the practitioner who often has only limited time to read widely within a new subject area or to assimilate research findings.

The role of the BCS is to provide advice on the suitability of books for the Series, via the Editorial Panel, and to provide a pool of potential authors upon which we can draw. Our objective is that this Series will reinforce the drive within the BCS to increase professional standards in IT. The other partners in this venture, Prentice Hall, provide the publishing expertise and international marketing capabilities of a leading publisher in the computing field.

The response when we set up the Series was extremely encouraging. However, the success of the Series depends on there being practitioners who want to learn, as well as those who feel they have something to offer! The Series is under continual development and we are always looking for ideas for new topics and feedback on how to further improve the usefulness of the Series. If you are interested in writing for the Series then please contact us.

It is increasingly being recognised that data is one of a company's most valuable assets. This means that more attention is being paid to the role of data administration — ensuring the protection of the corporate investment in data, making the best use of the available data and resolving conflicts between different sources and uses of data. Based on practical experience of data administration, the authors provide comprehensive advice and guidance for others wishing to follow the same route.

Ray Welland
Computing Science Department, University of Glasgow

Editorial Panel Members
Frank Bott (UCW, Aberystwyth), Dermot Browne (KPMG Management Consulting), Nic Holt (ICL), Trevor King (Praxis Systems plc), Tom Lake (GLOSSA), Kathy Spurr (Analysis and Design Consultants), Mario Wolczko (University of Manchester).

Preface

This book is based on our experiences in introducing data administration into a medium-sized organisation, from the very first tentative steps. Its role continues to grow and change as it develops with the business. We do not pretend to present a definitive view, with a rigid pattern which must be followed to achieve success. The book describes what has been learnt along the way, and how we have compromised and adapted. Its aim is to fulfil two main purposes. Firstly, it gives an outline of what data administration involves, and how it can fit into an organisation and help to support it. Secondly, it gives our practical experience as a guide, and in some cases as a warning! We hope that this book will be of interest to those reviewing the concepts of data administration, and those contemplating its introduction into their own organisations. It aims to show them the benefits that can be achieved, and to encourage systems professionals and management in both the IT and user communities to go ahead. In particular, we hope that our views, advice and practical examples will help and encourage data administrators, as they tackle the day-to-day issues which the role encompasses.

Acknowledgements

We would like to acknowledge the help and support we have received from various quarters. Firstly, Rolls-Royce Motor Cars Limited, for providing us with the opportunity to develop Data Administration, and our colleagues there, in particular Martyn Rowley, Pete Burgess, Phil Ashton, Tim Whitehead and Eric Butters.

The following companies gave us useful advice and encouragement when we first began to look at data administration:

Rolls-Royce PLC
British Gas (North West)
ICI Chemicals and Polymers
Jaguar Cars Limited

Special thanks go to Janet Banks for her hard work and patience in typing the text.

Last but not least, we would like to thank our respective spouses, Jeanette and Richard, for their understanding and support while we were writing this book.

1 Introduction

It has been said by some leaders of industry and commerce that data is the second most valuable asset that an organisation possesses. The first is people, a view it is difficult to find fault with. This analysis is interesting, when we take into account the fact that attaching a monetary value to either is not an easy thing to do. People have knowledge, experience, potential and many other qualities which defy quantification. In many ways the value of data is equally unquantifiable. An organisation will indeed possess many other assets which are far more accommodating to those wishing to attach a value. Machinery, buildings, tools, furniture, cash investments, and many more, are in fact valued very carefully and appear in company balance sheets. It is easy to see why the majority of people within industry fail to recognise the value of data to the organisation: it is intangible and its financial value is thus difficult to establish. Fortunately, the importance of data as an asset is being recognised more widely now. However, there is a long way to go before its value is accepted spontaneously.

Our perception of data has evolved over the last three decades. Early large scale data processing sought to copy and automate manual procedures involving compilations, calculations and selections. These simple operations on the data would normally be carried out by a clerk, long hand, with a typical end result being the production of a payroll or ledger. Data soon became recognised for its potential to provide information. Whilst the automation of clerical tasks was worthwhile, the data found more uses when stored and interpreted by someone who understood it. Throughout this period the daily operation of the business was becoming more and more closely linked with the storage and processing of data. There has been a clear convergence of business operations and information technology over the years, where data is the common denominator. The majority of organisations in business today rely on their systems and data to such an extent that they would be inoperable without them. Data has become the key to operating the business at a procedural level, running the business at a tactical level and directing the business at a strategic level.

Many organisations have become aware of the value of data through the introduction of major systems which effectively run part or all of the business. In many ways it is shock therapy to find that systems of this importance are worthless unless they have good data to work with. Quite often it becomes apparent that it is not the system but the people and the procedures that need to change.

It is no longer acceptable to operate to the less exacting standards of yesteryear, when data was not the key asset.

Many manufacturing organisations have graduated through various levels of sophistication. The most modern manufacturing philosophies cannot begin to operate successfully unless the accuracy of the data is proven to be above 98%. Accuracy figures of 30–40% were not uncommon several years ago when the value of data was misunderstood. Most large financial institutions now operate country-wide services which are extremely demanding in their accuracy. It would be intolerable to think that three out of five of us would have the wrong withdrawal debited from autoteller transactions because the data was processed incorrectly! Data is intangible. When we ask people to consider something intangible as an asset it requires careful thought to understand the value. The role of Data Administration begins with this challenge.

In most organisations it is easy to find a specific responsibility for the recognisable assets. The finance director looks after the cash, the personnel director looks after the people, the plant manager looks after the machinery and buildings, and so on. Who looks after the data? One of the difficulties we face is that data is something that belongs to the whole business and no one specific responsibility is apparently practical. After all, the Sales and Marketing function is hardly likely to be concerned about the daily delivery schedules of oil to the boiler house. Having accepted that data is a valuable asset (the second most valuable), a solution to this problem must be found. Data Administration can help, but only as a catalyst to stimulate the people throughout the business to be accountable for their data.

Data occurs within the organisation in a number of different states:

- standard reference data which is stable and changed only occasionally, e.g. tax tables;
- master file data where one value is held but is changeable, e.g. stock records;
- transient data which is volatile and subject to rapid changes, e.g. temperature sensor readings.

Regardless of the type of data we are dealing with, there are going to be people, procedures and systems dependent on having 'correct' data. In each of the examples given above, it is possible to predict the kind of difficulties which will be faced, should the data not be correct. In more extreme cases this could mean incorrect taxation calculations, inaccurate stock replenishments and valuation, or overloaded heating systems. We are therefore dealing with the same basic issue, data accuracy, but across a range of circumstances and types of data.

Data has a well-defined life cycle, as shown in Figure 1.1. At each point in the cycle there is the potential for this valuable asset to be devalued. Consider the following simple examples:

- During strategic planning it is very easy to misinterpret the data and cast it in a role for which it is unsuitable.

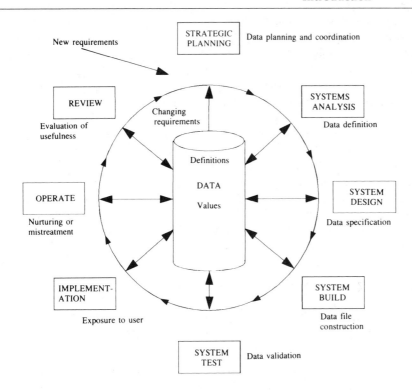

Figure 1.1 The data life cycle

- During analysis a piece of data may be assumed to have certain characteristics (e.g. length of ten characters) because its use to date has always been within this value. Later use could show that fifteen characters is required but the system is not capable of handling this.
- During design we may apply incorrect rounding to an arithmetic operation.
- During testing, software faults may be overlooked allowing possible data corruption in the production environment.
- If the piece of data is named ambiguously, then the user may well put it to some use for which it was never intended.
- During system operation, wrong values may be assigned to the data through procedures being incorrectly followed or other human shortcomings.

The point of this analysis is not to suggest this always happens and always will. We must recognise that there are many potential traps to encounter in using data as an asset. Data administration is a technique to identify and minimise the incidence of such difficulties.

Just as data has evolved as an asset from the early days of mass data processing to information for business decision making, evolution will continue to more sophisticated uses. As an asset we could make much better use of our data. But to achieve this there has to be a change in perception. Data is not the property and problem of the computer experts, it is the principal tool for most jobs and activities within the organisation. There needs to be a more open and co-operative approach within the whole IT community, that is, planners, designers, operators and users of data. This 'IT team' has a major role to play throughout the cycle shown in Figure 1.1 to ensure that the asset is put to good use and is improved continuously. More emphasis is needed on the importance of well-constructed, usable systems. The IT team must accept this task. It must also learn to look across the business and encourage the integration of business processes and IT systems to achieve a wider base of objectives using common data. Data Administration is a key player in the IT team and, judging by the rate of change in information technology the team needs to move fast. Technologies already being offered, such as artificial intelligence, object orientation and open systems will cause an IT explosion greater than anything seen before. Data will be more valuable and more critical to the business. It is our task to maximise the benefits that we can get from it.

The role of Data Administration

Data Administration has a basic mission statement which is

> TO ENSURE THE MOST ECONOMIC AND EFFECTIVE USE OF THE DATA ASSET

Naturally there is a great deal involved in carrying out this mission. The aim is the management and exploitation of the corporate data asset in order to maximise its value to the company. In Appendix 1 we have included a direction statement. Later on (p. 186), there is a discussion on selling techniques for data administration; the direction statement is one such technique. The statement considers various aspects of data administration such as:

- co-ordination and support of IT developments;
- systems planning to meet the needs of the business;
- effective use of data;
- effective management and control of data;
- maintaining the integrity of the data.

Data Administration are the planners, the catalysts and the co-ordinators. The full time protection and use of data is a matter for the entire data using community. Data Administration also needs to play a major part in policy making for data. The policies must finally be derived and delivered by the owners of the data. This is absolutely necessary to ensure that full accountability is taken by the data users for their own assets. The policy makers are a part of our IT team. Data Administration, then, becomes a focal point for the encouragement of excellence in data asset management. They are practitioners of 'quality' and are a very powerful weapon in the corporate armoury.

What is practical data administration?

Throughout the book we will be developing the theme of how to go about 'practical data administration'. Taking the outline aims and objectives covered above, there is an expansion of each of nine aspects of the subject. These are as follows:

- 'Getting started':   Advice on how to go about justifying and setting up a Data Administration function from scratch.
- 'User accountability':   Methods of building the skills and trust in the data using community to manage its own data where this is most effective — in its own functions.
- 'Data security':   Practical advice on both physical security, such as backups, and also logical security, which is the use of data for the right purpose by the right people.
- 'Data control':   How data standards and conventions can help to control the way data is conceived, designed and used, in a consistent way.
- 'Strategic planning':   A discussion on this very difficult subject. How to avoid rushing into reactive piecemeal systems development, and instead to plan out data needs carefully across the enterprise.
- 'Tools and techniques':   Looks at the impact of software methods and tools on the data administrator. We discuss how to gain most benefit from them.
- 'End user computing':   Explains the benefits and concerns of making data widely available for large scale manipulation. Advice is given on how to minimise the concerns.
- 'Problem solving':   Discussion of the role of the data administrator as a trouble-shooter in solving the various types of practical problem which will always occur whilst data is used.
- 'Awareness':   How to publicise the efforts of Data Administration and win support for something that is difficult (at best) for many people to understand.

Some basic terms

Many of the subjects discussed under the umbrella of information technology are littered with technical terms. We have kept these to a minimum, yet the glossary at the back of this book is still well populated. A few terms are used so frequently that a few moments spent on them here will be beneficial.

Starting with data itself. Clearly, from Figure 1.1 we are implying that data has a wide contextual meaning. Generally, we are discussing data definition, occurrence and meaning simultaneously, unless for a specific reason it is necessary to narrow the scope to just one of these.

Information technology (or IT for short) features regularly. We do not accept that it is synonymous with Computing only. The discussions in the book are relevant wherever data is used, using whatever processing medium is appropriate. Our reference to an IT department or function may be unfamiliar to some readers.

Many organisations have a 'computer' department or 'computer systems'. Others prefer MIS — Management Information Systems or Management Information Services. The old favourite, DP or Data Processing, is still very popular. From our point of view, all provide systems which use data.

We have used the term data administration consistently. Two other terms becoming more widely used now are data management and Information Resource Management (IRM) — all three are equally appropriate. Data administration, of course, is the subject of this book. Some readers may confuse the term database administration with this. In later chapters, we discuss the roles of both as they relate to each other and, whilst they share some similar objectives, they should not be regarded as synonymous in any way.

From within the systems development function, we refer to developers and development teams. There is an assumption here that analysts and programmers working in teams are used to develop systems. Sometimes we refer to application development teams. There has to be some latitude in these terms and you may well use designers, architects, engineers and other descriptive terms for the people who create systems. The arguments put forward are equally valid in all cases.

In defining some of the ways in which businesses describe themselves, we use enterprise, organisation, business and company synonymously. Functions and departments are subsets within these. Corporate systems is a term used to denote systems developed to serve the strategic needs of the business rather than the local needs of a department.

The last term we use frequently is 'end user'. This means the business person for whom the data was designed. In a sense all users are end users. The most important area where this is relevant is in Chapter 8 — 'End user computing'. The significance will then become clear. We are differentiating between the developers and the people for whom we develop systems.

Some background to the book

Data administration is still a mysterious term to many systems people, let alone the user community. There is relatively little in the way of education, training or text which can help the business with the development of vision to manage its data. This is certainly the fundamental reason for this book. The emphasis is on practical advice as opposed to theory. As practice is usually built on theory, we have made an effort to discuss both aspects and to illustrate the practice with our own experiences.

In defining the data administrator we have a mix of generalist and specialist, technician and business person, educator and listener. Data administration is a rich mixture of most aspects of systems and information technology. You will find that our views cover all of this. However, there is a difficulty; the data administrator has many roles and interfaces with many people. It is not our intention to describe the roles and techniques associated with these others, such as database administrators, systems analysts, programmers, etc. This has not been easy as the divisions are sometimes hazy. Our focus of attention, necessarily, is the data administrator.

Clearly, our intention is to describe data administration to you in such a way that you are encouraged to do it in your own organisation. Our experiences are quoted so that you may see the similarities and possibilities for yourselves. The difficulties faced have been explained carefully so that you may learn from them. In Chapter 11 there is an analysis of how a new Data Administration function might progress over the first few years. This will provide a useful yardstick. At the end of each chapter there are key action points which serve as a quick reference.

Those organisations which have gone down the data administration route have found that the natural tendency of systems people is to make it a technical subject. Whilst a high degree of information technology is involved, the social aspects are probably more important. If, as technical professionals, we are arrogant enough to believe that data is perfectly secure and well utilised whilst in our care, we must remember that our influence is minor. The business user is the key player, as this is where the data is first defined and where it is eventually used. It is the way in which the data comes through these aspects which will make it a valuable asset or a valueless overhead. You will find a lot of emphasis throughout on the role of the user in data administration. Quite simply, if we cannot get the 'people' aspects right, then data administration will not work.

The convergence of systems and technology within business operations bears a close analogy with the way the social and technical aspects of data administration are coming together in an interesting blend. The data administrator who can achieve this blend successfully is a very valuable person to have. Such persons are the ideal raw material for the development of hybrid management, the key people who manage the convergence, that is, the excellence of design technology with the fundamentals of running the business. We believe that our experiences and thoughts can help you to develop such people.

The book is, of course, written largely from experience gained in the last four years in a medium sized manufacturing company. The principles are equally applicable to service industry, finance, distribution, and so on. We must acknowledge that very large multisite operations (such as multinationals) will encounter practical difficulties with our proposals. Whilst the difficulties are by no means insurmountable, it would be wrong for us to pretend that we can offer 'practical' advice. The principles are sound but the implementation is probably different.

Data is, without doubt, a tremendously valuable asset. If anyone is unsure of this, get them to imagine that one day all of the data has disappeared. What would your organisation have to do to get it all back, and how long would it survive without it? Data administration is simple basic business common sense. Let us move on to see how to make a start.

2 Getting started

The main prerequisite to 'Getting started' is to have gained senior management support for the initiative. Data administration is good common sense; it is sound business practice; it is not a producer of high-visibility, high-profile end products. This makes the process of gaining that support all the more difficult. The standard method of justifying such an exercise is to look at cost savings. Once again, data administration is not a high-visibility cash generator. So how does one get started? Figure 2.1 shows the kind of process involved with some of the key inputs and deliverables.

First of all we must assume that the business managers agree with the premise that data is a valuable asset. That being the case, they will almost certainly agree that sensible steps should be taken to nurture this asset and to get the best value for money from it. At this stage 'sensible steps' will still be cost free where possible. The emphasis should therefore be on making better use of the data and facilities already in existence. The worst possible approach is to weigh in with demands for expensive CASE tools, dictionaries and automated security software.

In all probability, functions will already be in place to handle certain aspects of data administration. Physical data protection services are usually well formulated, development services will be operating and Database Administration will be functioning. A good starting point is to demonstrate the need to co-ordinate the worthy efforts of these groups so that a comprehensive data protection service can be achieved. Consistent and co-ordinated systems documentation (development and operation) is a feature which could be improved upon in many IT installations. Data Administration can be the focal point for specifying and promoting this (not necessarily producing the documentation). It is almost certain that no one person or group is drawing all data-related problems together. As with all problems, there will be a lot of commonality. Sharing problems and providing a wider-based solution is much more effective from the business point of view.

There are possibilities, therefore, to spend only time (a precious resource all the same) in setting up Data Administration. The early days are a period of gentle persuasion. Unless there is a disaster, including the loss of thousands of man-hours of data collection, the response will always be that the business has managed perfectly well without data administration, so why does it need it now? Data administration is evolutionary. A great deal of patience is required to establish the function.

RAW MATERIALS	PROCESS	DELIVERABLES	**Figure 2.1** The road to 'getting started'

- Data Administration promoter
- Senior management support
- Help of a champion

INITIATION AND EDUCATION

- Co-ordination of existing data-related functions
- Knowledge of other companies' approaches
- Reports and presentation selling the need for Data Administration

- Data administrator

SET UP A TRIAL DATA ADMINISTRATION PERIOD

- Objectives of trial
- Plan for trial period

- Initial plan
- Requests for assistance

CONDUCT TRIAL PERIOD

- Data-related documentation
- Data models
- Problem solutions

- Results of trials

JUSTIFY FULL IMPLEMENTATION OF DATA ADMINISTRATION

- Report and presentation on what has been done and its benefits
- Organisation implications

- Knowledge of status of systems in the business

IDENTIFY A DATA ADMINISTRATION STRATEGY

- Data Administration tasks to be done
- Deficiencies which need rectifying

DO IT!

Moving towards data administration

The selection of the promoter will have a significant effect on the outcome. Qualities of persuasion, patience, communication, logic, consultation and planning will succeed where haste, belligerence and bombast will fail completely. If the function is totally new to the organisation, it represents change. Change is feared and requires careful handling in order to implement it successfully.

An early goal to aim for is a pilot project to test the relevance and payback of operating data administration. To reach this point, a period of careful selling and lobbying is needed. A useful ally can be found in IT consultancies, who will often succeed in getting the process started because they are independent. The most lucrative selling points will be associated with the following:

- solution to difficulties in sharing data;
- breaking down function and political barriers in using systems;
- solving known business difficulties using systems and data;
- contribution to competitive edge;
- promotion of business efficiency and growth;
- better business decision making;
- easier and more successful change;
- systems longevity, reduced maintenance, faster development.

Some or all of these common difficulties will be prevalent in almost all businesses. Data administration can be offered, not as a panacea but as a way forward to encourage the business to help itself to overcome these difficulties.

Some prerequisites

In order to gain further credibility, it will be necessary to seek out other comparable businesses where data administration is practised. Because it is a wide-ranging subject, it is likely that all businesses will adopt some of the practices we are discussing. Few are completely successful with comprehensive data administration. Nevertheless, a lot of helpful information can be gained by looking at the ways in which other organisations have set up the function, what they do, who does it and what successes and failures they have experienced.

As with most new initiatives, data administration really does need a champion. The IT director or senior MIS manager is not necessarily the best choice, although it goes without saying that these people must support the idea. Ideally, the champion will be a very senior business figure who can state in simple non-IT terms that data is a key resource, requiring some specialist attention to protect it and maximise its payback. Thinking back to the key selling points, there is not one senior business manager who would not wish to have all of those at his or her command.

Initial marketing of data administration

At this point the promoter needs to write what may be the most persuasive and lucid report of his or her career. This should be backed up by a formal presentation. Much will rest on whether the first effort at marketing the idea succeeds. It is precisely because data administration cannot offer an instantly demonstrable payback that the salesmanship has to be first class.

Another useful approach to the marketing of data administration is to write down the implications of not adopting it. As we said earlier, the obvious response would be that it hasn't been needed so far. It is necessary to look below the surface of that over-simplification. Is it true that the following apply?:

- A single version of each data item exists in common format within different systems.
- Procedures are in place to prevent proliferation of multiple formats.
- Data is always clean, accurate, timely and usable.
- Cross-functional systems exist which are not constrained by requirements.
- Data is always backed up and secured for all systems, following agreed policies and procedures.
- No security breaches are ever noticed.
- System designs always have the required data elements after implementation.
- There is no uncontrolled data redundancy.
- Changes to procedures upstream do not materially affect the data delivered downstream, rendering it unusable.

If the answer to these questions is yes, then congratulations, you have no need of (further) data administration. If not, then there is a case to be made for instituting the service, either as a new function or as an additional responsibility to an existing one.

The proposal should make it clear why data administration is desirable, who should provide the service, how much it will cost and what the objectives of the function will be. In Appendix 1 we give a sample direction statement which indicates the kind of objectives the function may have. The proposal is very much a make or break stage. Success here will provide a platform on which to develop a formal service quite quickly.

A trial project for Data Administration

Progress towards a dedicated Data Administration function within our organisation took a positive step forward after this stage, with the decision to initiate a trial project. The purpose of this project was to examine some of the data administration issues in depth. One person was dedicated to the project for six months, full-time. The stated tasks for this period were to produce data flow diagrams representing the company's major system and also one of the major new developments, to determine how data flow could best be used in the company, to investigate how data authorship (responsibility for creating data) and ownership (overall responsibility for the data) might be controlled and to further data administration in its wider context. To an extent, the objectives of the six-month project were fairly arbitrary. The selection was based on the issues relevant at that time. It is advisable to aim for two or three key objectives which are likely to produce visible results and, hopefully, a tangible benefit. The following are possible areas which come to mind:

- Incomplete backup and recovery procedures. Usually these can be sorted out and audited to show evidence of good custom and practice.
- Unclear authorship responsibilities for a containable system. Authorship is a fundamental principle of data administration. It seeks to assign responsibility for all items of data to accountable individuals so that data accuracy is assured.
- Demonstration of existing data redundancy.
- Solution of a number of smaller data-related problems to show a benefit.

However, as we will see, starting out with some objectives may only be the catalyst for commencing activities on a wider scale.

Perhaps the most fruitful outcome of the project was the achievement of its aim of furthering data administration in the company. This led directly to the formal adoption of a Data Administration function with a recognised scope, on a permanent basis. A substantial number of the other specified tasks, however, were not fully accomplished — for very good reasons! Once people in the business became aware that here was a dedicated resource concerned directly and solely with data, changes in priorities took place. Requests for the services of this limited resource, on a wide variety of issues, came thick and fast, some of them concerning topics of such criticality to the business that they were seen as more pressing than the original brief. Perhaps we were too successful too soon! As it had always been accepted from the very beginning that Data Administration's role was a service to the business, the objectives of the six-month project were amended to reflect the concerns of the user community, and the changes in priorities were ratified by senior management.

Conducting the trial project

The following is a brief rundown of the activities during this period, which may not, of course, be applicable to other organisations. However, it will give some idea of what can be achieved from virtually nothing. Initially, some time was required for familiarisation with data administration techniques and policies. General texts on the theory of data administration principles, and some of the recognised techniques, were studied, as well as the practical side of documenting company data using data flow diagramming. There was also some familiarisation with the dictionaries which already existed in the company, principally the integrated data dictionary forming part of the mainframe database management system. The amount and type of initial education required will depend on previous exposure to databases, dictionary usage, data flow, data modelling and data analysis. Indeed, this relevant experience is a factor for an organisation considering setting up a similar pilot project, and may influence decisions as to the personnel involved as well as the objectives and timescales.

One of the earliest visible results from the initial project came in the documentation of controls and procedures for drawing up data flow diagrams. This helped to ensure that there was some consistency between diagrams representing different areas of the business which might be produced by different application development teams or user areas. Education in the creation and use of data flow diagrams was given to IT system developers. This proceeded alongside the introduction of a systems development methodology, in which the data requirements are paramount. Substantial effort was required in introducing these techniques, which were new to the majority of systems development staff. Development teams still require a significant amount of help to get started on data-related deliverables, to overcome difficulties and to ensure a firm base for their development.

A significant investigation undertaken as part of the initial project was a review of some of the key items of corporate data which had caused, or were expected to cause, problems. This review brought to light numerous major items of company data which differed between systems. It revealed the problems that might be envisaged in the future because of inconsistency and lack of data integrity across systems. Many of these problems were caused by the historical development of individual business areas, where systems were developed to address the needs of their particular areas but did not consider those of other areas. While departments and systems work independently, this has little effect, but once the data is transferred elsewhere, or needs to be used in conjunction with other data, the effect can be significant and unexpected. A simple example will demonstrate this. An engineering system which supports the requirements of designers may carry a very specific description of a part, a long field length allowing for this. However, if that description is passed on to another system, where the description is not a critical field but merely one of many, it may be found that only a shorter field length has been allowed. The description may then be automatically truncated, rendering some descriptions misleading or totally meaningless, particularly where the most precise part of the description falls at the end. If the transfer of this piece of data is to take place, and if the second system is to benefit from a satisfactory description while not requiring the full engineering description, some readjustment must take place. In this case, some standardisation of descriptions can be introduced and a meaningful description specified within an appropriate length for the second system. The differing requirements of both systems can then be served.

Further problems were uncovered due to lack of understanding, again coming to the fore because of the increase in data sharing between departments. Some common terms, such as 'order number' were found to mean significantly different things in different areas, ranging from the order number for an order placed with a supplier to our customer's own reference number. On the other hand, different names were sometimes used in several systems to represent exactly the same item. In some cases, the same data item name was interpreted differently. For example, 'lead time' needs to be defined explicitly to show exactly what constitutes the time — does it include transfer lead time, purchasing lead time, manufacturing lead time, or all of these? And what elements go to make up the time? A manufacturing lead time, for example, may include set-up time, stocking time, processing time, and so on. Lead time values also differed between systems, sometimes being in months, sometimes in days, sometimes in work days. Another source of confusion concerned the different bases for costing, based on different formulae relating to frozen, pending, or historical standard costing rates.

There were also some difficulties caused by the manipulation of data by different areas. For example, some of the data added by engineers, such as the batch quantity and the processing method, were amended by material planners, who apply different criteria influenced by economic batches, inventory costs and storage concerns. Sometimes this resulted in the shopfloor having a choice of two sets of values, a confusing situation to say the least. In this case, the correct source of the data for shopfloor use had to be determined and the shopfloor given only the authoritative values for its particular uses. Some integrity problems were caused by simple operational difficulties, where the information in one system was not being updated or transferred at the right time. This led to differences between the systems, and problems in validation and in reconciling different amounts.

These investigations clearly demonstrated the fact for interested management that these types of situation might have been avoided had some of the basic data administration principles been applied. All these problems involved data definitions, authorship, standardisation and informed use of data, not to mention the absolute necessity for a corporate and not a parochial view. These were some of the points emphasised at the end of our six-month project, supported by some of the examples given above. They were familiar to user management and were recognised as having significant impact on the business, and a negative effect on business development if left unresolved. This view of the state of the data in the company became a major plank of the business case for the continuation of data administration as a formal service. An outline of how data administration could improve corporate data for the future was put forward. This included taking the decision that changes would not be made retrospectively, so that data formats would not be changed except when it was necessary to remedy a particular problem. However, Data Administration could clarify misunderstandings and simplify integration and data sharing. This would be done by examining and documenting data definitions to eliminate misinterpretations. Furthermore, data administration principles would be adopted for future developments, both of new or existing systems, and the guidelines would be better defined and monitored. In this way, gradual improvement in the state of the data and in its ability to support the expanding needs of the business could be envisaged, albeit on a far-distant horizon.

As well as these investigations into data concerns, work began on the original objectives of the six-month project. This started with an attempt to draw up data flow diagrams covering the company's major system and reconcile them with the overall company diagram. This high-level view was already in place, having been drawn up some time previously. However, before this task was completed, resources were diverted to two newer IT projects just commencing. Data Administration was still in the 'trial period' but was already developing into a popular resource for major projects, and was plunged straightaway into 'real-life' data administration. Both these projects involved reviewing their effect on data in existing systems and highlighting any potential problems. The first project concerned a new system which was planned to operate in close conjunction with an existing system and which would have repercussions for other areas and systems. The second project involved replacing two database systems with one. The major issue here was the authorship responsibilities, which needed to be assigned between several different departments, i.e. who would be responsible for different data values. These were agreed early on in the project, allowing for a smooth implementation and use of the new system.

The initial objectives of the six-month data administration project were further sidetracked by a request to investigate a key piece of data in the business and some of the difficulties being experienced with it. This involved tracing the flow of the data through the business, discovering that it was used in some way in virtually every department. The changes made to it en route were documented, together with an assessment of how well it met each department's needs. Data flow diagramming was used to document the path of the data and the processes performed on it or with it, and a Data Administration report was published with recommendations for further action. This report helped to advertise the Data Administration function as a source of independent review for this type of problem, able to examine the implications of cross-functional difficulties.

Deciding to go ahead

At the end of this first, busy six months, we took stock of the situation, primarily assessing what had been done and what could be done in the future. The main questions were to determine whether data administration could benefit the business if introduced on a formal basis, which areas could best be approached by some form of data administration attention, and what benefits could be gained by the business. In other words, this was the point at which the continuance and further expansion of the Data Administration service had to be justified. It is extremely difficult to quantify the benefits of data administration, since the costs of redundant data, for example, are hard to measure, particularly of redundant data that may be prevented in the future. Any benefits will also be quite slow in coming, and the data administrator will have nothing dramatic to show for considerable efforts. Hopefully, there will be a gradual improvement in the health of the data and a significant increase in its value as a corporate resource. Of course, the state of the data is more likely to be noticed when it is unreliable and undermining the business than when it is in a well-managed condition and taken for granted.

Formal review

A review document was produced which covered the company's reaction to data administration, a view of its scope and complexities, and the achievements so far in assistance on different projects, data flow diagramming and problem investigation. The principal conclusion was that the six-month project had barely scratched the surface of what could be done. Data administration had a growing and key role to play in company IT development. There was a long list of areas where it was felt that data administration input was either necessary or advantageous. These conclusions were presented to senior management, who agreed that the project had demonstrated not only the need for data administration, but also its ability to have a beneficial effect on the business. Two areas were judged particularly suitable for Data Administration involvement. The first was the investigation of problems encountered by the business which were related to the use of data or other data issues. The second concerned the introduction of standard, soundly based data policies to ensure consistent development and implementation, so that these types of problem could become a thing of the past.

The future of the Data Administration function was undoubtedly helped by the fact that the senior management technology policy committee had already recognised the potential benefits and had already asked for various projects to be tackled. Data Administration involvement was sought in a major investigation into the possibilities for computer integrated manufacturing in the business, a project which was high on the list of priorities. This type of large scale information engineering brings into play some major data-related issues: how data is used for information purposes, which areas of the business need what information and from which source, plus all the usual issues of authorship, definitions, and so on. The data requirements of a wide range of users, from shopfloor personnel to business managers, were investigated. It is significant that Data Administration input was sought in this important business development at such an early stage in the life of the function. This shows the commitment that had already been gained from key senior management at this stage.

Selling Data Administration futures

As well as this major project, Data Administration produced a list of items that warranted attention, as follows:

1. Identify the company's data.
2. Produce a high-level data model.
3. Draw up an inventory of existing information.
4. Determine where end user computing should fit in.
5. Improve the management of data redundancy and the use of shared data.
6. Establish a data policy to include the objectives and functions of Data Administration, defining responsibilities, etc.
7. Document corporate data on a central dictionary.
8. Improve the understanding and communication of what data is available.

In essence, the remainder of this book follows our paths in investigating the theory of performing these activities, and documents the amount of success or failure we have achieved in these efforts. At the end of this initial period, we had crystallised our thoughts on how Data Administration should operate within our organisation, where accepted guidelines could be followed and where they would need to be adapted. In this, consideration was given to the existing structure of our organisation, and the climate of opinion in the company. It was decided to present these views in a formal way, in order to establish the foundations and scope of the Data Administration function firmly. A document entitled 'Data Administration Futures' was issued, outlining these foundations and the suggested way forward, giving specific areas in the business which were viewed as priority areas for Data Administration involvement.

Initial positioning of Data Administration

An essential point was to set the ground rules for how the Data Administration function would operate and liaise with other groups. In fact, it was decided to continue in much the same way as initially organised for the six-month project. This means that the Data Administration function is based in MIS (Management Information Systems), a situation arising from the fact that the original impetus for data management came from MIS management. There are advantages and disadvantages in this situation, and much has been written on the proper situation and best reporting structure for Data Administration. This is discussed further in Chapter 11. The Data Administration function needs to be free of pressure from any one area and must have sufficient influence across the whole business. Without this, it will be unable to bring about the necessary changes, and with them the benefits to the business. Undoubtedly, a position in the framework of MIS has the advantage of a wealth of easily approached technical expertise on information systems, database architectures and dictionaries. Nevertheless, there can be conflicts between the more traditional roles in MIS and a data administrator considering the logical view of data, looking to future business requirements and an overall view of data and system use.

In our own organisation, MIS has responsibility for mainframe systems but only for part of the networked systems. Some networked systems, including key areas of corporate data, are the responsibility of users in the business community. The data administrator must work with all parties, and a position in MIS can sometimes be a hindrance. This is particularly true if users believe that the views held by the technical or application development group in MIS with which they have contact are the 'MIS views' which will automatically be reflected by Data Administration. It is a constant battle to rid people of this impression, and, of course, it leads to an unenviable position within MIS when an opposing view is taken! It is important to remain independent and neutral, bearing in mind the overall interests of the company and its data whenever conflicts loom.

Wherever the actual position of the Data Administration function may be, the scope of its activities must be clear. These may impinge on the realm of the database analyst, systems analyst or designer, strategic planner or information user. It is important that clear limits and guidelines are set in order to maximise resources and co-operation between groups. Decisions on this will vary depending on the organisation concerned, its structure, size and IT resources, and of course the situation which exists when data administration is proposed. Many organisations give Data Administration the responsibility for data dictionaries, being a key tool and source of control in data administration activities. However, this may already be controlled by the database group, particularly where it forms part of the database management system. The impact of any changes in responsibility should be weighed carefully. At all costs, the emerging Data Administration group must avoid taking on more than it can handle successfully. It should also beware of various responsibilities which it may find unexpectedly pointed in its direction, particularly those which have no obvious 'home' or which are not particularly popular! It is vital to take on only relevant tasks which can be successfully accomplished before more are added to the workload. Otherwise, there is a risk of failure and the early demise of a well-intentioned but over-loaded data administration effort.

First impressions

It will probably be found, in these initial stages, that the profile of Data Administration is too low for it to be fully effective. It is necessary for Data Administration to become known in the business, particularly from its various activities and from the willingness of user managers to involve it in their IT affairs. In Chapter 10 we discuss some of the methods that can be used to promote Data Administration in the business and to get its activities more widely known. One of these is to adopt a logo, which we did very early on. Memos carry the logo whenever we respond to any information or request on a variety of topics. Data Administration must put forward its views on a number of subjects, sometimes where it is not expected. One of the main problems was, and still is, keeping tabs on the wide variety of developments taking place and bringing their full data implications to the notice of relevant people. This is especially so in a distributed environment, where the MIS function in which we are placed has limited input to certain projects. Development may be considerably advanced before Data Administration is invited to assist or advise, or is simply informed of what is happening. Sometimes a casual comment may provoke our naturally inquisitive nature and lead to the provision of details which are significant for corporate data. However, most projects must be considered by a central senior management group, which must approve all resources for IT-based projects. This committee, therefore, has a wide view of developments in the company and a long term view of where we are heading. It is essential that this committee appreciates the value of Data Administration and where its involvement will be appropriate and beneficial. This group recommends that particular projects should be referred to Data Administration, or have some assistance from it, and can set the priorities as it sees fit.

An essential ingredient in the success of a Data Administration function, and whether data management principles will be able to work or not, is the awareness and support of senior management. They need to understand what we are trying to achieve, how we can influence IT developments in a helpful way, and how we can support the business productively. After all, we all have the same aims — to achieve maximum success for the business. Once senior management appreciated the role of Data Administration, we found that suggestions and requests for our involvement far outstripped the limited resources available. For some projects, we have confined our involvement to support of the relevant people. We can assist and guide them in production of data models, data definitions and data flow diagrams, or highlight potential integrity issues or data problems to widen their view from a purely local view to a corporate one. In these cases, we do not produce the actual deliverables required by the systems development methodology ourselves. The deliverables, such as data models or diagrams, are, however, monitored and registered centrally by Data Administration. In this way, individual developments fit in with the corporate plans, and future projects have the benefit of centrally documented material. This supportive rather than active role has been the approach taken overall, given that, even simply within the scope of MIS-based projects, a very small Data Administration group is attempting to support six project teams which are actively involved in development work across the whole spectrum of business operations — finance, engineering, manufacturing and marketing. Outside MIS, numerous equally wide-ranging and significant information systems are growing and developing. These, too, need to be included under the data administration umbrella if we are to have any hope of achieving our aim of being a consistent, valuable data resource across the business.

A realistic look at our resources led us to adapt our view of data administration to work within the existing organisation structure, working with development teams, user managers, the technology policy committee, and quality assurance. The aim is to direct these existing structures to include data administration mechanisms and adopt a data-related point of view.

We have to raise the awareness of data as an asset and bring data to the forefront as a consideration in all system development — something to be considered as a priority and not something which must fit in to a system structure. The system must bend to the needs of the data to support the business, not the other way round. We realised that a tremendous amount of support would be required from the business if Data Administration were to achieve its objectives, and decided to recruit friends to help us in all the major business areas. This was the beginning of the system controller concept, which is discussed in the next chapter.

Summary

The first six months of Data Administration seemed a hard time — a challenge to learn new methods and techniques, to become accepted in MIS and in the business, and to prove our worth to people at all levels. There were doubters, and cynics, and those who just opposed anything new — and there still are. Once

Data Administration is accepted as a formal function, it does not get easier. There is always more to learn, more developments to keep abreast of, more people to persuade to toe the corporate data line. There are the disappointments and setbacks — the 'ones that got away'. But if we never set foot on the mountain, there is no hope at all of reaching the summit. The following chapters give a view of how we are attempting to climb the mountain, in the hope that our practical experiences will both advise and encourage others sufficiently to take that first step.

Key action points

- Select an influential and supportive promoter.
- Research the theories of data administration, and how other companies have adopted it.
- Set up a pilot project to test the theories and reveal potential benefits.
- Make a substantial and persuasive case for data administration in the business.
- List the tasks that need to be done, and recommend the way forward by means of a formal document and presentation.

3 Data administration in the user community

Earlier we discussed the origins of data administration in a business that is forced into taking a critical look at how it handles its data as a key asset. Like all good medicine, it is unpleasant at the time but makes life much easier in the long run. In this chapter, we will be looking at the single most important move forward in data administration. That is, getting the people in the business to be accountable for the data, to use it as a tool and to protect it. There is a tendency on the part of many IT professionals to look at data administration as a technical subject and philosophise over the merits of dictionaries, CASE tools and methodologies. It is out in the business at the sharp end that data administration will live or die. As businesses become more dependent on data and systems, it is all the more important to sound the death knell for such statements as: 'Data — that's something to do with MIS isn't it?' Of course, not all organisations are affected by major philosophy or policy changes to their business operations. For them the selling of data as an asset will be all the more difficult. Nevertheless, they will not have to look far to realise the value of data.

It is by pinpointing specifics that the message can be pushed home. Where would the designers be without their drawings, the accountant without her ledger, the storekeeper without his stock records? The value of data is soon apparent once the amount of laborious effort to recreate it is considered should it be lost some day.

'Data administration in the user community' captures the essence of what we are trying to say. Without the support of data users of all grades, jobs, shapes and sizes, data administration cannot work. This is the major challenge to practical data administration — one that we examine here with the introduction of the System Control concept.

Quality assured data

These days many organisations are seeking to gain approval to BS5750 (or ISO9000). This is a British Standard which lays down criteria for the operation of a business such that it has the framework and capability of supplying a quality assured product to its customer. The ISO9000 accreditation is an international equivalent. This need not be constrained to manufacturing or engineering companies. There are many definitions of quality, but a simple and concise one is the provision of a product or service that is fit for the customer's purposes.

This, of course, implies that the customer is satisfied with the product's presentation and appearance as well as its functionality. In many organisations now, the concept of customer satisfaction is being incorporated within the infrastructure. Imagine a design department delivering a drawing to a toolmaker (within the same company). The toolmaker is a customer of the designer, who supplies the toolmaker with a product (drawing). Why should the quality of that product be any less than something delivered to a 'real' customer? This is the essence of quality assurance. If we now apply the concept to data, we can see that there are many customer/supplier relationships in action every day. In IT functions we are aware of the need for quality assured software, and some development departments go to a great deal of trouble with their quality assurance procedures. Where quality falls down is in the day-to-day use of data. The many users of data in the company probably don't readily acknowledge it as a prime asset, as we have already said. What incentive is there, then, to ensure its accuracy, timeliness and integrity? The challenge is to give data an equivalent standing in the organisation to other, more tangible, assets. We must aim to institute a customer/supplier relationship which requires a customer to accept only data that is fit for its purpose, and a supplier to deliver only data that is known to be fit for its purpose.

It is worth examining how some of those relationships may work to demonstrate the need for system controlling — the concept we propose to facilitate our aims.

Customer/supplier relationships

In the days of single mainframes supplying all of the data for the organisation, the customer/supplier relationship was simpler. The supplier was the DP department. It is probably true to say that systems were also developed to service the needs of one particular function, e.g. Payroll, Accounts, Production Planning, etc. To an extent, the quality of the data received was directly related to the quality of the data put in by the same function. This scene is much changed now. Most organisations will be operating at least one mainframe or large mini. In addition, there will be a proliferation of PCs. Many companies will be operating networked systems, distributed processors and client/server architectures. In other words, the mechanisms for creating and moving data around make it much easier to provide data across a wider and more participative spectrum. Systems development has also moved into enterprise-wide computing, promoting data sharing and integration. This all makes it much more involved to pick out customer/supplier relationships.

For example consider Figure 3.1, which depicts the flow of data around a modest computing network. There are many potential relationships here; the principal ones are shown in Table 3.1. Let's pick out some of the more critical relationships:

- If the product costings are wrong the new price catalogue may not reflect accurate prices. Sales revenues may then suffer: If the prices are too high,

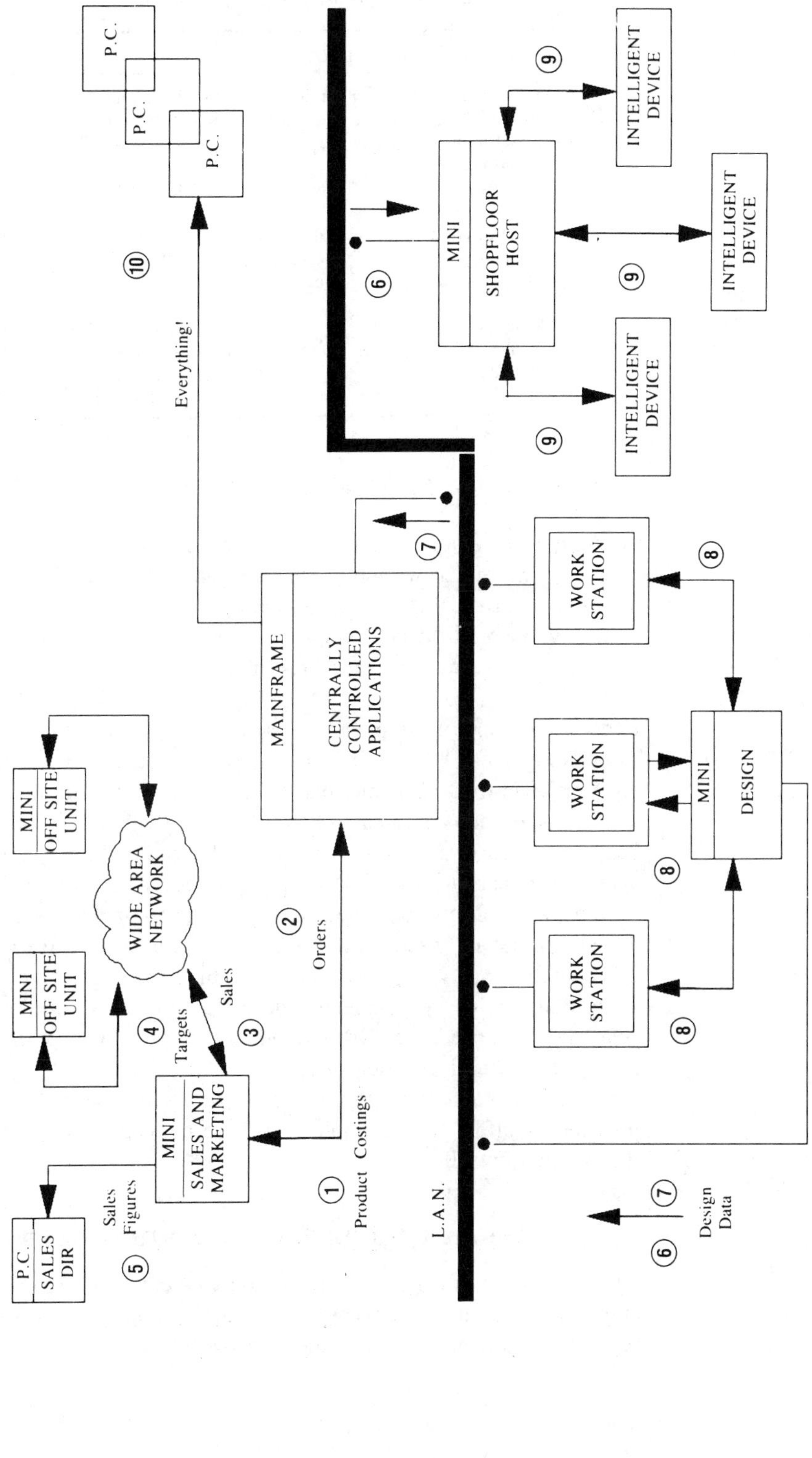

Figure 3.1
Customer/supplier
relationships with
data

Table 3.1 Customer/supplier relationships with data

Customer	Data	Usage	Supplier
1. Sales and Marketing	Product costings	Price catalogue	Cost Accounting
2. Production Planning	Planning orders	Material requisitions	Sales and Marketing
3. Sales and Marketing (corporate)	Sales figures	Market surveys	Offsite unit Sales Office
4. Offsite unit	Targets	Sales planning	Corporate Sales and Marketing
5. Sales Director	Sales figures	Budgeting	Sales and Marketing
6. Shopfloor	Design data	Robotic operation	Designer
7. Material Planning	Design data	Bill of material analysis	Designer
8. Design Chief	Design data	Shared designs	Other Designers
9. Shopfloor Controller	Completion data	Shop planning	Intelligent Device
10. End users	Almost anything	Spreadsheets, graphics, etc.	Almost any system

less parts will be purchased and if the prices are too low, parts could be sold at a loss.

- If the designers pass the wrong dimensions to an intelligent device the parts will be machined wrongly. This wastage will be very expensive.
- If the end users (i.e. the business people using the data to carry out their job) receive incorrect data, manipulate it and make key business decisions based on it, who knows what may result?

Every single one of these customers will expect good data. How many of the suppliers will look beyond their own use of the data to how it will affect someone else on the network? The question facing Data Administration is first of all how to get this attitude accepted and then how to put in a structure to encourage it. The surest thing of all is that it will not just happen of its own accord. The simplest approach could be the use of a 'data police force'. Aggressive auditing, spot checks of procedure, inquisitions over problems, and so on and so forth. This happens to be the worst approach if you want success. Because the use of data is so wide, it is essential to have a general buy-in to the principles being offered. As in all good total quality environments where the accent is on the involvement of all concerned, we need to get the individual data user to adopt the principles. This is an extraordinarily difficult task.

But all is not lost. There are a number of key people in the business who will provide the effort to help implement these policies. The central figure here is the system controller.

System control for data administration

Of all the people within the organisation who can influence data administration at the sharp end, the system controller is the main one. We will discuss the others presently, explaining the interaction between them.

System controlling is all about being accountable for a particular system, group of systems, or even part of a system. We have found that application systems form the best arbitrary boundaries. Needless to say, though, the requirements of a system controller looking after a CAD (Computer Aided Design) application will be quite different from those of the payroll system controller. What follows is a general outline of what a system controller is and what (s)he should do.

The role has been developed out of the knowledge that the best usage and sharing of data is invested in the people closest to it; not a central MIS function, not a small central Data Administration function, but the systems' users. In developing system controllers, we are creating a new and powerful peer group within the user community. This is a group whose members will share mutual responsibilities and may even need to work closely together on integrated systems. Let us start with a definition.

> A system controller is: 'A member of a business function who has responsibility for maintaining data administration principles relating to the data created or used in his or her area.'

Of course, the system controller's specific responsibilities are for the applications which serve his or her own function, but, very importantly, they also cover the data passing through his or her applications, which originate elsewhere. The role itself can be described under five major headings - Data Security, Data Integrity, Standards and Procedures, Documentation and General Duties.

Data security

In Chapter 4, we discuss at length the requirements of keeping data secure. The system controller will play a major part in this by:

- reviewing and implementing central and local backup and recovery procedures (e.g. for PCs);
- storing data securely in magnetic or paper form;
- educating others in his or her area on local security policies;
- reviewing data sharing or transfers from his or her applications for co-ordinated backup and recovery across multiple applications or machines;
- controlling signons and access to data from his or her applications;
- investigating access violations on his or her applications;
- being aware of Data Protection Act requirements in his/her area;
- ensuring that the data that (s)he is responsible for is only used elsewhere in the appropriate context.

Data integrity

Chapter 5 explains the detail of this aspect of data administration. In essence the system controller's role involves the following:

- making sure that the right person creates/maintains data at the right time using the right part of the application;
- maintaining a clear statement of authorship for all data items, i.e. who creates the data;
- checking the accuracy of data within applications;
- correcting data where necessary;
- solving problems where data is unusable or corrupt in some way, or where data is needed which is not currently supplied.

Standards and procedures

This involves the following:

- Providing procedures for creating/maintaining/using data in his/her area.
- Implementing standards consistent with corporate standards to facilitate integration and data sharing. This is particularly important if PC data is being shared around. The level of corporate control on PC data is usually very low.

Documentation

For his or her own area the system controller should provide the following:

- Up-to-date system documentation. This will no doubt be a tailored version of the material produced by the development function, in many cases issued as a User Guide.
- Procedures (as above).
- Authorship/ownership lists.
- A view of data used in his/her area. This is where a simple data flow diagram will come in handy.
- Uses of data in end user computing.

General

In addition to all of this, the following are some general tasks that the system controller should perform.

- Along with the development function, maintain close ties with package suppliers to influence product development and quality of support.
- Be the instrumental user in new system design or modification of applications.
- Monitor corporate directions, plans and goals for his or her area which will influence the role of the systems.
- Encourage effective and more beneficial use of the data in her/his area and promote that data outside her/his function.
- Be Data Administration's 'man on the spot'!

Table 3.2 Typical system controller profiles

Application system	Typical controller	Some special responsibilities
PAYROLL	Payroll Administrator	Data privacy and data accuracy
PERSONNEL	Personnel Manager	Data privacy and Data Protection Act
DESIGN (CAD)	Section Leader	Design integrity for downstream users
PRODUCTION ENGINEERING	Section Leader	Link between design and manufacture
MANUFACTURING	Materials Manager	Inventory levels, delivery efficiency
ORDER PROCESSING	Sales Office Manager	Timeliness of orders
PARTS BUSINESS	Senior Parts Planner	Link between parts and manufacturing
QUALITY CONTROL	Senior Technician	BS5750 audit worthiness
ACCOUNTING	Management Accountant	Accurate balance sheet figures
SALES MANAGEMENT	Sales Office Manager	Link to long term production planning
FIXED ASSETS	Financial Accountant	Depreciation and link to management accounts
MAINTENANCE	Chief Maintenance Engineer	Link to production planning
PURCHASING	Senior Buyer	Supplier performance and negotiating data

Oh! and by the way, the system controller will need to carry out his/her 'real' job as well. This can be the major sticking point in establishing system controllers. However, systems and procedures have become so intimately linked that key users can be established for the application. In our experience it has not been a problem to select and install these people. It is quite likely that someone is already fulfilling a role along these lines without the formality. The formality is necessary, however, to push the concepts of customer/supplier, quality assured data and data administration. Inevitably, the question of which applications warrant such attention will be raised. Our experience suggests that any system which is vital to the daily running of the business and/or shares data with other such applications should be 'system controlled'. This may in fact only leave out personal and end user applications. So be it! A typical profile for a manufacturing business would be as shown in Table 3.2.

The question of the seniority of the system controller will also be raised. On the one hand, (s)he must have sufficient authority to prevent or persuade other functions to change the way they operate. On the other hand, (s)he will need to have a detailed working knowledge of the system. Practically, this will result in senior staff and middle management levels becoming involved. Each system controller will specialise in certain aspects of the business application. This is where it is important to select a practitioner who understands the application. As Table 3.2 shows, all the controllers will have some aspect of their application which makes it unique and critical. For example, the payroll administrator must maintain absolute data privacy and accuracy. The quality control technician, on the other hand, is concerned with audit trails and traceability, so that when an audit is conducted by a third party (as in obtaining an ISO9000 accreditation) all the data can be reproduced to demonstrate quality principles.

So far, then, we have considered the system controller as an individual. There

Figure 3.2 System controller relationships in the IT community

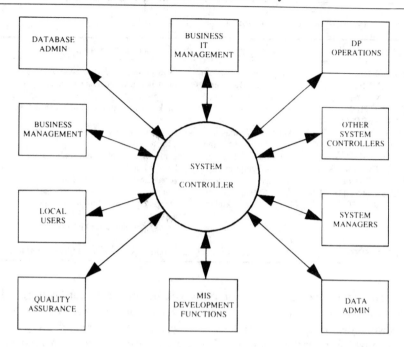

are a number of working relationships which need to be discussed in order to understand how the user community can operate as a team to achieve our goals of data administration.

Teamwork for data administration

Figure 3.2 illustrates the relationships in the teamwork approach. Here we explore the roles of the individuals and the special relationship needed with the system controller.

Business information technology management

In any sizeable organisation there will be some form of senior body responsible for IT directions and decisions. In some cases, this may be the IT director alone or a policy-making unit of managers. Whoever it is needs to maintain a dialogue with the system controllers. There should be a two-way flow of ideas. What is required is a progressive development of the controller's application area. Central MIS functions apart, it is the system controller who should try to influence the decisions, based on his or her detailed working knowledge of current applications, standards of data integrity and usability. Reciprocally, the policy makers need to understand the practical aspects of running applications in that area and take account of this in package selection, hardware policies, operating decisions, processing or database distribution and much else. Most importantly, information technology planning can only benefit from teamwork.

A team of central MIS, system controller and policy unit is a powerful one. Where no central MIS function exists, a void can develop between planners and practitioners which can only be filled through system controllers bridging the gap between practice and policy.

Data processing operations

There is an assumption here that there is some form of centralised operations function, as in a mainframe environment. Both the system controllers and operations share a common bond. Both are at the sharp end. When the system developers have moved on, it is operations and the system controllers who have to make the system work in practice. If the system controller has accomplished the role described, then operations will be fulfilling the policies that (s)he has set for data protection, access and control. The most likely incidence of some active collaboration requirement will be in solving problems. These problems will stem from failure to recover, access violation, data corruption and general operational setbacks which threaten the viability of the data. In many organisations there may be a third player in this team, the central MIS production support function.

The most effective approach, in general terms, is to make the system controller responsible for policy, with the guidance of MIS development staff who are responsible for implementing and supporting the policy, and to make operations responsible for carrying out the duties specified in pursuit of the policy.

Other system controllers

It is highly likely that all IT functions will run multiple applications unless there is only one large specialised application. Following the logic described for system control, there are likely to be multiple system controllers. Each will need to fulfil the role described for their application area, but questions remain about integrated systems and shared data. Does the data administration responsibility fall down the cracks? It can do, which is why this particular relationship is probably the most important of all those described here. As systems become more integrated and the message about sharing data is picked up, inter-application data administration becomes more vital. There are all manner of horrifying things that can happen to data in this limbo state, some of which are described in parts of this book. Associated with these, we discuss ways of combating this through procedural and administrative techniques.

The system controllers, assisted by Data Administration, must sort these problems out. Most of the difficulties which will arise are related to use of the data. If data transferred from A to B is inaccurate, not timely, non-standard, corrupt or unusable for any other reason, the system controllers of A and B need to establish the way round the problem. It is to be hoped that Data Administration need do nothing more dramatic than facilitate the exercise. Real accountability for data administration in the user community comes from system controllers working individually and in teams. When the system control concept becomes accepted, you will find that the incumbents will encourage each other and build the relationship without too much outside interference. However, one piece of interference which will help is the staging of a half-day get-together once every six months or so, in order that the system controllers can meet and compare notes away from the daily grind. This is particularly true where they are geographically separated as in multinational organisations.

System managers

It is possible that this role is not a familiar one to many organisations. The term tends to be used to denote the individual who is assigned the responsibility for running a particular processor.

Naturally, this tends to gravitate towards smaller departmental and office machines, as the larger kit is handled by specialised technical functions. DEC (Digital Equipment Company) certainly use the term for the management of their mid-range systems. The kind of responsibilities designated to the system manager will include operating, scheduling, backup and recovery, physical security, access security, documentation for the machine, maintenance contracts, etc. — in other words, anything to do with operating a specific processor. As we have said, the system controller is concerned with the quality and use of data within applications running on the machine. There is of course a temptation to select an individual and combine the two responsibilities. This can work for smaller machines, limited applications, or low numbers of users. It is generally *not* a good idea. There are those who like to pull wires out of boxes, solder joints and dig into operating systems. There are others who enjoy working with applications in a business function. The two are not mutually exclusive but neither are they particularly complementary.

Having established that they are separate functions, the roles can be differentiated as follows: system controllers establish the data administration policies; system managers implement and operate them. This is comparable to larger scale operations functions such as mainframe computing centres.

Bear in mind that the policies will relate to physical security (backup and recovery, archiving, etc.) and logical security (access, passwords, signons, tailored menus, etc.) and these are the areas that system managers can impact. Interestingly enough, outside the scope of data administration, system managers are likely to form a peer group which benefits from sharing techniques on operating systems, file placement and other technical issues.

Data Administration

Having established the system controller concept, put people in place and encouraged collaboration between them, it would be nice for Data Administration to put their feet up. This cannot be so! It will be a rare IT function indeed that does not experience data-related problems. Data Administration must be there to help. This is especially true where the difficulties lie in integration issues in which it is difficult to establish the exact location and cause of a problem. Apart from problem solving, it is a good idea for Data Administration to offer auditing facilities. This is a most useful service, since the system controller, being involved in the detail, may find some difficulty in taking a more detached view. A slightly wider view of the application from fresh eyes can often yield results by questioning some of the data values and relationships. This will require Data Administration to be sufficiently knowledgeable about the application. In a computer-based audit function this needs to be so. The audits need to identify levels of data accuracy, data integrity and completeness. In addition to these services, Data Administration has a lot to offer just in terms of moral support to the system controllers.

MIS development functions

This is one of the classic relationships, that of the end user. There are any number of jokes and references to the role of the user in systems development, most notably: 'The system would work fine, if there weren't any users.' Back in the real world, the role of the user is critical. Many system developments do fail to achieve their full potential because the development functions do not utilise the resource fully. Most end users are extremely knowledgeable about their business; they do understand the data requirements; they can operate screens effectively; and they are sensible enough to leave the complexities of database techniques and programming languages to the experts.

As professional system developers of some years, we have to acknowledge that the user is a much misunderstood and unjustly maligned phenomenon.

The system controller role can provide a solution to this dilemma. What we have in effect is a 'super-user'. This does not imply special powers, but a deeper involvement. Let us review the aims of a system controller: protection of data, better utilisation of data, control of data quality and integrity, specification of new data, sharing data with other functions. All of these aims influence the design of applications. We discuss the systems development life cycle later on, showing where Data Administration is active. System controllers are the data administrators out there in the user community. They do not only run applications, they specify them.

The system controller should be seeking to achieve the following objectives with the developers:

- development of enterprise data models to aid the strategic IT planning process (Chapter 6);
- development of detailed data models and system specifications for his or her application area (Chapter 7);
- design of appropriate physical security measures (Chapter 4);
- design of appropriate logical security measures (Chapter 4);
- new and better ways of manipulating and presenting data as information (Chapter 8);

- involvement in corporate IT planning through systems integration and data sharing (Chapter 6);
- solutions to application-related problems using data (Chapter 9).

This constitutes quite an onerous task and a huge responsibility. If the system controller is successful, then the developers get what they want — a user with whom they can work closely; and the business gets what it needs — applications which really work.

Quality assurance

In discussing this relationship, we are introducing a function into the business which is a specialised branch of data administration. Some companies already employ professional quality assurance engineers, mostly within engineering and manufacturing. In suggesting ways of instituting data administration into your organisation, it is necessary to propose a QA role. We will describe the function of a QA department and then explore the data administration issues.

A Quality Assurance function tends to be set up with the specific aim of providing an organisational framework which is capable of supplying quality assured products. This does not mean allocating policemen or inspectors to check everything that is produced, be it insurance policies or aeroplanes. Quite the reverse, quality assurance is all about getting the providers of the product to be accountable for its quality. Earlier on in this chapter, we discussed this concept in relation to data. Many organisations who seek third-party accreditations such as BS5750 need to set up some kind of QA function. The working tool of this function is something called the 'quality management system'. It is not a computer system but a framework. The major components of the framework are as follows:

- controls and mechanisms for designing the product or service;
- manufacturing controls and policies;
- purchasing controls and policies;
- effective correction of unacceptable goods;
- documentation policies;
- business procedures/departmental operating procedures;
- effective training.

Clearly, much of this is well beyond the remit of Data Administration. It can be seen, however, that it is seeking to provide controls over data, documentation policies for data, training in data, procedures to support the use of data and effective correction of unacceptable data. The parallels are very clear.

Where a formal Quality Assurance function does exist, it and Data Administration have a joint responsibility for the health of the company's data and procedures. Formal auditing is most likely to be required from QA functions, in which case system controllers and QA should work together towards continual improvement of data integrity and control within the business. Again, because the system controller has the detailed knowledge, (s)he is best placed to work with QA within the heart of the business applications.

Where a formal QA function does not exist, we can only recommend that consideration is given to setting one up, or something equivalent. An alternative does exist, which is to build a branch of Data Administration which looks specifically at computer-based auditing. The role would involve sitting down with the system controller and going through his/her written policies for security, data accuracy checking, system operation and data handling. The whole aim of QA is to encourage continual self-improvement, so this exercise must be seen as a positive improvement program and not a 'big brother is watching you' threat.

Local users

This is a relationship which can offer great comfort to both local users and MIS. Here is a fact: some users are scared of development functions; they see them as ivory towers staffed by overpaid people practising black arts. Another fact: some developers believe users have no place in the scheme of things and would really much rather not deal with them. Whilst this state of affairs is deplorable and indefensible, we might as well acknowledge it. We must look for ways of giving users more IT awareness and encouraging teamwork between the functions. The system controller role is fundamental to this. The earlier arguments for an effective system controller/developer relationship are echoed here. The system controller can act as the super-user and buffer.

As long as we are careful not to cut developers off from all users bar one, this arrangement can work well. The system controller is seen as 'one of us' by both camps and, while we chip away at the long term goals of better working relationships, the immediate goals can be achieved. For the local users, the system controller is their expert on the spot. (S)he has application knowledge, IT capability, influence over central development functions and a friendly face in the world of computers. In their turn, the local users are enacting the policies set out for them by the system controller.

Business management

The system controller is likely to be a fairly senior practitioner. It is not advisable for her/him to be part of the senior management team whose responsibilities are more strategic. The relationship between this level of the organisation and the system controller is, however, very important. Much of the system controller role described so far is creative: development ideas, local methods of operation, data sharing between functions, etc. There comes a point, however, when the system controller will need a helping hand from above. The most obvious area is investment. We have explained that the developers and the controllers will form an alliance to create better applications. No doubt, the financial aspect will be called into play. This is where the system controller and his or her local business management represent their function together. Other areas where this brand of teamwork will pay off are: cross-functional problem solving where a little corporate pressure needs to be brought to bear, selling difficult local policies, especially where changes of job are involved, and gaining collaborative effort from other functions.

Very occasionally a question of data sharing may reach a sensitive level where two system controllers feel they cannot take the decision about whether the data can be shared, should be shared or is legally able to be shared. The best examples involve the use of personal data outside of, say, Payroll/Pensions/Personnel, where contravention of the Data Protection Act is possible. There does have to be some senior decision taking to adjudicate in these cases.

Database administration

This is a relationship which should not need to concern the system controller very much. We are using the term database administration to cover those activities that are directly related to database, e.g. design, sizing, operation. It should be possible for the system controller to conduct the majority of her/his business through operations, development teams and Data Administration. Contact between database analyst (DBA) and system controller will be most likely in the event of a 'clean up' exercise on the database, to remedy some corruption. If it is necessary to analyse database records manually for inaccuracies or corruption, then the system controller is the best person to assist the DBA. Database Administration has a much more significant role in interfacing with Data Administration during the development of the system.

System control: strengths and weaknesses

In this chapter we have looked at the need to make the business — the whole business! — accountable for its own data. Each individual who processes data and passes it on elsewhere has a responsibility to ensure that only 'quality assured' data is provided. Because this is a tall order, we have proposed the role of system controller. This is a critical role out in the user community, someone who will in effect be a local data administrator. This is a fine idea but, as always, there are some drawbacks to be overcome. In summary we will examine the strengths and potential weaknesses of system controlling.

System controlling — the strengths

- The role itself is very diverse and good quality people are needed for it. System controllers need to be very able, dynamic and wide-thinking people. These qualities enable them to consider the operation of the business function, getting the best out of the system and the data supporting it.
- The system controller, by definition, needs to know his/her own application and business area fully. Someone who has operated in that function for some

time, especially using the application system, has all the local knowledge needed.

- If the role is sold well and the organisation decides that system controlling is to be a formal task, a fairly senior person may be selected. This is good, as system controllers do need influence both within and outside their immediate functions.
- System controllers become very involved and attached to their applications. The resulting detailed knowledge and enthusiasm gives data administration a real chance in the user community.
- System controllers can operate on distributed systems equally as well as on mainframe or corporate systems. Remote systems which are out of the limelight of corporate control need the special attention that system controllers can give them.
- System controllers must be part of the fabric of the department in which they work. This gains them co-operation and respect which in turn makes the adoption of data administration principles that bit easier.
- The role is sufficiently important to consider a formal job definition of system controller. This is one way to develop hybrid IT/business people with benefits for the application, the business, the data and any longer term drive towards hybrid managers.
- The system controller approach will herald the start of the business becoming aware of its data and the good housekeeping practices needed. It is a genuine 'quality' approach in that it places accountability firmly where it belongs and has a real chance of getting results.

System controlling — the weaknesses

Thankfully they are few; however points to watch out for and guard against are as follows:

- Selecting an individual to be a system controller for the wrong reasons, which are: light workloads, nobody else is prepared to do it or, historically, this person has been most involved with it. None of these are remotely good reasons.
- Selecting too senior a person. A major part of the role is attention to detail. Senior people, especially strategists, cannot spare the time for this.
- Becoming dependent upon one capable person to control and manage systems (see discussion on system management role, p. 30).
- Allowing split loyalties to compromise the system control effort. The individual concerned will, at times, come under pressure to carry out other functional duties at the expense of system control. Before succumbing to this, the situation should be properly addressed and priorities decided.
- Organisations which are geographically split and operate applications on multiple sites will find it difficult to work with one system controller. If possible the controller should be mobile and operate on multiple sites. Where those

sites are multinational, we have a real problem. Under these circumstances teamwork will be necessary with perhaps a system controller plus key contacts. The weakness in this may be the dilution of accountability. It is still possible for the system controller to carry out much of the role, especially the electronic aspects using the system. The human interaction part of the role will be more difficult.

To conclude this analysis, there is no doubt in our minds that system controlling is the way forward for data administration. Realistically, there are difficulties ahead, as the above argument clearly demonstrates. It is not an easy role, but it is most certainly a fulfilling one, given a chance. For those of you starting from small beginnings in terms of data administration, this could well be the single most important step you take. If it is successfully implemented in the business, everyone stands to gain, including the business itself.

Key action points

- Identify and develop a quality relationship between suppliers of key data and their customers.
- Implement a network of system controllers covering the organisation's key systems, to enhance data administration within applications and across application interfaces.
- Foster a teamworking relationship between the main players and the system controllers to strengthen the joint accountability for data.

4 Keeping data secure

It is self-evident that if the data resource is viewed as an essential asset in the company, it must be available when and where it is needed. Yet it is amazing how regularly that availability is left open to chance by the casual measures taken to secure and protect it. Disasters always happen to someone else!

Although it is not normally Data Administration's role to secure the data resource physically, it is part of its responsibility to take steps to ensure that the data is there when needed. Policies for backing up and restoring data need to be put in place and followed rigorously as progress is made in any system development. Once a system is operational, procedures for achieving these policies should be followed as a matter of routine. Data Administration must be satisfied that no part of the corporate data resource is at risk. Normally, however, the function should not be involved in backup processes itself, as this would detract from the other tasks required of it, particularly when it is only newly established.

Data Administration can, and must, ensure that the task of securing the data is given the attention it needs. As a neutral party, it can stand back and review the corporate data scene, highlighting where company data is vulnerable and where action is needed to remedy the situation. That action must be obligatory — it is not an option!

Data Administration's responsibility lies in being satisfied that corporate data is not being compromised in any way. It is an important part of data administration's role to ensure that adequate steps are taken by the relevant parties to avoid this. This applies to both physical and logical security aspects. Physical security ranges from the security of machine rooms and equipment, the regularity of security backups of data, physical storage of backup media, avoiding damage or corruption to diskettes, and so on. By logical security, we mean controlling access to the data by using various hardware and software measures. This includes the use of passwords and access control facilities, for example. In this way, we prevent the use of the data by those who have no need to use it, and we protect its integrity.

The data administrator is necessarily interested in both sides of data security, as lapses of whichever type, whether intentional or not, can threaten the validity of the data held on a system. The two different aspects are closely linked, although specialist groups may handle security tasks related particularly to one type or

Table 4.1 Responsibilities in data security

	Data Administration	Security Co-ordinator	System User Manager	System Controller	Quality Assurance	Data Store Management	Database Group	Application Development Group	Technical Operations Group	User Management	Users
Corporate policy	•	•								•	
Overall security plan (practical)	•	•	•	•	•	•	•	•	•	•	•
Audit of backup/recovery procs.	•	•	•	•					•		
Legal/confidential/sensitive	•	•		•						•	
Data storage		•				•			•		
Access control		•		•			•		•	•	
Archiving issues	•			•	•	•					
Password maintenance				•			•		•		•
Risk assessment	•	•		•			•	•	•	•	
Physical recovery		•				•	•		•		
Training/Education	•			•							•
Telecommunications		•							•		
Networking		•	•						•		
Software		•	•				•		•		
Hardware		•	•						•		
General data issues	•			•	•		•				
Procedures		•		•	•						•
Backups		•	•	•				•	•		

the other. Table 4.1 shows the responsibilities of different groups in handling different activities related to data security.

Responsibilities for data security

All these activities to ensure data security imply liaison between different areas and close co-operation between interested parties, as well as some high-level management decisions. The system controller must work closely with the system user manager or IT department, depending on who actually controls the machine, to make sure that sufficient backups are taken to cover security needs. The data store management has a duty to hold the material properly and provide it in a fit condition when necessary. The system user manager or IT department, however, must supply satisfactory material in the first place. The system controller's policies must cover the provision of backups in sufficient quantity to recover the system, establishing where a full backup is required, or whether interim partial backups (e.g. of updates) are sufficient. The system user manager will set up the procedures to ensure that backup routines are carried out to achieve those policies. The application software must also be adequately protected. The system controller should advise management of any risks being run, perhaps because of technical difficulties or lack of resources.

The Quality Assurance function also has a role to play in checking that any general company procedures for backups or security are met. These are *minimum* requirements, but of course a system controller may decide that his or her system needs more regular backups. Quality Assurance will check not only that the procedures are in place, but that they are being followed actively. It is too late to find out that they are not when a security tape is needed!

Different technical groups can supply the expertise to put software measures in place to control access, and can then monitor their effectiveness. Security needs to be considered as an intrinsic part of any project and should form part of the standard review of any hardware and software which may be introduced into the organisation.

Management has an essential role to play at a policy level, in determining the minimum acceptable level of security and the amount of resources available to achieve this. The level of security, and its accompanying costs, must be appropriate to the perceived business risk.

Data Administration's role is to view the security of corporate data overall and to act as a catalyst to improve the situation if necessary. We must promote a realisation of the value of data, and encourage system controllers and user managers to protect data held on their systems adequately. As well as this, we can put forward information on legal issues, such as the Data Protection Act. Other than this, it is not our role to become actively involved in security activities. Data Administration needs to provide the forward-thinking approach to a situation which may never happen. If it does happen, though, the business will benefit from the arrangements and documentation put together during a less stressful period. In the next sections, we look at some ways to address physical and logical security issues, and Data Administration involvement in them.

The need to review security

It is, hopefully, a standard part of both operational routine and development procedure to make sure that adequate backups are taken of a computerised system and its data. But in saying 'adequate', an element of subjectivity has already been introduced. Sometimes, what was considered adequate at the beginning of a system's life may no longer be satisfactory as the system itself takes on more data, more importance and a more central role in the business. This is particularly the case as the amount of integration in the business increases, resulting in more interdependency between systems.

Quite often, it is enough for the Data Administration function to ask some questions about backup procedures, their regularity, and so on, for the application team or user manager to realise that the data is not in fact sufficiently covered. The mere fact of alerting them to this, and hopefully spurring them into action, may be of inestimable value. It may mean that data rendered inaccessible or unusable for whatever reason can be more easily and quickly restored. It is all too easy for an application development team to move on to other projects or further enhancements, assuming that everything will be handled satisfactorily, when the system may prove more vulnerable than had been thought. A system methodology which covers security issues within the deliverables can go some way to ensuring that basic security mechanisms are given full consideration and are implemented.

It is an inescapable fact that a system is rarely put in place and left to tick quietly away over the years, although our more problem-free systems may lull us into believing that nothing will ever go wrong. A system continues to develop and grow, and the more valuable the data it contains, or the position it holds in the business, the more secure it must be. For this reason, the security of all data should be reviewed regularly. The Data Administration function is in an excellent position to do this. It can review each system independently, assessing its relative importance in the business and the strategic value of the data it contains. It is not limited to the view of an individual system, as an application team might be, but takes a corporate view of the data as a whole. A system, which in itself may be relatively unimportant, can take on an important corporate role where it is the provider of some data to another area. It might be a system holding relatively low-priority data, perhaps a PC-based system. This is in fact of the utmost value if a major system is dependent on some of that data, sometimes just a single item of data. It may also be that the department operating such a low-key system is unaware of its strategic importance and is therefore completely oblivious of its obligations to the corporate data scene. On the other hand, some departments may consider their systems to be of the utmost importance, whereas in fact they are not. Perhaps they duplicate data held elsewhere in a system which is considered the authoritative source for that data. Sometimes this arises for historical reasons, with one system being overtaken by later developments but still maintained, occasionally with resources spent on it which are totally out of alignment with its current value.

It is up to Data Administration to view the data resources of the company objectively, and to establish their relative values to the company's business. This can involve stepping warily through a minefield of departmental rivalry, attempting to define the significant data, even where the originating department is unaware of its significance. Once the priority systems are established, their security arrangements can be reviewed and any potential problems or gaps highlighted. Once again, this may be a delicate task, as people are notoriously unwilling to be told that their systems are insecure and that they are running unnecessary risks.

In many cases, greater security will mean spending more resources. An evaluation of the risk, together with an assessment of the value of the data, needs to be performed before the business decides whether to upgrade its protection or live with the risk. Whether this risk assessment is a structured, mechanical process, perhaps using a risk assessment package, or a more loosely based value judgement, will depend on the organisation and its assets and needs. The basic approach is similar whether the organisation seeks to merely obtain a view of the risk potential or to place actual monetary values on possible loss. The value of the system must be weighed in terms of physical loss, and also of data loss, corruption, loss of service or continuity of production, for example. Against this, threats to the system must be analysed, ranging from any software weaknesses, malicious damage and 'hacking', discontented or inexperienced staff corrupting the data, to the ever-present nightmare of fire or flood. The potential weak spots of the system should be pin-pointed, and, by measuring all this information, a picture of the risks can be drawn up. At this point, it is possible to determine whether those risks can be reduced. The business may decide not to introduce measures to reduce the risks, or it may not have the resources to do so. At least, in this case, the business is now fully aware of the potential risks and can review them from time to time. These activities and decisions need to be at a corporate level, rather than simply left to local management.

Where gaps in security can be easily plugged, most people are more than willing to do so, once they realise any dangers. After all, if the worst does happen, they will be taking the responsibility, as well as sorting out the mess. Data Administration must ensure that all company systems are reviewed, not only those managed by the IT department but, in particular, distributed systems managed by the users. In some companies, all IT systems are managed centrally by the IT department, and there is more likelihood that a standardised security policy will be set up and followed. Where this is not the case, Data Administration's job will be more involved, as different areas may follow different standards and policies. If a good rapport has been built up between Data Administration and user areas, particularly with the system controllers, this will pay dividends here, as it will be seen as helpful rather than critical involvement.

Figure 4.1 Data
Administration's role
in the data security
review

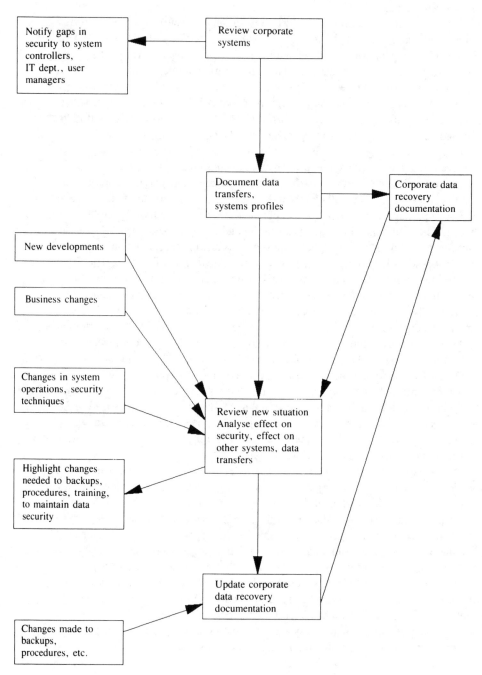

Data Administration's duty to analyse the company's systems and initiate improvements in data security does not stop after an initial review. The situation needs to be reviewed constantly (Figure 4.1).

When Data Administration learns of changes to a system, new developments, or a different emphasis on the company's business, it needs to consider: 'What does this mean in terms of data security? What effect will there be on other systems?' And, following on from these questions: 'What needs to be done to maintain a satisfactory level of security?'

In our own case, the system controller has yet again been charged with some responsibility here. (S)he needs to recognise the value of the system to the business as a whole and to other systems and the way data flows between that system and others. The system controller must ensure that the system is adequately protected by the backup routines and recovery procedures, and keep Data Administration informed of any significant changes in the system. Where there are changes to the data held, for example if a manual system becomes incorporated into a computerised one, this can affect the value of the system significantly. The system may then acquire new responsibilities to all systems downstream which need access to that data. If the system is unavailable or corrupt, how long will the other systems be unusable? How will the business continue to function? Will there be just a localised impact, or will it affect the normal running of the business?

Data Administration's security review

Data Administration has taken a central role in our own business, initiating a corporate view of data security. Firstly, individual systems were investigated, as it goes without saying that each individual system must be protected against loss and corruption. It must be possible to restore each system satisfactorily on its own. But, of course, 'satisfactorily' is a subjective word. In our view, 'satisfactorily' is to a point where the business can continue to operate with minimum disruption. In other words, the strategic value of the system has immediately come into play. A system which is essential for the efficient day-to-day running of the business must be recovered as near as possible to the point of failure, and with minimum delay. A system which has less strategic value, and whose loss will cause less immediate impact, may have less need to be restored to the precise point of failure and with such speed. But beware! A system which has little *immediate* impact may none the less have a *significant* impact. Any data loss may be critical, particularly when it is not fully appreciated until after the event. It is important to know exactly what data has been lost so that allowances can be made for it.

It is a good idea to have a clear idea *before the event* of how the department or business might continue to function if the system were lost. Should transactions be noted down manually, for later input, or would that be inappropriate? Would it be sufficient to input a new 'snapshot' of how things stand when the system is restored? Would this be possible? Can the business tolerate the gap in records? Will the incompatibilities simply pan out over a period (how many days/weeks?)

and can the business afford to ride that time, during which the data is not 100%? Answers to all these questions will depend on the systems and organisation involved. In manufacturing, policies are aimed more and more at 'just in time' and 'just enough', requiring a high level of data accuracy in inventory or purchase control. The amount of leeway once enjoyed has been whittled away. In shopfloor transactions, catching up with a string of earlier transactions would involve a lot of unnecessary effort. A 'snapshot' view of work in progress so that the latest shopfloor movements are captured would be sufficient. This approach could cause chaos in the stores inventory, however, where discrepancies would linger and cause problems in stock control, purchasing and manufacturing. A library system needs to input all returned books and loans to the system later, but it must have a procedure to ensure that this is done in the correct order, so that the latest data is not over-written. Where difficulties are envisaged, standby systems and fall backs such as an uninterruptable power supply may be introduced. In financial areas, any loss of system can have a critical effect on transactions. Banks need up-to-date, accurate pictures of accounts, and with this in mind they invest a lot of resources in running parallel systems to avoid total dependence on any one machine. Any business area needing real-time access to data, such as an on-line reservations system, will be unable to tolerate system failure. Business practices requiring data accuracy help to give us the competitive edge in manufacturing. The more dependent we are on data accuracy, though, the more essential it is that our information systems are backing us up with reliable and accessible data. These are business issues, and the Data Administration function cannot attempt to resolve them without the active participation of the business areas. However, Data Administration can be instrumental in instigating and co-ordinating solutions. Both Data Administrators and system controllers need an understanding of the issues and the impetus to encourage satisfactory protection for corporate systems.

The data security review in practice

All these issues were borne in mind during our Data Administration review of strategic systems. There was some debate over which systems were or were not 'strategic', but the Data Administration policy was simply: if in doubt, include it.
   The basic guidelines were that the system must be included if it was:

- essential to the running of the business in its own right; *or*
- linked to a system essential to the running of the business (i.e. a data transfer in or out).

The concept of a 'link' was similarly wide. This was not necessarily an on-line electronic link, but could be any transfer of data, even including inputs based on a printed report from a system. For example, the Accounts Department may expect a computer-printed report from the Purchasing Section, from which it extracts figures and inputs them to the accounting system before producing its own reports. This can then be viewed as a significant input. A rough guideline is the inconvenience that other systems or areas would suffer if the data were unavailable.

Rolls-Royce Motor Cars Limited has a wide variety of links across different hardware platforms, and to and from outside agencies. These use different software, on-line links, downloads and uploads between mainframe and personal computers, transfers across the local area network, and so on. Any systems can be added in to the review for completeness, and it is safer to include extra systems rather than leave out a border-line case.

This review aimed to build up a picture of the complexity of the IT systems framework and how it supported business processes. The purpose of this was to draw up a centralised documented picture to assist a recovery co-ordinator during a systems failure. Hopefully, it will never be used! If it seems a lot of effort to perform this review when it may not be needed, there are some positive benefits to be gained along the way. It allows us to recognise our weaknesses and take steps to improve them before it is too late. A project like this has a higher profile and therefore more impact than merely advising an individual user manager. Our procedures, backup policies and potential risks are documented for all to see. Higher-level management also become more aware of the IT complexities and any risks being run.

The effort involved in documenting the IT security picture can also be offset against the knowledge gained during the research — not only for the Data Administration team but for application development teams and system controllers who need to provide information. Sometimes they may be unaware of other systems that are dependent on their own system for a particular file or some elements of data. In some cases, jobs have been run for years to provide data, the reasons for doing so having been long forgotten. It is normally only when data is missing that it is realised how critical it is. This exercise provides an opportunity for timely realisation.

Even those of us working in MIS were surprised by the number of links and their complexity uncovered during the review. It is inevitable that links will increase in the future, as the distributed network grows and management requirements expand to cover information from a variety of sources. The aim now is to improve business operations by using the most relevant data, regardless of source. The days when data belonged exclusively to a single department are being left behind. Many departments now use a variety of systems on a day-to-day basis. The manufacturing shopfloor, for example, uses not only a manufacturing system, but quality, human resources and production engineering systems. Future uses will include tool management, engineering and financial systems. The traditional foreman's role, based in one manufacturing area, has developed into that of a team leader, heading a variety of manufacturing activities and managing personnel with a number of different skills. This approach to manufacturing requires the support of a complex data 'work bench', pulling together all the necessary support information from a variety of sources across the business.

Many areas currently use information 'downloaded' from various feeder systems, provided perhaps on a weekly or monthly basis. The requirement for this to be more immediate is sure to grow, and the technology is there to achieve such growth. In other words, our users are going to expect data at their fingertips from several disparate sources, and the internal workings to achieve this are of no interest to them. They do not care where the data originates; they simply want reliable data that is accessible on demand. It is therefore an eminently sensible step to document our current IT systems network, and to continue to update it in the light of future developments.

Strategic systems recovery documentation

For the 'one in a million' chance that it may be required, the recovery co-ordinator will find the following information available:

1. A 'map' — a diagrammatic representation of the systems, showing their relationships and type of hardware platform. This allows the links between systems to be traced, to discover which systems are affected by a particular failure (Figure 4.2).
2. A 'matrix' — an overview of system A's relationships with systems B, C and D, giving the regularity of the interfaces and their type, e.g. on-line, daily, nightly, weekly, monthly, annual, irregular, manual (Table 4.2).
3. A 'profile' of each system, giving the basic information required, e.g. hardware platform, basic schedule with backup routine, type of recovery documentation and media, any essential information for recovery, and, most importantly, the links in and out of the system — details for these links show when they take place, what type of data is involved and where it goes to and comes from. The business implications of a system or data transfer failure are noted (Figures 4.3 and 4.4).

The aim of the information presented in the profile is to give the recovery co-ordinator guidance on how far the knock-on effects of the system failure may travel, and how critical the problem is. Is some data due to reach the affected system? Should this be held temporarily somewhere? Will it be lost otherwise, or is it recoverable without action? Is the system due to pass data elsewhere (system B)? If so, system B's system controller must be notified. Will this be critical? Is there even a knock-on effect from system B to system C? Has faulty data been passed through already, due to some corruption? The variety of recovery situations which might occur is endless, and hopefully these will only be theoretical questions. We cannot hope to answer all the possible questions. These will depend on the specific incident and the effects not only on the data, but on machines, buildings and personnel. However, this information will allow someone to make a quicker, more informed response than might otherwise happen. In the heat of the moment, it would be easy to forget some of these data issues. The effect might

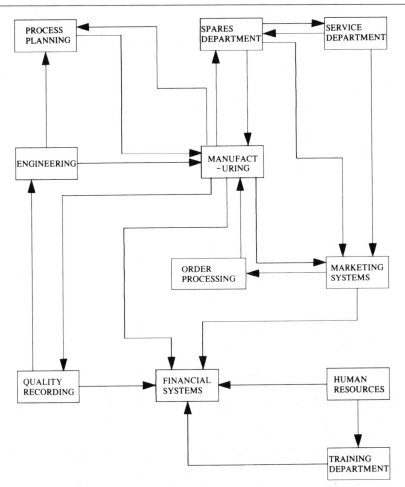

Figure 4.2 Simplified version of a system map to show links between systems

only become apparent weeks later, when the original system, machine or disk has been fixed and is working merrily away once more.

It might then be discovered that another system's data is out of alignment, or that inaccurate data has been passed and used unknowingly by some other area. The resulting data integrity problems could have a significant effect on the business. Imagine the problems on the shopfloor if some of the manufacturing processing information has been missed. The machine shop would be making parts to the wrong method or specifications, with resulting problems for the assembly line, or rejections at the quality control stage. No doubt this would lead to rework, loss of time and material, and consequent loss of money. If some of our supplier or customer details are lost or not updated, we may ship the wrong goods, at the wrong time or price, to the wrong address. This involves both loss of money and loss of supplier or customer confidence in the company. By being aware of

Table 4.2 Systems matrix to show frequency of links (simplified example)

Data Transfers To → / From	Process Planning	Engineering	Manufacturing	Spares Dept	Service Dept	Order Processing	Marketing	Quality	Financial	Human Resources	Training Dept
Process Planning			O								
Engineering	D		W								
Manufacturing	D			D			D	O	D		
Spares Dept			O		D		W				
Service Dept				W			M				
Order Processing			D								
Marketing						D			D		
Quality		W							W		
Financial											
Human Resources									D		M
Training Dept									A		

Key: D daily; W weekly; M monthly; O on-line; R on request; A annual.

the data transfers which take place regularly, we can assess which ones may be impacted by a system failure and check that data integrity has not been affected. Updates may have to be rerun to maintain the level of accuracy, and the data may need to be checked for its reliability before pursuing normal business. In this way, we can establish whether costing information was transferred from system A to system B before or after system A suffered problems, and whether the information is correct and in line on both systems before we use system B to update price catalogues to be sent to customers or dealers world-wide. We do not want to wait a month, or even longer, before discovering that catalogues just distributed carry incorrect prices, leading possibly to a financial loss for the company.

The information drawn together by Data Administration is not intended to replace the more technical information held on individual systems. Indeed, it is a fundamental requirement of this 'strategic recovery plan' that each individual system must have satisfactory backup and recovery procedures. This includes the provision of safe storage and logging of backup media, and complete system documentation.

If the need arises for a backup tape, software installation procedure, user

SYSTEM NAME

HARDWARE PLATFORM

DATA LINKS (ON THE SAME PLATFORM)   } detailed on
DATA LINKS (ACROSS DIFFERENT HARDWARE PLATFORMS) } second sheet

---

SCHEDULE

Backups, updates from other systems, transfers to other systems
Dependencies — what must be done before transfers or updates

This is not a full operational schedule, but guidelines on system
availability, dependencies, backup routines, etc.

Special timing requirements
(particular point in the day, particular week in the month)

Backups — medium, frequency, incremental or full, name of jobs

Details of database journalling, rollback facilities, etc.

RECOVERY PROCEDURES

Contingency procedures — where these are documented and held
Backup procedures

Failure documentation for batch runs, if available

These items should not be detailed in this document, but should
be referred to by name, with location. They should be kept in a
secure area in case they are needed.

Backup log details — where backups are logged, and where the logs
can be obtained.

HARDWARE/SOFTWARE REQUIREMENTS

Details of hardware/software requirements for the system — either
in detail or showing where these details are documented.
This will include details of processor requirements, disk space,
database management system, programming languages, suppliers, etc.

NOTES

Any special information relevant to a recovery situation.

Figure 4.3 Basic information required on a system profile

procedure or whatever, it must be *available*, kept securely, clearly marked and
ready for use. It is useful, in this respect, to ask someone neutral to inspect
recovery procedures. This might be personnel from the Internal Audit function
or from MIS, who may vet a user department, or, more formally, an external
body such as a mainframe supplier or a consultant may be asked to perform an
audit. These people will not have the extra grains of information which are carried
in the heads of people working daily with the system, but which may prove a
critical gap if not available. Inevitably, one or two people become closely
associated with running machines and backups in individual departments, but any

Figure 4.4 System
profile — second
sheet

LINKS AND DATA IMPLICATIONS
SYSTEM NAME: A

SYSTEM A TO SYSTEM B

SYSTEM A TO SYSTEM C

SYSTEM D TO SYSTEM A

For each link, the following information should be given:

> Type and frequency of the link or transfer
> Data details, e.g. type of information involved
> Business implications — effects if the link does not take place,
> with an estimate of manageable downtime if possible.

The information provided should be sufficient to assist a
recovery co-ordinator in assessing the impact of a system failure
and in planning the recovery. It should enable him to prioritise
the recovery of several systems, if appropriate.

recovery instructions should be interpretable by someone outside the organisation
with relevant skills. If this is not the case, security arrangements must be reviewed
urgently.

Storing the data

The preceding statements make the assumption that there is a satisfactory place
to store backups and other materials needed for recovery, somewhere secure even
in case of fire or flood. The measures taken here will depend on the type of
business, its potential loss, and the amount of resources available for disaster
contingency. Some businesses will require off-site storage, and will maintain a
contract for instant replacement facilities for machines lost. For other companies,
this will be beyond the resources available, and out of proportion to the criticality
of their systems. Once again, having acknowledged the potential risks, this is
a high-level business decision. However, even in the simplest organisations, some
of the places regularly used to store backup material should be ruled out, such
as in the same room as the computer equipment. There is no need to tempt fate,
after all! The minimum requirement is a dedicated area with the correct conditions
for storage of computer media and sufficient security to ensure that everything
is where it should be, if needed. In addition, this store should house the other
requirements for recovery. These include details of hardware and software
requirements, details on machines and machine room access, the strategic recovery
documentation detailed above, logs of security backups, contingency procedures
for all machines and additional user material for recovery, if any was established
as necessary during the strategic recovery plan review.

Logical security

As well as the physical side of data protection, the other aspect of security must be addressed — logical security. This means ensuring that the right people use the right data, and that unauthorised people do not have access to the data, whether to update it or merely to view it. It is important that people have confidence in our systems, and particularly that information that they may provide will not be abused. As well as being an understandable requirement for business data, there are also legal obligations. The Data Protection Act requires proper care to be taken of personal data, and the Computer Misuse Act defines the obligations to prevent 'hacking' and unauthorised use of data. The Data Protection Act requires data users to operate correctly with regard to personal data, including the assurance that data is used only for the proper purposes for which it is registered, that it is accurate and up to date, and that it is held securely. This need for security means that the data user must ensure that the data is protected against unauthorised access, disclosure, alteration, or loss, whether accidental or malicious. The Act states as a legal obligation the principles that we should be applying to the data in any case, if we value the data resource. The Computer Misuse Act deals specifically with unauthorised access either to data or to software, and malicious intent will need to be proved for a successful prosecution. This makes it all the more important that the organisation has adequate computer security, with a recognised policy of which all employees are fully aware. It can then show that security measures have been considered and applied. This will not only make it more difficult for the offence to be committed in the first place, but will increase the likelihood of the offender being caught and prosecuted successfully. The Act itself is a deterrent, but the stringent use of available security features is a more powerful one.

The type of data used in the business will, to some extent, determine the amount of protection needed, but in most cases a business will want to ensure that competitors do not have access to data, and also that internal systems such as Payroll and Personnel are off-limits to the merely curious as well as the criminally inclined.

Once again, Data Administration has a role to fulfil in making people aware of their obligations and helping them to meet them. Any potential weaknesses can be highlighted, and these are sometimes more easily spotted by a neutral body than by someone working with a particular system every day. In most cases, logical security will be handled by technical means which are the responsibility of other groups, such as operations departments, system user managers and database administrators. Systems can be protected by a variety of access control mechanisms, depending on the type of hardware and operating system. IBM systems can be protected by the use of RACF (Resource Access Control Facility) or ACF2 (Access Control Facility); Digital's VAX/VMS software uses a variety of security features, from login controls, captive accounts, access control lists, and different levels of protection and privilege for files and directories. These controls need to be considered during the design and implementation of the system.

Once set up, access control devices protect access automatically, flagging up and logging any violations. These violations need to be investigated. Sometimes a genuine need to use the files is discovered, and access can then be given to the user.

Logical security can also be built into the system at the development stage, so that different security levels of user are presented with different menus. In this case, enquiry functions may be freely available, but the casual enquirer is unaware of other screens which are inaccessible. Higher security levels can only be reached by the use of system sign-ons and passwords. Protection must be built in to reject passwords entered incorrectly, usually allowing the user only two or three attempts at the password before withdrawing the sign-on. Setting up different security levels is a balance between providing maximum access to the data, and therefore maximum business benefit from it, and protecting it sufficiently to preserve data integrity and maintain data privacy where required.

Any security features available, either as part of the database management system, built into the system design, or used in conjunction with the operating system, should be used to maximum value. Whatever features are involved, the system controller has a major role to fulfil in determining who needs access to which files or screens, and for what purposes — enquiry only, or the ability to add, modify and delete. The system controller needs to document who is allowed to do what, and may organise this according to those groups of people who need to perform the same, or similar, functions. This can be documented in a matrix format, and it will need to be maintained regularly (Figure 4.5). New employees and changes in job functions must be reflected in it, and staff who leave must have their privileges removed. The system controller also needs to ensure that passwords are changed on a regular basis and that they conform to some basic criteria (Figure 4.6). This can be done routinely and automatically where users and security levels are held on file, which is more satisfactory than leaving it up to the individual. Passwords may be randomly assigned by a computer program, which means that the more obvious and easily broken variations, such as a wife's or husband's name, are not used. The system controller is then responsible for advising users of password changes. Unless the system controller is controlling the security programs personally, the technical function which controls the passwords should be notified of any changes or deletions so that these can be implemented. Alternatively, users may select their own passwords, but password control software should be in place to ensure that they are changed regularly and pass the same basic criteria.

Access control is a routine part of the system controller's role, and one that must be performed scrupulously in order to maintain control over access to the system and data, and its use. This will help enormously if there are any data problems. For example, if data is misused, or wrong values are input, the system controller will know who may have been responsible, and the field of enquiry will be narrowed significantly. Any reported violations must be followed up and appropriate action taken. The job functions which have access to the different processes within a system must be reflected correctly in the operating procedures

Figure 4.5 Security matrix reports to assist access control

USER GROUP ID	USER GROUP DESCRIPTION	RESPONSE NAME	RESPONSE DESCRIPTION	SECURITY CLASS
02	STOREMEN (RESPONSIBLE TO: MANAGER GAUGE STORES)	AGAU	GAUGE ADDITION	207
		RCAL	GAUGE CALIBRATION REVIEW	207
		GRET	GAUGE RETURN TO STORE	207
		GREP	GAUGE REPORT REQUEST	210

RESPONSE NAME	SECURITY CLASS	01	02	03	04	05	06	07	08	09	10	11	....	99
AGAU	207			X										
"														
"														
GRET	207			X										
GREP	210			X					X	X	X	X		
"														
"														
"														
RCAL	207			X										
"														
UREP														
VCAL							X							

Figure 4.6 Some
suggested criteria for
password use

— LENGTH – AT LEAST 4, NOT MORE THAN 8 CHARACTERS
— SHOULD NOT CONTAIN SEQUENTIAL CHARACTERS,
     e.g. 1234 or 4321
— SHOULD NOT HAVE CHARACTERS ALL IDENTICAL,
     e.g. AAAA
— SHOULD NOT BE ENTIRELY NUMERIC
— SHOULD NOT BE RE-USED WITHIN A GIVE TIME PERIOD,
     e.g. within a year
— SHOULD BE CHANGED WITHIN A GIVEN TIME PERIOD,
     e.g. every 30 days
— EACH CHARACTER SHOULD ONLY BE USED ONCE OR TWICE
— SHOULD NOT BE IDENTICAL TO THE TERMINAL ID
— SHOULD NOT BE SOMETHING OF PERSONAL SIGNIFICANCE
     WHICH MAY BE EASILY GUESSED,
     e.g. family names, dates of birth

of the department. This ensures that the data is handled by the right people. The management of logical security thus ties in with the system controller's task of providing procedures and user guides for the system. The need to take security seriously must be emphasised to staff, and the system controller can include this as part of any user training and ongoing education. Users need to be aware of their responsibility for actions under their sign-ons. They must be encouraged to keep passwords to themselves, log off when leaving their work areas, and so on. Data cannot be protected sufficiently where users do not regard it as a valuable asset and do not appreciate their responsibilities towards maintaining the value of that asset.

Unauthorised access from outside the company

Another form of unauthorised access, to which some businesses are particularly susceptible, is that of someone outside the organisation tapping into the company's data. There have been numerous reported cases of this, affecting businesses and national organisations.

The company needs to analyse its risk and the likelihood of being affected in this way, and evaluate any steps that can, or should, be taken to counteract this threat. Dial-back facilities can be used to lessen the security risk from remote users. The user cannot dial directly into the network from a remote terminal; after the initial call, the line will be dropped, and the system will call the user back to establish the link, using predefined numbers. This type of security system helps to protect the vulnerable area of links on networked systems; and organisations with networks, remote sites or users need to be particularly aware of the risks here. This is an area which requires a technical solution, and the company needs to keep abreast of developments which can handle this type of security problem at a cost corresponding to the risk. As with other technical developments, such as changes to database security features, technical support groups need to evaluate possible solutions. However, the allocation of resources to data protection, whether software, technical devices, or physical storage, becomes the responsibility of the business management, who need to weigh up the potential risks to the business of not improving data security.

PC security

PC-based systems create special headaches for the system controller, as they are potentially more vulnerable. The system controller must satisfy himself or herself on issues of physical security, which is more of a problem than with less portable hardware. As with any system, backups should be taken regularly and deposited safely. A locked box on the user's desk is no deterrent, and no sensitive data should be stored in this way. Indeed, if the system carries sensitive or critical data, the system controller might well challenge whether it should be PC-based at all. Is it too vulnerable to abuse, or theft? Does the system really require proper audit trails and more sophisticated access security routines? Of course, many PC-based systems hold only data of local importance and word-processing or spreadsheet packages which do not necessarily have the value of corporate data. The system controller needs to be satisfied that the security of PC systems is sufficient for the data held, bearing in mind any sensitive data and its protection from unauthorised users. If (s)he is not satisfied, it is up to him/her to take steps to change it. However, some improvement in PC security can be made, simply by educating the users to the dangers of PC abuse. The system controller should insist on the correct use of passwords, regularly changed, and of filenames, and should ensure that regular backups are taken and stored securely. Users should appreciate the possibilities of disk corruption. Even if the data is not of any great value, it is annoying, to say the least, to lose any significant amount and have to start again.

PC systems have suffered particularly from viruses, which may be brought unwittingly into the system by using corrupt software. This has resulted in some disastrous system corruption and data loss. The organisation needs to have a policy for vetting software before use to avoid this problem. Disks may be checked by a central technical support group. Alternatively, a checking program can be installed on the user's PC, so that the user can validate any software. The user must be made aware that it is essential to follow any such rules, for the benefit of him/herself and others.

Hopefully, the system controller's drive towards better appreciation of the data asset and raising the users' awareness of their responsibilities to data in their daily activities will lead to improved understanding of the need for data security. This will then be reflected in improved data handling techniques across all hardware platforms, and better protection for our data throughout the company.

IT security policy

It is helpful to pull together all the security issues that need to be addressed and to develop some overall company policies for them. A policy document can be issued which clearly defines these policies so that everyone in the company is aware of them and of what their own personal responsibilities are with regard to data security. This document is likely to come from Senior Management, with particular input from the IT department's management on technical issues, but it is essentially a business policy statement and must have the support of business areas. Data Administration involvement in drawing up the policy document is crucial in ensuring both that data administration requirements are addressed and that any guidelines can be implemented practically.

The IT security policy document should state the company's general policies on such things as accessibility of data, confidentiality, adherence to legal requirements, accuracy and integrity. These are the basic principles which the business adopts, and which form the backbone of systems development and usage. There should also be a statement outlining the responsibilities of different areas and personnel for IT security, ranging from IT developers, technical and operations staff, to users and auditors. The roles of Data Administration, system controllers and system user managers should also be defined. The policy document should then give guidelines and standards for IT security in different areas. These should include the use of PCs, standards for backups on different hardware platforms, different backup media, storage of backup media, testing/auditing recovery procedures, access, recovery documentation and passwords. The details of the policy guidelines will depend on the IT environment and are not intended to give explicit rules for every situation. However, they should lay down the basic ground rules for each hardware platform and development, testing and production environments. The policy should point to further sources of information or technical expertise where necessary. It is also a good idea for a glossary of terms to be included to avoid any misinterpretation. Figure 4.7 gives an example of the topics which might be covered in an IT security policy document.

Summary

IT security is an issue which is only too easily left at the bottom of the pending tray. It always seems more important to start on the next piece of development work, and move on to the next business issue, than to review and improve security for existing systems. But it is one of those things which should not be put off, and Data Administration has to try to encourage people to tackle it. Drawing together the documentation on strategic systems is one way to focus people's attention on security. It should make them realise their responsibility to their own and other systems, as well as their dependence on other areas. There may well be a moment of panic when they realise the gaps in their security. The strategic systems review provides the impetus to acknowledge the deficiencies and analyse the risks. They can then be accepted and allowed for, or measures can be taken to counteract them. IT security policies provide a framework for good overall protection, with standards and methods which become understood and accepted across the business. It is impossible to cover all the angles for any possible disaster situation, data corruption or loss, or criminal access to a system. However, sound

```
IT SECURITY POLICY DOCUMENT

A. SECURITY POLICY OBJECTIVES AND SCOPE

B. OVERALL SECURITY POLICY

    1. GENERAL POLICIES
            accuracy and integrity
            legal issues
            confidentiality
            data usage

    2. RESPONSIBILITIES

C. GENERAL SECURITY PROCEDURES/GUIDELINES

            risk assessment
            contingency policy
            logical access
            physical access
            networking and communications
            office automation
            end user computing
            auditing
            education and training in IT security issues
            Data Protection Act, Computer Misuse Act

D. SPECIFIC SECURITY PROCEDURES/GUIDELINES

            mainframe
            mid-range
            PCs
            network

E. GLOSSARY
```

Figure 4.7 IT security policy document — outline

knowledge of the data network and cohesive and consistent policies and procedures will at least give the best possible base for a successful recovery.

Key action points

- Identify the responsibilities for the different aspects of data security.
- Carry out a Data Administration security review.
- Act as a catalyst to encourage the production and maintenance of comprehensive documentation for the backup and recovery of strategic systems.
- Ensure the formulation of policies on passwords and access control, and the development of security matrices to assist this.
- Stimulate the development of a company-wide IT security policy.

5 Controlling the data resource

One of the Data Administration function's major tasks is to control the data resource so that the organisation derives the most benefit from it. To be fully effective in this, Data Administration needs to come in to a 'green field site' at the very beginning, setting up data administration policies and mechanisms for implementing them. Systems would then be developed using these mechanisms and adhering to the policies.

However, for most of us the realities are somewhat different, presenting us with a greater challenge and the likelihood that the solutions will be something of a compromise. Nevertheless, if we can establish our ideals, there is a chance of working towards them and ensuring that our problems are not increased and that at least some of them may be eliminated in the future.

What is data control?

Data control assumes knowledge of what data is available and how and where it is used — the more superficial knowledge of the data which can be represented in the top one or two layers of a data flow diagram. For genuine data control, however, a deeper knowledge of the data is required, including the detailed definition of each data item. This is then followed up by a rigorous application of the standards relating to the data to give a consistent view across all systems, with the data being more understandable and accessible because of the standardisation imposed on it. Consistent data will enhance our ability to take opportunities for integration, simplifying the effort involved in this process.

By clarifying what data is available and being more cautious as to what is or is not allowed, the amount of redundant data and the possibility for errors in using data can both be reduced. More importantly, as the business strives to operate in a distributed environment, mixing different systems as the business need for integration grows, this type of control improves our flexibility and the way in which IT systems can adjust and support the changes in the business.

The ideal in data control terms is to have data of a consistent format, regardless of system or hardware, that is compatible between different systems. This means that a piece of data in one system has the same physical characteristics in all other systems, and that it carries the same name and actually represents the same thing. The data should be so clearly defined that there is no room for error. However, this is rarely the case, and, in fact, is virtually impossible where different hardware, operating systems or application software must be considered. It is often found that the names of two data items are the same, or so similar that the conclusion is that they represent the same item. This is not always the case. On the other hand, some data items which do indeed represent the same thing have been given different names, sometimes leading to confusion with another data item, and in any case making it more difficult to make the connections between different data sources.

This situation is inevitable, given the historical development of IT systems, many of which were developed separately, to fulfil a particular business requirement in a single department. Once the data needs to be used over a much wider area, disregarding traditional organisational boundaries, the problems start to emerge more clearly. There may be many connecting interfaces, which are mechanisms for moving data between systems. These are like a translation device, telling the system to use 'x' in place of 'y'. This allows the use of data between systems, but makes the process more involved and open to error. Conversion programs such as these need to be maintained long term, but are often neglected in project development plans and tend to fall between the responsibilities of different development teams. They are apt to be forgotten over time, creating further sources of error. How much simpler if 'x' had been used throughout in the first place! There are further problems if 'x' is ten characters long, and 'y' is twelve characters long, perhaps because system A always assumes the first two digits, or refers to them in a separate field. Unless all the systems were developed together, with a common view of all the data items, there are bound to be such problems.

Data Administration tries to bring together this common view, discovering discrepancies which already exist and attempting to minimise further discrepancies. In many cases, database technology has already helped by setting up a data dictionary which records data definitions and ensures that data items with the same name in different systems have the same format.

The dictionary records the meta-data (data about the data), and is actively used in processes on the database. But this may not be enough, now, because of the way our systems and businesses are developing. Our data dictionary covers only database systems, operating on the mainframe. It therefore excludes non-database mainframe systems (e.g. file-based), distributed network and PC-based systems, and package-based systems, which may have their own data definitions and minidictionaries. A substantial part of the corporate data is therefore not included, and not controlled from a common point. Furthermore, even in the database systems which are covered by the dictionary, identical names and formats have not been used consistently, having been set up by numerous database analysts and systems analysts.

Perhaps at this point the data administrator may be tempted to forego ideals on data control, and leave everything to chance, knowing full well that sooner or later the systems developers will discover the benefits of data control when it comes to further systems integration. However, this is clearly not the most positive attitude for a data administrator to have! There are several things that can be done, and the sooner a start is made, the better, since IT development is constantly going ahead and Data Administration needs to influence it as early on as possible.

Steps towards data control

Firstly, it must be recognised that it may never be possible to achieve overall consistency but that there must be a decision point after which guidelines will be followed to strive towards the goal of consistency, and these must be followed as closely as practicable. New developments must be reviewed in the light of the guidelines and must follow them, unless there are strong reasons against it. Data Administration needs to be convinced of these reasons and to support them. It may be necessary to introduce or adapt systems methodology so that data administration requirements for data control are built into the working practices of the development team. This allows for the production of relevant deliverables, which can be documented, discussed and approved as necessary. Systems methodology is examined in more detail in Chapter 7.

Developments in user areas, which may not follow the MIS systems methodology, must also meet the data standards and Data Administration must work hard to encourage users in this direction.

Secondly, the guidelines must be clearly established and mechanisms need to be put in place to ensure that they are followed. This will involve close collaboration between Data Administration, system developers and database analysts, at different stages in the development cycle (Figure 5.1).

The system developer will determine the system requirements, drawing up a logical design supported by data requirements, down to the fields required on the system. The developer will be expected to conform to data standards and to use the data dictionary where possible to assist in selecting data items.

The database analyst translates the logical design into the physical database design, taking into account performance issues, data access and any limitations caused by the database management system or dictionary. The DBA will work from the logical design and data item requirements drawn up by the development team but it may need to create additional entities or reallocate key fields in order to produce the most satisfactory operational system.

The data administrator has a job to perform at both stages. In the logical design stage of system development, (s)he needs to ensure that the design team have defined their data requirements adequately. The Data Administration function will be aware of any existing or developing systems which may have common data and should advise the development team on these. The team, however, must describe its requirements fully and unambiguously to allow Data Administration to do its job. Data Administration then needs to liaise with the database analyst, particularly on any refinements needed to the logical design in order to complete the physical design.

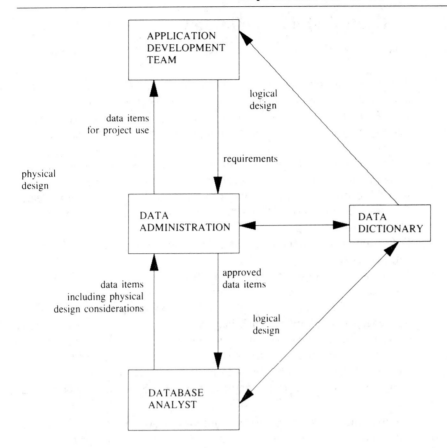

Figure 5.1 Data control sequence during application development

The database analyst is responsible for implementing the best possible physical database, fitting in with existing dictionary definitions, other database systems, and operational considerations. However, the DBA may not be aware of systems on other hardware platforms which the data administrator may need to consider, particularly with a view to future integration or data-sharing issues. It is the data administrator's responsibility to consider these, particularly in a distributed environment where major corporate systems are controlled by user departments, rather than by a central IT department.

In some organisations, Data Administration and database analysts are very closely linked, sometimes under the same manager. However, it may not be ideal to have Data Administration so closely allied to the physical side of design. In our own organisation, joint policies have been developed, with the agreement of Data Administration, database analysts and system developers, to try to limit the proliferation of different names and formats, to promote consistency and reduce redundant data by limiting the need to hold data twice simply to cover technical system requirements.

Control of data definitions

The sequence of events for data control during system development runs as follows:

1. The systems development team work on the design. One of its deliverables according to the system methodology is 'data item definitions'.
2. Data Administration checks existing systems to see if similar corporate data items already exist. If so, format, name, length and other characteristics are checked.
3. Where there are similarities, they are referred back to the development team, to see if an existing definition can be used. If the data item is actually something different, a name may be chosen which differentiates more clearly from existing data items. This stage helps to clarify the exact descriptions of the data items.
4. Data Administration approves names and formats for use and informs the database analyst.
5. The database analyst implements the physical design, referring to Data Administration where changes are necessary, or where synonyms, etc., are to be used. Definitions are added to the dictionary.
6. Any changes or additions which may take place during development must go through the same checking process. This is sometimes difficult to achieve, as there are sometimes frequent changes during the development stage, but the procedures need to be followed to be effective.

Figure 5.2 shows the Data Administration routine for checking data items.

Of course, the checking process will not always go smoothly, and although there are guidelines to check against, it is an inescapable fact that principles may have to be foregone for a variety of reasons, some of them purely practical. One of the tools available for simplifying and increasing productivity in programming is a program generator, which uses data item definitions entered by the developer. In some cases, existing names cannot be used because they are too long for the program generator being used on the project. If there are already two names, which one should be used? If a package is being implemented, or customised, the supplier's definitions may be unavoidable. However, progress can be made towards standardising the data, which means that problems are being reduced rather than increased.

Data Administration checks existing data items, looking first at the major company system if there is one or at a closely linked system in the same area of the business. In our case, the manufacturing system dwarfs other systems and is therefore usually taken as the base, but a marketing system might be checked first against other marketing systems. If there are already two existing data items, the development team will be requested to use the most closely linked one, unless this would cause problems because of name length or format. If one system is known to have a limited life, it will not be considered as important to match with

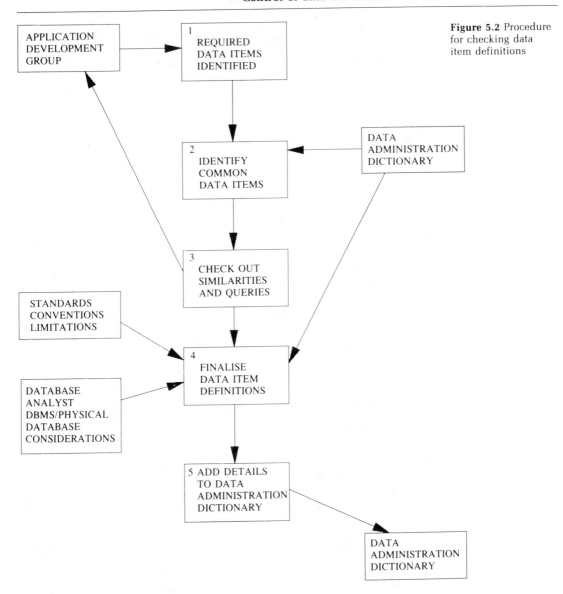

Figure 5.2 Procedure for checking data item definitions

data definitions from this system. Future integration possibilities are also borne in mind.

In other words, it can become a very subjective judgement, in which knowledge of existing data definitions and of corporate data as a whole, plus any future developments, all have a part to play.

The checking process needs to follow any guidelines or conventions that have been introduced. For a site with multiple systems on several hardware platforms, it will first be necessary to research any existing standards and discover the similarities and the gaps in conventions in use. This becomes the first compromise in data control, as a decision may need to be taken to follow a less than ideal convention simply because it is the most prevalent or is held in the most dominant system. It is necessary to fit in with what already exists, and most businesses could not even contemplate the remedial action required on existing systems if standards were to be enforced retrospectively and rigorously. This could involve database restructures, changes to hundreds of programs, screen designs and stationery, and the cost and effort required, not to mention possible disruption of the system, would be enormous. Any known corporate directions on hardware or software policy must also be considered, so that any standards established will not be obsolete in the future.

It may be that only the most rudimentary general guidelines can be drawn up because of the variety of software used and the amount of development work which may make it impossible to adhere to rigid guidelines.

It is useful, nevertheless, to establish the general principles and determine how rigid a structure is suitable for the particular business environment. A mechanism for checking proposed data definitions at an early stage in a project is invaluable in alerting Data Administration to potential problems before it is too late. This needs to be done before any programming or physical database design takes place, to eliminate the possibility of rework and to ensure that clashes with other systems or projects are avoided.

Data control guidelines

As a general guide, the following areas are those which need to be reviewed before establishing data control guidelines. The amount, content and rigidity of those guidelines is a matter for the individual business, taking into account the scope of IT systems, database management systems, dictionary support, and so on. These suggestions should, however, give some pointers towards what to consider and which questions to ask.

Naming Standards

The data item name should be unambiguous and unique, and should convey the essential content of the item. This makes it easier to see which similar items are contained in different systems and if any may be used in a new system, thus reducing duplication.

Are numbers or special characters to be allowed? With some software, this may not be possible. Should the most complete name be used, to aid understanding, or the shortest, to save coding effort? Should the most significant part of the name be placed at the beginning? How many segments can be allowed in the name, e.g. SUPPLIER-INVOICE-NUMBER or SUPP_INVNO?

The most important point in resolving these considerations, as far as may be possible given software or database management system considerations, is that consistency should be the aim, together with clarity and understanding.

Data item definitions

The data item definition needs to adequately and unambiguously define the character and use of the data item as a part of corporate data. There needs to be a clear description of the data, which will again help to reduce confusion and unnecessary duplication. Data formats need to be clearly defined, recognising that systems supporting different areas may have different requirements.

The basic formats need to be compatible if the potential benefits of systems integration are to be achieved easily. This becomes more difficult in distributed environments, where systems may be based on different hardware and software. However, the data administrator will try to reach agreement on lengths and formats for data items and ensure that these are used wherever possible, with an eye to future development and integration. Proprietary package software, however, may not conform and this needs to be considered during the software selection process. This is discussed further in Chapter 7.

Standard formats can be agreed for basic fields used in several systems, such as dates, or user references. The data definition should include the item's structure: its length, alphanumeric or numeric, decimal places, any signed values, any constraints, valid values, etc. Standard formats may be possible for quantity or dimension fields, or for monetary values, but in these instances one system may require a more precise value than another and, therefore, a different field structure.

The data item definition needs to fulfil the needs both of the application software and any data management languages, and the data administrator's requirements to work towards a consistent, fully documented and accessible range of corporate data. Any standards put in place must be followed, and consequently must not be set up if they provide only a straitjacket within which IT systems cannot develop and serve the user community properly. Co-operation must be gained from systems developers, and standards must be such that they support and simplify development, rather than hinder it. Documentation, particularly when held on a centralised dictionary, should provide a useful tool during systems development and should be seen as an integral part of development work.

Synonyms and homonyms

The data administrator will need to recognise and document where synonyms and homonyms form part of corporate data, and this is often established as part of systems analysis work. Two data items may carry different names but in fact mean the same thing: they are therefore synonyms.

Conversely, the same name may represent two different things: these are then homonyms. Clearly, possibilities for confusion exist here, and clear definition of the items can help to clarify this. These situations may arise either because of different usages for similar terms within different areas of the business, or because synonyms have been introduced to the database by developers on different systems. A data dictionary can help to differentiate between homonyms, and allows cross-reference between synonyms. A policy needs to be agreed on the extent to which synonyms will be allowed in the corporate systems, so that consistent standards apply across all developments, and care needs to be taken in obtaining specific descriptions of these items. Homonyms can be even more elusive, but the problem can often be resolved in the data item name by making it more explicit, e.g. differentiating two varieties of ORDER-NUMBER by extending them to PURCHASE-ORDER-NUMBER and SUPPLIER-ORDER-NUMBER.

Once again, in resolving these problems the objectives must be clarity and consistency. The business must use the correct data for the correct operations, and Data Administration can assist this process, together with precise input from the systems developer.

Acronyms

Information technology is riddled with acronyms, to the extent that the meanings behind the initials are often a mystery. However, acronyms should only be used where there is no ambiguity, and where there is not likely to be any confusion or doubt, even in the future when other 'buzz-words' have come into the business. In manufacturing, reference is made to 'big MRP' (Manufacturing Resource Planning, i.e. the manufacturing system as a whole) and 'little mrp' (material requirements planning, i.e. one element of the manufacturing system). Initially, only 'little mrp' existed, and there was therefore no confusion. Now, however, people do not always differentiate clearly between the two, and this can lead to misunderstandings.

Numerous terms are widely accepted and are incorporated into data item names without any problem. For example, Master Production Scheduling is one activity within the cycle of MRP — the scheduling of the major components for the product. Its acronym MPS occurs frequently as MPS-SCHEDULE-DAYS, and so on.

Acronyms are useful, therefore, where they are understood without any problem in the context of a particular business environment. Where they are likely to lead to confusion rather than simplicity, they should be avoided. Data Administration is in the right position to decide this, and should give guidance to system developers on which acronyms may and may not be used.

Standardised abbreviations

A central list of abbreviations should be drawn up and introduced by Data Administration. This can help to achieve consistency in data item names, for example where NUMBER is always represented by 'NO', and options of 'NUM' or 'NBR' are not allowed. It is useful to have guidance on commonly used words, but it is not always necessary to have an extensive list. Books are available which

ADJ	adjustment
ALT	alternate
AMT	amount
ASSY	assembly
AVG	average
CAT	category
CUST	customer
DEPT	department
DESC	description
EMP	employee
IND	indicator
INV	inventory
MFG	manufacturing
MTD	month-to-date
OP	operation
PCT	per cent
QTY	quantity
SCHED	schedule
SEQ	sequence
UOM	unit of measure
YLD	yield
YTD	year-to-date

Some of these abbreviations are particularly appropriate in a manufacturing environment.

Figure 5.3 Examples of acceptable abbreviations

give definitive abbreviation lists, but often all that is required is sensible interpretation and avoidance of ambiguous abbreviations which could be confusing. This will depend on the business context and the most commonly used entities within particular systems (Figure 5.3).

Outside standards

Do standards from outside bodies, such as ISO and ANSI, need to be adopted? This will depend on the possibility of links to the outside world, and the parts of the organisation which are affected, or which may be affected in the future. If such links are envisaged, it will be important to take outside standards and developments such as Open Systems Integration (OSI) into account. Adherence to these standards will make it easier for the business to develop in the future and to take advantage of IT opportunities.

Data Administration needs to be sure that data requirements which may result from future developments have been considered and can be fulfilled. If a business objective is for more effective tooling provision, this might require the transfer of tooling data to suppliers, and, following on from this, the need for compatibility with the supplier's system. Significant data compatibility issues need to be resolved within the accepted standards for technical data interchange, using IGES (Initial Graphics Exchange Specification), for example.

Many organisations are moving into electronic data interchange (EDI) in non-technical areas such as orders and invoices. When EDI is being established in the business, policies on EDI standards need to be put in place. Currently, different standards have developed in different business areas, but these are slowly being pulled together. The business requirements for EDI need to be considered carefully, while drawing up a policy on EDI standards, to ensure that the data can support the business processes in the ways demanded of it.

Further considerations for data control

The sections above dealt with the standardisation that can be built into data definitions to control the consistency of data throughout applications. These are the particular concerns of Data Administration. As well as these considerations, which are reflected in the meta-data, the implementation of a methodology-based system development and more structured procedures allow us to build in other basic methods of data control which can be considered at this stage. These help to enhance the quality of the data and should be considered as part of the system development stage. The implementation of these controls falls to the application development teams, and they are commonly used. Data Administration should encourage their use. The details of rules and checks should form a standard part of system documentation, and may also be documented by Data Administration on a central dictionary, forming a useful source of information on corporate data.

Audit trails

How should changes to the data be tracked and monitored? Changes to data in a financial system, for example, may need to be strictly reported, with a requirement for tracing transactions back to their source. An inventory system in a manufacturing environment will require a more limited audit trail.

Validation checks

It may be possible to build into the application software some rules for data validation at the point of data entry, to help in the process of data control. These may be quite basic but can improve data accuracy enormously by preventing inaccurate data being entered on the database.

Validation checks can include checking that the field is present and is the correct format (e.g. alphanumeric characters in correct positions, length correct), and that its contents are within a specified range (e.g. range of permitted order numbers, or allowable dates). This can help to remove some of the simplest errors. There may also be a check digit, built into a number, which is calculated mathematically when the number is generated and can be rechecked by the program whenever it is entered. Further checks can be set up to flag abnormal amounts, such as quantities or monetary values entered outside a given range. They can also prevent null values, or allow only unique values, so that duplicate employee numbers, for example, cannot be entered. These constraints put in place during system development help to maintain data integrity, and are similar to the 'business rules' checks which the analyst may design into the system, whereby some fields may only be entered based on certain conditions, such as the existence of another field. This ensures, for example, that an employee's address cannot be entered without the employee's number. The quality of the data is also maintained by referential integrity, whereby a department code cannot be added to an employee record unless that code already exists as a valid department code on the database.

Validation checks, whether based on simple rules derived from the data definition, or on more complex knowledge of the business, are a useful control at data capture.

Verification

Verification can also ensure that the data is as accurate as possible at data capture. This can vary, depending on the method of input. Keying by a dedicated data preparation department, involving thousands of key depressions per hour, is verified by a second operator overkeying the original input. Any discrepancies are then noticed and amended before input to the computer system. However, increasingly, the operator is now the sales clerk, stores supervisor, or payroll assistant, inputting their own data rather than writing it out and sending it for keying. These people are, of course, aware of the meaning of the data and should recognise unusual values and query them. Nevertheless, there is still room for error, and mistakes in keying, and where these are critical, steps should be taken to avoid or highlight them. This may involve production of an audit trail so that mistakes can be rectified, but perhaps the most useful resource in some circumstances is the verification of deletes. In this case, when deleting a record or part of a record, the operator is prompted to check his or her actions and is given the opportunity to back out. Some fields may require over-typing, for example a number field, before the action is carried out. Of course, this slows down the process, and the requirement for verification will depend on the data and the consequences of error.

Data dictionaries in data control

The active use of data dictionaries can simplify data control by fixing rules and constraints for creation or modification of data. Should systems be required to use the dictionary actively? This is discussed in more detail in Chapter 7.

Whatever the guidelines established, they need to be clearly disseminated to all the groups involved and should be formally documented and monitored.

Checking the proposed data items in a project leads to another part of the data administration armoury. This process assumes that Data Administration is aware of all the data items in the company, or at least those having corporate significance. This is quite achievable if all systems are held on a central database system with a centralised dictionary.

From our own experience, the dictionary may not include all the necessary corporate systems. The ideal would be an 'active' dictionary holding all corporate

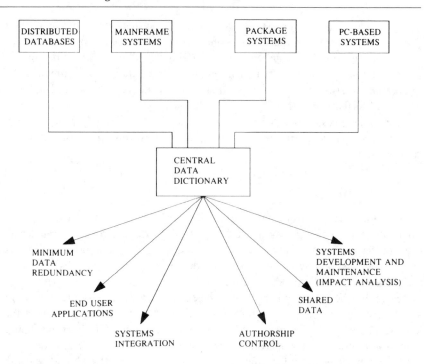

Figure 5.4 Managing the data resource with the support of a central data dictionary

data — one used actively during run-time and controlling database processing, rather than a passive dictionary which is simply a store of data. However, this is another case for compromise and, after much debate, a separate dictionary has been developed in our business for Data Administration use (Figure 5.4). This is being populated by data definitions from corporate systems and allows data item checking for development teams. The major disadvantages of this passive dictionary are keeping it complete and up to date and ensuring that the correct definitions are used. Mechanisms need to be put in place to catch changes to data definitions held on the various hardware platforms. Automated transfers of information are possible from the main database dictionary and from design tool documentation files.

It is not always easy to assimilate the information from different dictionaries which are created in different ways, particularly in a distributed environment using a variety of hardware and software. We may conclude that PART-NUMBER (Mainframe) can easily be compared with PART_NUMBER (Digital). It is less simple to compare data items where names are more dissimilar. Package software may have its own in-built dictionary, and use names and definitions that are only meaningful to the system software. In some systems, data items carry a short code in different files. These convey little direct meaning but relate to a global table with a universal definition. These present more of a problem in understanding throughout the business and in data administration-related documentation, but have an advantage in that, if necessary, changes can be made to the global definition, rather than to individual definitions. Program generator tools have their own dictionaries, with 'public' definitions across all applications, and 'private' definitions defined by an individual user.

If we intend to venture into the realm of computer-aided design tool databases and computer numerical control files, both of which hold valuable corporate data and both of which are in the forefront of integration possibilities, the situation becomes even more difficult. This is because of the complexity of the formats required to hold data relating to dimensions or mechanical operations such as drilling or grinding. The data administrator needs to approach all these areas, however, with the assistance of the specialists, both IT and user, and attempt to maintain sufficient detail on all the facets of corporate data to be able to support future development of the data architecture with minimal problems.

The difficulties of approaching a complete picture of corporate data and its definitions should not be underestimated. The business that can achieve it, however, will reap the benefits in future years, in its flexibility and adaptability to new IT and business opportunities. If all data definitions throughout all our systems can be brought together and made accessible, there is a firm basis for checking new developments and maintaining a consistent approach to data in the principal operations of the business. It will also bring benefits as the goal of systems integration becomes ever more desirable, and as the advantages of compatible data in simplifying the task are appreciated.

Checking data items is a major reason for maintaining some kind of centralised data administration dictionary, but there are other purposes which are also concerned with data control (Figure 5.5).

Once a system is set up correctly and its structure is properly controlled, the actual values input to it must also be controlled, otherwise it will be worthless to the organisation. The dictionary supports the implementation of data authorship responsibility, which is a major part of the Data Administration function and one which must be actively supported by the user community. It must be recognised that the business needs to know who inputs the data and that users must accept their responsibility towards the data. Authorship for each corporate data item is assigned to an individual, or group of individuals, such as 'production engineer' or 'export sales manager'. This individual is responsible for creating the initial value of the data item and is therefore responsible for its accuracy. This helps to ensure that the data is input by the right people and that the accuracy of the data values is maintained.

It is important that people recognise the value of their role in ensuring that data is input correctly and on time, and that no data is omitted where it should be included. This may well have no significance in their own area, but it may be vital to another department further downstream. The system controllers need to educate their users not only in regard to working accurately with their system, but also in respect of the reasons why their input has a value to corporate data as a whole. The stores clerk who guesses at a figure, or leaves it blank, may not realise that (s)he affects the integrity not only of stores inventory but also of requirements planning, purchasing and financial systems. As our systems become more integrated and as more data flows around the organisation, the more

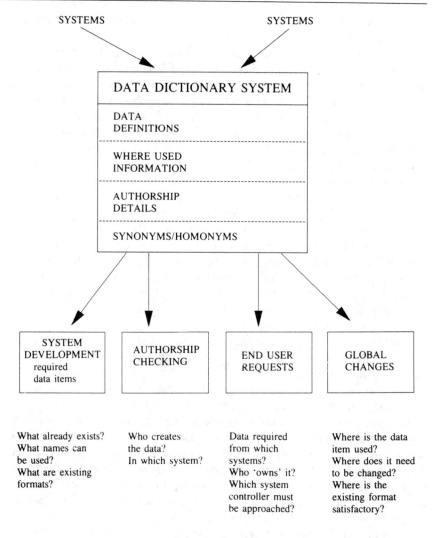

Figure 5.5 Use of the
Data Administration
dictionary

important an appreciation of authorship and data integrity becomes. It is a vital
message to get across: data integrity depends on the accuracy of us all. We all
need to be fully aware of our own input to the value of corporate data, an essential
step towards improving its quality and effectiveness.

Responsibilities for data values

Formal responsibilities for different jobs should be available in system operating
procedures, and the data administration dictionary's authorship details should
reflect these accurately. In assigning a 'prime author' for each data item, we can
establish where and by whom the essential values of the data resource are entered

into the company's systems, and where the responsibility for that part of the data resides.

The authorship details are not assigned at a personal level, but by job title or function. For example, 'QUANTITY-RECEIVED' in the stores department might be the responsibility of the stores clerk; 'START-DATE' for a new employee might be the responsibility of the personnel assistant. It is the responsibility of the system controllers to assign the authorship labels, as they are closely involved with both the system and working practices in their areas. They also have a responsibility to ensure that working procedures are in place, so that these two tasks complement one another. The dictionary system is used to provide information for the system controller to work from, and later to document authorship details and maintain them.

Data Administration provides assistance for the system controller by giving advice on assigning authorship details and using the dictionary to provide data item information to help to do this initially, and to review it later from time to time. Appendix 3 gives some Data Administration guidelines for assigning authorship.

It is important that the flow of data through the business is documented with the points along its path where it is created, changed or deleted. The origins of the data items are particularly significant, and the area responsible for creating the data must be recognised in the company. Setting out the authorship responsibilities in a dictionary helps to achieve this, and any disputes must be resolved along the way.

In some cases, two departments may believe that they are the originator of some item of data, but only one should be accepted as the authoritative source for that data in the business. As a by-product, it may even emerge that the two separate sets of data are maintained unnecessarily and that some data duplication can be eliminated. The authoritative source is the 'prime author' for that data item, and other 'secondary authors' may need to be determined, for example in the event of the data being changed significantly.

It is important to know where and by whom data values are input, in order to be able to come to grips with any data-related problems; our first point of reference will be the creator of the data, and the accuracy of the data input at that stage. The dictionary is a valuable pointer for this information.

Accuracy monitors

As well as investigating data accuracy via the authors when there is a problem, there are more routine data accuracy checks which can be performed, and which give a measure of how effective training and procedures are. They can also highlight system errors. The system controller should be encouraged to set up data accuracy monitoring, first deciding which are the critical data items input in the area.

The data values of these items can then be checked routinely to see if they are correct. The system controller's local knowledge is needed to do this; (s)he knows the system and can devise a way of checking the data against known values, or against another computerised file or paper-based information (e.g. orders, invoices). This type of checking is also done by Quality Assurance, who, as part of a controlled audit programme, will follow the path of particular data through the company's processes. In our case, Quality Assurance performs a range of control part audits, following a part number in different IT systems and checking that values in engineering, manufacturing, inspection and financial systems accurately reflect the physical part on the shopfloor. These values must also be consistent in other documentation such as drawings, shopfloor paperwork or invoices. The system controller should perform these checks more routinely and regularly and can set up automatic procedures to do this, possibly with the help of the IT department. For example, routine jobs can be run to analyse certain fields on the database to see if they contain a null value if the system controller knows that there should be a value. Alternatively, values lower or higher than a selected value can be printed out for detailed checking.

In some departments, a simple spot check of paper forms against the data actually entered can be a useful monitor. Any discrepancies found need to be tackled either through amended procedures, education and training, or possibly through adjustments to the system. Where validation rules can be recorded in the data dictionary and actively used to check data before it is added to the database, this provides a positive form of data accuracy checking. The quality of the data in the system will benefit accordingly.

In some cases, if there is a serious fault, or after an initial check has revealed a lot of discrepancies, it may be necessary to organise a major 'clean up' of the data, with a special exercise to correct inaccuracies, as well as fixing the fault which caused them. After this, the data should be monitored regularly to ensure that the errors do not recur.

In most environments, this concept of data accuracy monitoring is not difficult to convey and is easily appreciated by users and system controllers. After all, inventory checking, stock taking and Quality Assurance audits are well-known events. The same principle is in use: being certain that the values seen on the computer screen can be trusted and used as a dependable basis for decision making or day-to-day operations.

Summary

In this chapter, we have considered some of the possibilities for controlling the data resource, in an effort to improve the quality of the data while maximising the means at our disposal to do this as automatically and consistently as we can.

All the data control mechanisms put in place, both during the system development phase and while the system is being used, are working towards improved management of the data resource. This resource is one of the key assets of the organisation and needs to be in good condition to support the varied requirements of a developing business. If it has been managed successfully, it will be a major aid in the process of system integration and will adapt readily to the wide-ranging uses required of it. The ultimate aim is to give the business community a wide, consistent and compatible pool of data which can be used throughout business activities with confidence and with increasing benefit to the organisation.

Key action points

- Draw up guidelines and standards which must be followed by system developers.
- Check data item requirements as part of system development, to control data duplication and encourage integration by using common data definitions.
- Consider the need to comply with outside standards, particularly in the light of any plans to use technologies such as EDI.
- Develop the use of software controls and dictionaries to manage the data resource.
- Establish the principle of authorship responsibility and document individual systems with the authors of the data.
- Encourage routine data integrity checking to maintain the value of the data.

6 Strategic information systems planning

Strategic information planning can present data administrators with their greatest frustration. This is an activity which the purist would see as the essence of good planning and organisation. It offers a genuine top–down approach to planning information systems which has its roots in the basic business objectives. Starting with a business mission statement, it breaks down in a structured way to provide a logical and reliable basis upon which to construct systems. In practice, it is very rarely anything like this. For many reasons it becomes impossible to achieve this purist dream and this leads to disappointments for the Data Administration function, which likes to see clear, structured models of the business.

Strategic information systems planning is a major component of the wider aspect of business strategic planning. Whilst we do not describe the latter as such, the steps advocated are appropriate for fulfilling 'business' objectives as well as information objectives.

In this chapter we take a look at the theory of strategic information planning, why the theory cannot work in many enterprises, and how it is possible to gain some benefit from adopting a more pragmatic approach.

What is strategic information planning (systems planning)?

Imagine for a moment a completely 'green field' company setting up from scratch. Let us say that the newly formulated board of directors sits down for the first time with the remit to start up their new company. They will establish some very basic criteria, which are represented in Figure 6.1.

It should be possible to ensure that all plans and strategies are consistent with the goals. The new company should have clearly defined objectives, with the correct level of resource and prioritisation of events. All of the functional strategies should be complementary. If this happy state of affairs did exist, the strategic information planner would indeed find job satisfaction. (S)he could then adopt a perfectly purist and text-book approach to planning the systems to support these complementary business strategies.

Possibly the single most important criterion for the systems planner is the clear statement of the business objectives. This applies equally to any business enterprise, from dairy farming to aero-engine manufacture, where information and data are

Figure 6.1 A typical business planning process

the raw material for systems. The objectives will necessarily vary in degree of detail. For example, a human resources function may provide a set of objectives of the following kind:

- All employees must belong to one discrete working unit and be transferable between working units.
- The identification of an employee should be by means of a unique personal identification number.

- All personnel data should be held on (and accessible from) a central database (e.g. payroll, pensions, training records, personal data).

In an engineering environment perhaps some of the objectives would be as follows:

- All components and assemblies must be uniquely identifiable.
- All components required for product lines X, Y and Z must be designed using CAD (computer aided design) in digitised geometry format within twelve months of product concept launch.
- Computer aided design systems must be fully integrated with computer aided process planning systems to ensure data integrity between separate engineering disciplines.

And the list goes on. Each function within our 'green field' company will set down objectives of differing complexity and substance. The systems planner will then piece together a picture of how information systems can be conceived to achieve all of these objectives in a mutually beneficial way. The overall aims of the systems planner can be described as follows:

- Gaining a thorough understanding of the whole business and its objectives, so that information systems will reflect those objectives and will help in achieving them. This is particularly true where disparate functions have joint responsibility for objectives.
- Making the link between the business and its goals and the systems development function, whose role is to help to achieve those goals with information technology. In our green field site, the systems department would start from this position.
- Setting up long term and short term systems development plans consistent with those of the business.
- Developing an architecture for a systems network which will support the whole enterprise, crossing functional boundaries as required, i.e. the concept of systems integration begins to take shape.
- Establishing a framework for databases which can serve as much of the enterprise as necessary without incurring disproportionate cost and complexity.

In order to carry out this task the systems planner would follow a logical and rigorous approach, as described below.

An idealistic approach to strategic information planning

Figure 6.2 illustrates an approach to systems planning. Here we expand on these steps.

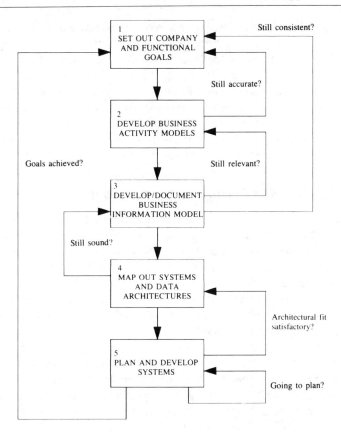

Figure 6.2 An ideal approach to systems planning

1. Set out company and functional goals

Ideally, this should be as simple as lifting the company's corporate and functional objectives from a business policy document. For strategic systems planning, it is necessary to expand and interpret the objectives so that they become more slanted towards information systems purposes.

From one of our earlier examples concerning the unique identification of components and assemblies, we may also need to establish the following:

- Assemblies should be distinguishable from components.
- Drawing numbers and part numbers are synonymous and should always be the same.
- Modification to an existing design or use must result in new versions of the part being created.

In other words, for this particular objective, it has been necessary to question vigorously the real meaning and impact in terms of information systems. The output from the exercise is a list of criteria on which the information systems will be based. Clearly, there are going to be a large number of objectives to deal with, especially once all functional areas are subjected to this decomposition process. Some structuring of the objectives will be necessary. Having obtained a structured set of objectives, great skill is required to marry those which are mutually related. This is one of the key skills of the systems planner and (although it may not be clinically demonstrable) provides one of the most valuable paybacks that the company will gain from its systems strategy. The following discussion on the business activity models will demonstrate the structuring of the objectives, which allows the marrying process to take place.

2. *Develop business activity models*

In the derivation of our new company criteria (Figure 6.1), we established the structure of the business and the objectives of the functions within that structure. The business activity model seeks to describe what those functions are going to do. This, too, is a top−down decomposition (like the derivation of lower-level objectives). Figure 6.3 demonstrates a very simplistic business activity diagram based on a new venture recently started in our home area. We can use this example to illustrate the way in which a systems planner will analyse the business through structured levels of activity detail.

Once we are confident that the activities shown in Figure 6.3 are indeed the business activities for which systems need to be planned, the decomposition can commence. From this we establish that 'manage materials' really means predicting when new materials will be needed, buying them as required, and keeping some form of record of how much is available. These can be taken as objectives for the 'manage materials' activity (Figure 6.4).

It may be necessary to break down the function shown in Figure 6.4 even more, to a third level. For a more complex business than our example, several more levels of decomposition are likely. In addition, the level at which very simple instructions are reached will be much lower. The lower level of detail provides the kind of criteria we would use in analysing a specific system requirement.

Figure 6.3 First-level view of company functional structure

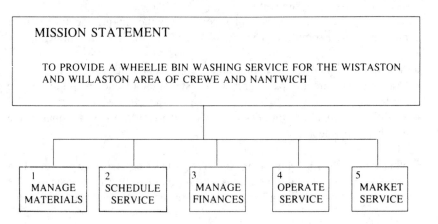

MISSION STATEMENT

TO PROVIDE A WHEELIE BIN WASHING SERVICE FOR THE WISTASTON AND WILLASTON AREA OF CREWE AND NANTWICH

| 1 MANAGE MATERIALS | 2 SCHEDULE SERVICE | 3 MANAGE FINANCES | 4 OPERATE SERVICE | 5 MARKET SERVICE |

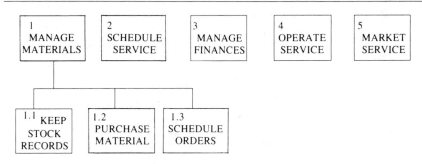

Figure 6.4 Second-level view of company functional structure

If the business activity model in our example were to be completed, it would contain something like four or five key activities at the third level for each first-level activity.

Many of these business activities may require no support from computerised (information) systems at all. However, it is still important for the systems planner to understand all of the business functions and the relationships between them. Each of the activities described, at all levels, will have its own objectives, with varying levels of detail.

It is entirely likely that the objectives for lower-level activities will be derived from and related to higher-level parent objectives, in the same way that lower-level activities are derived from parent activities. Once the activities and the objectives have been mapped out in structured fashion, the marrying process can begin. Here we are trying to ensure that any goals we set for, say, the financial systems will be compatible with those for materials management systems. Purchasing and stock handling will have significant ramifications for the financial business activities. This may seem quite obvious; nevertheless our systems planner needs to understand the total picture. Given a thorough grasp of the business structure, its objectives and its activities, the systems planner can start to deal in information. The next stage of the systems planning process is to derive the information needs of these activities.

3.   Develop and document business information model

This process seeks to analyse the business for specific subject areas about which information or data will be needed to allow the business activities to take place, and for the objectives to be achieved. It is probably easiest to take each activity and establish the 'things' which make that activity describable. These 'things' will be defined as business entities. Each activity needs to be examined with all of its derivative activities to extract the entities about which information needs to be kept (Figure 6.5). This is called 'entity to activity matching'.

As the exercise progresses the entity list will grow. However, it will become apparent that the same entities are in fact used time and time again in different areas of business activity. An entity such as 'PART' can crop up in several areas. From these humble beginnings, we can piece together a complete inventory of all the business entities needed. Upon examination, many entities will be found

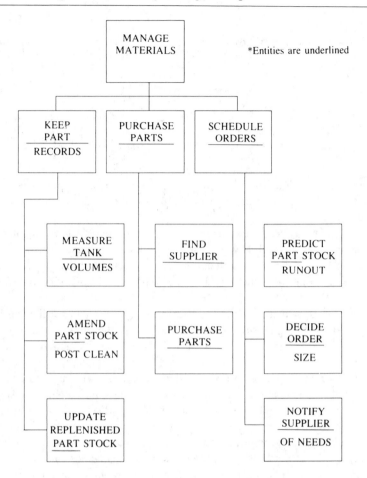

Figure 6.5 Entity to
activity matching

to be variants of the same basic entity, e.g. PART = STOCKED PART, REPLENISHMENT PART, PURCHASE PART. For our purposes, they are all parts.

In our example some of the business entities may turn out to be:

PART	SCHEDULE
ORDER	CUSTOMER
SUPPLIER	ADDRESS
TANK	INVOICE

Each entity will bear some description to furnish the systems planner with a thorough understanding of all aspects of the business. This should include a list of attributes for that entity, the key piece of identifying data, the area of the business responsible for it and some guidelines or rules about its use. A suggested description for TANK from our entity list might be as shown in Table 6.1.

Once we have a description of all the entities and understand their role in the

Table 6.1 Entity description table

Entity	Attributes	Key	Area responsible	Rules/guidelines
Tank	Plant ID no.	Plant ID no.	Maintenance	Numeric 9(3) 001–999
	Volume			Numeric 9(4) 0500–9000
	Make			Char (10)
	Allowable content			Char (20)
	Period of inspection			Numeric 9(1) 0–9
	Material			Char (15)
	Measurement type			Numeric 9(1) 1, 2 or 3
Comments	Plant ID number is unique and will be assigned on commissioning			
	Volume indicates manufacturer's stated volume in litres			
	Make will indicate the manufacturer's name, abbreviated if necessary			
	Allowable content is maximum safe volume in litres			
	Period of inspection is the number of months between inspections			
	Material is a description of the material abbreviated if necessary			
	Measurement types are 1=DIP, 2=SIGHT GLASS, 3=GAUGE			

business, a start can be made on mapping out the way those entities are used throughout the business activity model in a simple matrix. The information needed is where the entity is created, updated, used or deleted. These are the earliest efforts at establishing the principles of prime authorship and accountability discussed at length in Chapter 5.

Table 6.2 shows an extract from a function/entity matrix. This shows a number of business functions which use the entities. The next stage is to develop the entity/relationship model. This model tries to connect together entities which are in some way logically dependent on each other, if at all. The convention adopted here is:

———————————	One to one
——————————→	One to many
←——————————→	Many to many

In our example, each CUSTOMER will have an ADDRESS and a number of

Table 6.2 Function/entity matrix

Entity	Function			
	Amend records post-clean	Organise schedule	Notify customer	Find supplier
Part	Updated			Created
Supplier				Created
Schedule		Created Deleted	Used	

Figure 6.6
Relationship between
'customer' entity and
other entities in the
business information
model

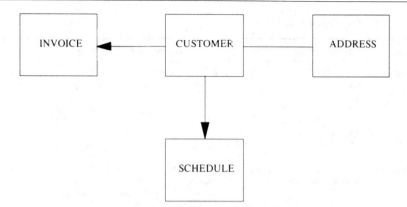

Figure 6.7 Entity
relationship diagram

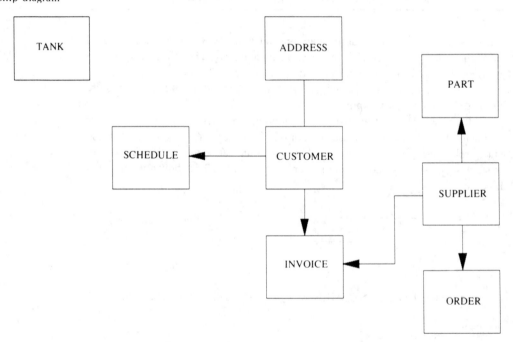

SCHEDULE dates. The customer will also have a number of INVOICE(s) (perhaps some paid and some not!). Diagrammatically, this is as shown in Figure 6.6.

Figure 6.7 shows what a complete entity relationship diagram for the example might look like using the entities listed earlier. There are assumptions in the diagram such as that a part will only be purchased from one supplier. At the systems planning stage, it is reasonable to have assumptions, but they must be consistent with the objectives.

At this stage of the proceedings, the systems planner understands the structure of the business, the objectives, the activities, and the basic building blocks of data used in the business. Getting the building blocks right at this stage is important because so much will depend on this model. Later on we will discuss the aspects of the data and systems architecture which are changeable. A business may change the way in which data flows around it regularly. It may change the database designs occasionally. But, unless there is a radical change in the business, the entity model will be enduring. Getting it right at this stage can save a lot of rework later on.

We are now in a position to look at systems and data.

4.   Map out systems and data architecture

Strictly speaking, there are two significantly different processes here, in sequence. The data architecture needs to be established, then combined with the business activity model (and the objectives) to lead into the derivation of a systems architecture.

Ideally, we should be able to look at the way in which data is structured for the business and the way in which data flows around the business, without burdening ourselves with the concept of a 'system'. A system, by its very definition, seeks to impose boundaries and functionality which add nothing (at this stage of the process) to the total picture sought by the systems planner. The structure of the data began to emerge in our last process ('Develop and document business information model'). The entity diagrams describe those major objects about which data will eventually be maintained. However, this kind of model best describes the way we look at the data 'at rest'. For systems to work, data needs to be 'in motion', in other words found, transmitted, manipulated, shared, archived, viewed, and so on.

The combination of the view of the way data is kept 'at rest' and how we view the data 'in motion' will give the data architecture needed to develop systems.

To see how the data is used 'in motion' requires a data flow diagram. Again, this is a proven structured analysis technique which takes the business activities in the original top−down/decomposed form and establishes the flow of data in and around them. For the moment, it is perfectly valid to assume that data will be stored (at rest) for each entity in the model, and that data elements (attributes of the entities) will flow around the business and be used by the activities.

It is reasonable and advisable to develop a data flow diagram levelled in the same way as the business activities. The higher levels are simplistic but they allow a progression to more detail in a structured and consistent manner. As an example, consider the following extract shown in Figure 6.8 which decomposes activity 2 'Schedule service'.

By examining all three levels it can be seen that the systems planner is still looking at generalisations, in terms of stores of data, activities and dataflows. As analysis progresses (hopefully beyond the systems planning stage), the stores will become real files (and a schedule may become several different files

Figure 6.8 Data flow
analysis for 'data in
motion'

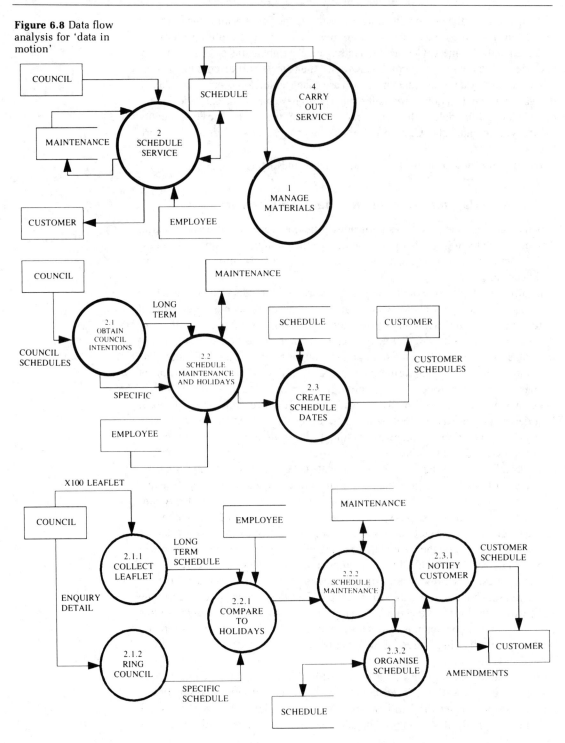

of schedule data). The activities will certainly become more detailed than 'organise schedule' (2.3.2 on the diagram) and the packets of data such as 'long term schedule' will be broken down to discrete data elements.

From stages 1, 2, 3 and 4 we now have an impressive portfolio of information to take us into the next step. To recap, the portfolio is:

Business organisation structure
Business activity diagram (Figure 6.3)
Business and functional goals/objectives
Business information model
● Entity descriptions — Table 6.1
● Function/entity matrix — Table 6.2
Data architecture
● Entity model — Figure 6.7
● Data flow diagram — Figure 6.8

Now we can start to sub-divide the business functions and data architecture into 'systems'. There are three principal objectives in doing this:

● To group business functions logically to form the scope of the system. From the systems planner's view, this makes best use of the data achitecture.
● To come up with an initial view of how systems can be deployed to help achieve the objectives of the functions within the scope, paying particular attention to systems operating across business functions. This is again the notion of planning for systems integration. It really is much easier at this stage!
● To provide a sensible approach to sequencing and prioritising the systems. Some systems will undoubtedly be fundamental to the operation of the whole enterprise, others will aim towards a narrower and perhaps more specialised function.

The level at which the systems will be specified is high. Without completing detailed systems analysis, we can only work with the generalisations mentioned earlier. However, they are perfectly satisfactory to enable us to develop a systems plan.

By examining the needs for storing, manipulating and reporting the information in our data architecture, we can obtain a systems equivalent. Our earlier example may look something like Figure 6.9 when completed. From this, it can be seen that a scheduling system will be needed and is likely to be central to most other activities. In order to schedule, data is needed from the council, and from maintenance records and employee details. The scheduling system will certainly need to interface to whatever arrangements are made for customer liaison. Also, the maintenance and personnel systems will generate transactions of cost to the business. This small representation shows how the systems planner will establish the role of the system in helping to achieve business activities and goals. At this stage it will suffice to have an outline scope for each system and its major

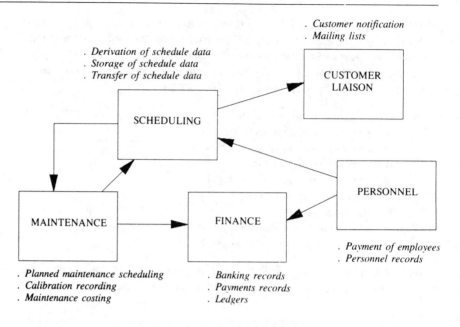

Figure 6.9 System architecture for Wheelie Bin washing

. *Customer notification*
. *Mailing lists*

. *Derivation of schedule data*
. *Storage of schedule data*
. *Transfer of schedule data*

CUSTOMER LIAISON

SCHEDULING

PERSONNEL

MAINTENANCE

FINANCE

. *Payment of employees*
. *Personnel records*

. *Planned maintenance scheduling*
. *Calibration recording*
. *Maintenance costing*

. *Banking records*
. *Payments records*
. *Ledgers*

interfaces. We can begin to see how these systems should be sharing data and where that data logically resides.

In a 'green field' situation, all the systems will emanate from the one planning process and it is a matter for business management to establish their relative importance. Again, some of these decisions will be taken for you, in that some systems are 'core'. For example, any company selling a very complex product to very few customers is more likely to require design and manufacturing systems in advance of sales and marketing support, whereas the converse is true for simple products in large and complex markets. This is, of course, if resourcing and prioritisation are an issue, as they are for most of us.

For each system derived in this fashion, there will be some basic information to push forward into the detailed analysis and design. Minimally this should be as follows:

> system name;
> system description;
> business activities supported/objectives supported;
> key user area;
> entities created or used;
> principal flows of data;
> system interfaces;
> major system functions required;
> a view of complexity/cost/resource.

5.   *Plan and develop systems*

Assuming success so far, it should be a relatively straightforward matter to establish the sequence in which the business needs the systems and how much resource is allowable. There will be an anxious systems development department ready to dig deep into the detail, so control at this stage is vital. The real spend is about to begin! The role of the systems planner now changes to that of refinement and monitoring.

After several years (hopefully) it may be necessary to go through the process again. We do not intend to discuss planning or systems development here, although there is a discussion of practical approaches to development in Chapter 7. The data administration skills give way to those of general systems development and project management. However, we will look at the feedback loop next, which is the monitoring role of the systems planner.

6.   *The feedback loop*

Figure 6.2 described the ideal approach to systems planning. The whole process should really be covered in less than six months. In parallel with systems planning, a whole range of IT and non-IT activities will be taking place. These will include the selection of hardware strategies, communications strategies, development environments, software tools and languages, and many more not in the principal remit of the systems planner. Assuming we are ready to go when the systems plan is available, the feedback loop swings straight into action.

This allows us to check continuously that our original thinking was sound and that any changes in the make-up of the business framework are being taken into account. The following points need to be checked in detail:

- The business activity models must still reflect the way that the company is going to operate. In new or radically changing organisations, it is not uncommon for whole new functions to spring up over night (and others to become defunct), thereby introducing new and changed business activities. In performing these activities, the aim will be to achieve company objectives, and systems support will be needed. Are we still able to provide it within our current set of models and plans?
- Is the information model still relevant for the new activities, containing all the required entities, and capable of supporting the business? We said earlier that the basic building block of the business information model — the entity — is enduring and unlikely to change, but it is certainly not impossible. If there is change, then the data architecture may also need to change.
- Does the data architecture (models of data at rest and data in motion) reflect the information needs of the business? As soon as the basic building blocks change or new activities manipulate the data differently, then the architecture is compromised. A change to the entity model can be very costly where the

database structure has already been established. Less dramatic is a change to the flow of data, as long as the data is in existence somewhere in the architecture. If the architecture is still sound, however, the next step is to consider the systems being developed.

- Are all developments keeping within the agreed architecture? Everything we have discussed so far has been the fruits of a careful planning process with a deliberate global view. To introduce a little system on one side, not originally considered and needing unplanned data entities, will start to rot the fabric of the architecture. Once it starts it will go on! Needless to say, the plans for developing the systems will need constant monitoring.
- Do the systems we have carefully planned and developed actually help us to achieve our original objectives? Alas, too many organisations find that this is not the case. This usually leads to expensive re-writes of systems, or a continual enhancement programme.

So far, then, we have established an ideal way of planning systems. Not many organisations will be in a green field situation and the theory might not work in its entirety, but the approach is still valid even for partial systems building programmes. The practice, though, can differ considerably, and there are plenty of reasons why it can't always work as the text books would like. In the next section, we discuss a more practical approach to systems planning.

The realities of strategic information planning

As mentioned earlier, strategic information planning is a dilemma to the organisation which wants well thought-out and architecturally sound systems but which wants them now! Quite often the first priority is convincing the company to make a start. In the 'green field' situation described earlier there is a fighting chance. With suitably IT-orientated senior management and a persuasive IT chief, the mechanism can be sold. As we move away from 'green field' to progressively more established systems users, the benefits of 'going back to the very beginning' may seem obscure.

At this point, we need to bring out the concept shown in Figure 6.2, which demonstrates graphically that systems plans must be allowed to change with evolving data and information architectures, which in turn are changing to mirror new business activities and objectives. In the majority of organisations there is plenty of change happening at this level and to pretend it won't affect the systems is the first step to IT obscurity. Statistics quoted in some of the popular computing periodicals suggest that 80% of organisations do not get value for money from their IT strategies. Inadequate systems planning is a major contributor.

This state of affairs comes about simply enough from a belief that systems can be developed at sufficiently low levels of detail for a finite user group, and that even without rigorous systems planning they will be architecturally sound and serve the whole enterprise. Not true! How many times have systems departments been criticised for producing systems which look good but don't actually do what was requested?

Quite often the problem lies not within the depth of the code of a particular system, but rather in the fact that the enthusiastic systems analyst has not been encouraged to concern herself or himself with the global philosophy of the business objectives and the ways in which they might change. This reality is one of those infuriating facts of life: 'Yes, it seems to be a sensible thing to do, but we'll just start the development anyway and then see if we are on the right track later on.' Later, we will examine some specific recommendations on ways round this, but in general terms the approach has to be as follows:

- Get senior management involved in it, not as an IT activity (as many senior people are still suspicious of IT), but as a business planning activity. At the end of the day, the systems are merely tools to help to achieve the business plan. If one of these people can be a champion for the exercise — all the better.
- Approach it as a team. The team will need careful selection to get the right balance of visionaries and pragmatists. The IT specialist can go through the mechanics but it needs individuals with business knowledge to achieve the goal.
- Set a finite timescale of between three and six months for a whole business — scale this down for obvious sub-functions where very clear boundaries exist. Beware of the risks of creating artificial boundaries, as this will lead to sub-architectures within the business framework, and they will quickly grow apart.
- Get the right level of detail. No more than, say, four levels of business activity diagramming should be developed. The results must be documented in a digestible form, otherwise the fruits of these efforts may simply gather dust.
- Be very clear about why a strategic information plan is necessary. If it is explained as an ivory tower IT department idea, it is dead. It is a fundamental business activity. Yes, we do want to end up with a stable, well-constructed set of databases and systems, but they will do nothing for the business if jointly they don't achieve the business objectives.

With any luck, the first hurdle (of at least starting the information planning process) can be negotiated. But ever close at hand will be the spectre of the point solution. Point solutions are systems designed to fulfil a very specific need for a very specific area of the business. They are usually narrow in scope and take no account of the broader strategic information systems plan. They are always very high priority and there is often a great deal of pressure to implement them. Quite often they are developed in the full knowledge that they are temporary, although 'temporary' can be a long time for some organisations.

Point solutions can be developed for expediency. This can be a powerful motive, which even a governing body committed to systems planning may find difficult to overcome. If the business is crying out for a system and the case is pleaded sufficiently well, in all probability it will be developed. This tends to be a fact of life which systems planners have to accept. The best we can do in these circumstances is to have the systems planner work closely with the development team. (S)he must attempt to guide the design along the line of closest fit to his or her view of the global systems and data architecture. This will inevitably lead to conflict, as point solutions invariably call for their own database architecture. No amount of argument will stop some data duplication being introduced.

If it were simply a question of extra disk space, this might not be so important. The data may have two 'prime authors' and may be manipulated differently. Very rarely will it say the same thing. Which value do we take to be true? If one of our point solutions tells the board of directors that stock is going through the roof and another point solution says it is within acceptable limits, what do we do?

Another less palatable reason for point solutions is parochial glory. Certainly, in this country, business tends to be viewed as series of functions which share the same roof. In the best case those functions interact efficiently, following some clear instructions for the good of the whole. In the worst case the functions operate entirely independently and perhaps even score points over each other. Perhaps you have heard comments such as the following in your own business?:

'Why don't sales stop over-selling the products we have no stock or supplier for?'

'Why can't design give us something we can make without all these problems?'

'How come personnel think we have five people when accounts say it is six?'

Happily, not many organisations suffer the worst case, but how many operate as a fully co-operative and integrated whole? Quite often, the functional blindness we all encounter is not malicious at all but is part of the fabric of the organisation as it has evolved over many years.

Even if all goes well and agreement is reached on the need for a systems plan, it is not a simple matter to produce it. The approach described earlier looks fairly straightforward, but it would be interesting for an organisation which is contemplating a systems plan to examine the credentials of the people who will be tasked with it. There is no wish to sound elitist here, but the quality of thought and vision required is quite high. Systems analysts brought up in the tradition of developing systems from the aspect of the point solution just described (and sadly there are many more than we would like) do not make good systems planners. By definition, those key business people who demand point solutions will struggle with global planning. Perhaps even the basic structured tools and techniques utilised in the examples will be totally unfamiliar to many IT and business people alike. So another reality we have to face is that there are some very basic skills needed to accomplish such an activity. You may not feel you have them. This should not mean that a system plan cannot be attempted, but it does mean that you need to be realistic about the depth and quality of the result.

There are, of course, ways round this. Many organisations employ specialist consultants to produce the plan, and this can be money well spent. Of course, the commitment has to be there to implement the architecture proposed. It must not be compromised immediately with point solutions, which may even be underway whilst the consultants are devising the plan. There may be several people currently in the organisation talented enough to do the task given some training in the tools and techniques of systems planning. However, these people must aleady possess the width of vision necessary to understand the complex relationships which exist across the whole business. There are also software tools available which purport to accomplish the task for you. Bearing in mind the old adage that a tool is only as good as the hand that wields it, this has to be true of software for systems planning. The real quality comes from the vision of business functional breakdown and the setting of objectives. The derivation of entity models and data flow diagrams should be more mechanical. That is not to say that the tools which are available are not useful. Some of them are very powerful and it is for each organisation to establish its own policy for them. However, the discussion in Chapter 7 will be relevant, as it is possible to select tools which use the data generated by the systems planning process as the raw material for systems development.

The popular term is, of course, I-CASE (interlinking tools which automate several phases of the life cycle). Although there is still a great deal of sales hype about their capabilities, many I-CASE tools are moving towards a single business development modeller. But of course this all costs money! It can be very difficult to justify these costs, and to an extent we are asking our overlords to take us on trust in doing a strategic information plan.

Keeping the business model up to date is a perennial problem. We discussed the feedback loop earlier. Many organisations pride themselves on becoming project orientated. In many ways this is the right thing to do, but it must be remembered that projects tend to have defined starts and finishes. The project becomes the all important measure. Systems people like to work on 'projects' and become concerned at the possibility of doing something not related to a project. The spectre of maintenance rears its head. In a sense, of course, the feedback loop of systems planning is maintenance, but it is extremely important maintenance. When discussed in the context of this chapter, most people would agree that it is vital. However, when the dust has settled and the excitement of developing the systems begins, then being on a project is what counts!

In the absence of a full-time systems planning function, the continued employ-ment of a data administrator (acting in the role of systems planner) will pay dividends. Using consultants, as suggested earlier, may leave you exposed. There is no solution other than selling the concept of systems planning well enough and getting the right value attached to it from those who are sufficiently high in the IT organisation and the rest of the business. The model will become out of date very quickly in any business with a healthy attitude to continued improvement and change for the better.

One reality which most organisations will have to face is the purchase of package software. Here we are faced with introducing a 'misfit' into the carefully planned jigsaw. 'Misfit' is used to indicate that the package will almost certainly have its own architecture and therefore will not readily fit into another architecture devised specifically for a whole business. The package may well be a very fine specimen and be a perfect point solution in its own right. In some organisations

Figure 6.10
Integration versus
interfacing

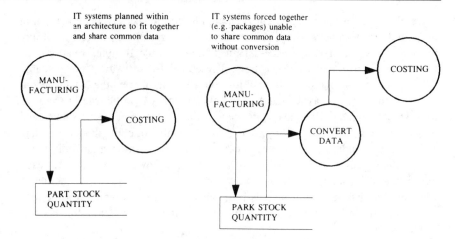

package solutions are the rule rather than the exception. This does not have to mean the total demise of the strategic information plan.

Indeed, to select the package in the first place it is highly advisable to construct the business information models as the 'ideal' and use this as criteria for selecting the package. At the other extreme, if one single package becomes the major force in the business, then a strategic information plan can be derived using this model as a basis and building the rest of the architecture around it. However, slotting packages into an independently prepared architecture will require a lot of patching up and building of bridges between systems. Where the ideal would be integration, the practice may be interfaces and conversion (Figure 6.10). This will introduce extra development, extra maintenance, increased possibility of corruption and perhaps data duplication. But, again, this can be an acceptable overhead in certain circumstances.

The systems planner can work around packages, but these can make life very difficult. The biggest danger is that the packages become the point solutions (and consequently receive due attention) while the patches and bridges become 'maintenance'. That is when the trouble starts along the road to systems integration. Who will stand back and look at the patchwork quilt? The system planner can, but what incentive is there? Packages are a means to an end (the systems plan), not a series of ends in themselves. Many organisations find themselves with the latter.

It would be naïve to assume that the carefully prepared systems plan is always the best solution. There will be many occasions when two systems should be developed, rather than the one depicted in a strategic information plan, utilising two similar databases rather than one complex one. The reasons for this apparent about-turn can be as diverse as geographical, disk space cost, processor preference, development time, data privacy, etc. The reality is that a strategic information plan will give a theoretical best fit which in practice may need toning down a little. Beware the cynics who may question the wisdom of carrying out the process at all.

Our recommendation is always to go to the extreme with the plan and backtrack a little for practical reasons, rather than set out with the intention of moving towards the ideal architecture from a series of point solutions. The reason for this is simple. The latter path will never work. Of course, it is easy to challenge this statement and ask how much extra effort and resource is involved in going on the point solution route. The answer will not be easy to give. However, the statistics (if true) show that most systems require significant maintenance and overhaul 1−3 years into their life. We would contend that a likely cause is lack of systems planning.

A practical approach to systems planning

At the beginning of this chapter we looked at an ideal way of achieving the strategic information systems plan. This is what we should be aiming for, but the realities just discussed conspire to make the ideal solution a pipe dream for many of us. All is not lost; there are still benefits to be gained from a more pragmatic approach. By adopting the ideal approach where possible, supplemented by the practical approach, success can be achieved. The concepts are as follows.

Set up an IT planning document

In a sense this has to be the Bible for systems development in the organisation. It is a strategic document which arises from the business planning process and should be the sole repository of corporate IT aims and objectives.

It is suggested that a specially formatted document is drawn up which contains the corporate aims and objectives for IT. This must be a 'live' document to help control the use of IT within stated guidelines. Its structure should be along the following lines:

- subject activity policies;
- data architecture and objectives;
- processing architecture and objectives;
- communications architecture and objectives;
- functional long term systems plans (5-year);
- corporate IT policies

Subject activity policies include activities such as: automated manufacturing, international sales, office automation, material handling, teleconferencing, etc. It is possible to see the relationship between these policies and the functional objectives discussed in the ideal approach. The functional long term systems plans relate even more closely to these. Here we are concerning ourselves with the needs of recognisable parts of the business, e.g. accounts, maintenance, stores, etc.

Let us look at this document in a little more detail.

Subject activity policies

These need to reflect the agreed approach to providing information technology and systems for key aspects of the business. Again, we can use the functional breakdown to help.

Let us say that we have a number of recognisable business areas for which systems are needed. The aim of the policy is to provide a scope (distilled from systems planning) within which systems can be developed, in the knowledge that they will be architecturally sound. The policies will also reflect the business goals and objectives which gave rise to systems planning activity. Examples could be as follows:

- Tool manufacturing: A real-time control system will be created to control, monitor and cost all tool work undertaken. The system will produce planning layouts, monitoring reports and costing information, work in progress location and discrete job status. The systems will be departmental comprising a local processor with a number of satellite screens and will be linked to the local area network. Compatibility and integration will be necessary with the production engineering monitoring system and engineering administration systems.

- Demand management: A rolling eighteen-month forecast arising from sales and operating planning will form the basis of the high-level production plan. Forecasts will be provided from historical usage. Forecasts will be consumed by actual orders within the order time horizon.

  Demand management will be controlled via the master production scheduling module of the manufacturing system residing on the mainframe.

Data architectures and objectives

As shown earlier, the data architecture should show the organisation of the data both at rest and in motion. The data at rest is represented by the entity model and the data in motion by the data flow diagram. In addition, it is wise to produce a database architecture diagram. An entity model will show a logical view of the business; the database architecture will show the physical representation of that view.

For the planning document, it is not wise to incorporate too much detail. Entity diagrams and data flow in minute detail for each and every corner of the business will probably cover every wall on the site. Leave the detail for the systems documentation; here we are concerned with corporate level guidelines.

The objectives for the data architecture form a part of the document. If they can be observed, then systems planning can be worthwhile.

The objectives should lay down corporate rules for systems development within the architecture. The policies will cover controlled data duplication/redundancy, frequency of global reviews of the architecture, rules for establishing new or changed entities within the model, and rules for implementing changes to the flow of data. The overriding reason for all of these is to ensure that data is used effectively and that different systems development teams can work simultaneously on different areas of the model without compromising one another unwittingly. It is not uncommon for data flows to disappear suddenly, rendering a system useless, because the feeder system has been taken out of commission

Processing architecture and objectives

In this section we establish the policies for using certain types of data processing equipment. In larger organisations, it is very likely that a mix of equipment will be used. It may be necessary for reasons of purchasing, systems integration, design criteria, and many more, to specify the criteria for using certain kinds of equipment. A possible example follows:

● All corporate systems	Mainframe based — IBM or compatible operating MVS/ESA utilising DB2 or VSAM file structures.
● All departmental systems	Mini-based — DEC VAX UNIX or VMS systems.
● All shopfloor cell control systems	DEC or IBM (or compatible) PC where a choice of host is not predetermined by equipment specification, e.g. flexible manufacturing system.
● Personal computing	IBM OS/2 or DOS

Data Administration tends not to be too concerned with the way the bits and bytes are processed, but a processing architecture may influence the choice of file handling products. This will have an impact on other aspects of data administration covered elsewhere.

Communications architecture and objectives

Like the processing architecture, this will be of secondary importance to the system planners as regards 'data'. However, it is mentioned here for completeness. The objective of the architecture is to provide a framework enabling inter-connection of different types of equipment (discussed in the processing architecture). An architecture may be typified by such policies as the ones listed below:

● Local area network:	Broadband and Baseband Ethernet. Bi-direction data transfers using DEC and IBM proprietary software. Link to wide area network via X25. Personal computer attached via PCSA. Links to DEC terminal servers.

- Wide area network: Remote communications connectivity to IBM processors via IBM 3745 controller. X25 packet switching and OSI terminal servers.

Like the processing architecture, the impact of the communications architecture on the systems planner should be minimal. At the conceptual data planning stage, physical implementation criteria are not welcome. That is not to say that system planners can ignore them. We would suggest that this is a function outside strategic information planning which may have a bearing on final physical implementations, for example in distributed databases. If a data planning exercise indicates the likely use of distributed databases, then communication feasibilities will be important.

Functional long term systems plans

Going back to Figure 6.2, which shows our ideal way to tackle systems planning, stage 5 is 'Plan and develop systems'. This section of the planning document should be a definitive summary of what those plans are. A five-year planning horizon is suggested, although that is a long time in our business. The plans should also be detailed by function. The functional decomposition will have shown the structure of the business and it will be enough to record systems plans by high-level groups, such as Product Design, Domestic Sales, Purchasing, etc.

Since global IT solutions have been so carefully defined, it is important to ensure that the planning document covers the cross-functional systems and recognises the importance of development without boundaries. The plans may very well include enhancement to existing systems, and upgrades to bought-out packages, as well as brand new developments arising from changes to our business goals. By committing to implement the plans in a document of this nature (all of which are or will become architecturally sound), the risk of the point solution is lessened.

Corporate IT policies

Unlike the subject activity policies which are mainly aligned to areas of the business and business practice, these policies should reflect corporate decisions on information technology itself. The kind of policy here may cover EDI (Electronic Data Interchange), word processing, bar coding, product identification, robotics, security, distributed databases, and any other policy related specifically to the technology itself rather than to its application.

Set up a data architecture service

The diagrams and components of the data architecture will quickly dissipate and fall into disuse if they are not co-ordinated as a single business tool. Once a Data Administration function is established in your organisation, this can be one of its tasks. In Chapter 7 we look at using the tools of data administration. The collection of data flow diagrams and entity models resulting from systems planning and systems development need to be used as a working blueprint of the organisation to assist the systems planner.

When the systems planner sits down to look at the business structure and functional goals, (s)he must be intimately acquainted with the existing data architecture. Without this, the system developer may reinvent the wheel each time. It is the knowledge of what data the business relies on now, how it is stored, and how it flows, which enables the planner to look at optimal ways of utilising the resource for changed requirements. As we said earlier, the business will be structured on a certain number of key entities. Unless there is a radical change in the business these entities will not change much. However, the method of storage can and will change, allowing the database architecture to move with the needs of the global systems view. The data flows will certainly change regularly. But so long as the basic structure is there, the data, to all intents and purposes, can flow in whatever way it is needed to flow. Encourage your Data Administration staff to cover their walls with the company data architecture. Just like the old principle of sticking diagrams to the bedroom wall to help revise for exams, this helps the architecture to become part of the planners' ingrained knowledge. These diagrams should be as important to the business as the utilities drawings are to Plant Maintenance or the product designs to Engineering or the chart of accounts to Finance. Make them look like it. Where packages are routinely employed,it is worth instructing the data administrator to obtain documentation either from the vendors, or by re-engineering the physical model. The aim is to illustrate the whole organisational data architecture.

Document the prime systems architecture

We have discussed the inevitable pressures on systems planning. It does not have an apparent usable deliverable, unlike system development. If time and resource are constrained, it is worthwhile trying to document the prime systems architecture. Every organisation will have core systems. When we examine the functional breakdown, there are always some very basic requirements which must be fulfilled. It is almost certain that these core systems will account for the derivation of 95 % of the company's key data. So one way of living with time restrictions is to make sure that energy is only expended on those core systems. There are no mechanistic rules or heuristics for selecting them. They will be fairly obvious.

No doubt, with further analysis, other sub-systems would be needed for this business, but they would not necessarily affect the key data items and would serve to detract from documenting the core systems.

The core systems will also give rise to the principal databases to be employed in the business. Bearing in mind that one of our main data administration aims is to reduce data redundancy, we must make these core databases the subject of our attention. Parallel development of non-core systems could spawn non-core databases. It is odds on that one system will revolve around 'components', another around 'items' and another around 'parts'. They are all the same but it is too late once the databases are in the architecture! It is one thing to notice this problem before systems are developed, and another to worry about it when there are several gigabytes of data floating around attached to the non-core databases.

The unenviable task of the data administrator is to develop the core databases, whilst being aware of the needs of the peripheral systems. It is possible that the only recourse for the data administrator will be to notify senior IT management of potentially harmful non-core activity and to hope for the necessary veto.

Formalise integration

Systems integration always seems to crop up when discussing those aspects of systems development with which people encounter most difficulty. Here we are not interested in multitudes of technical software products and black boxes which offer painless integration. There is no such thing. We are talking about genuine data sharing across systems to meet global needs. One of the realities we discussed earlier on gives a clue: the concept of the 'project'. When analysed, the project has a stated scope and goals, and all the participants are fired up to achieve them. Let us just assume that we are in a non-ideal organisation where system planning is not top priority and point solutions are frequently observed. Projects will often be set up around the needs of a point solution implementation. In a reasonably organised project, there will be such tasks as 'identify high-level interfaces' or 'document interfacing systems'. The intention is good, that is, to develop the point solution, not forgetting that it may need to work with other systems. It is quite possible to be developing two simultaneous point solutions, both documenting each other as interfacing systems.

Somehow, though, the interfacing parts of the solution seem to receive the status of second class citizens. Quite often their development is the result of policies determined by the point solution.

In the simple example shown in Figure 6.11 we have three point solutions occupying the position of islands in the sea. Projects will undoubtedly be geared

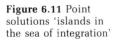

Figure 6.11 Point solutions 'islands in the sea of integration'

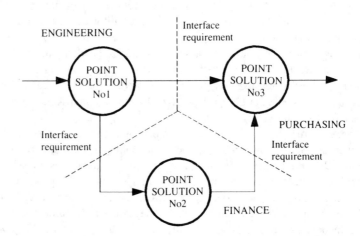

up to design perfect islands. The interfaces will be incidental, particularly where they cross functional boundaries. What we are proposing is to turn this argument on its head, such that projects are raised and conducted specifically to develop the interfaces. The islands can then be designed with clear input/output objectives to complete the bigger picture. Only by giving them the status of project will interfaces get the enthusiasm and attention needed to develop a fully linked systems architecture.

In order to make integration projects more visible, they need to be recognised as such. It is reasonable in the systems development methodology to conduct each development and/or integration project to stated goals and scope. Each type of development needs its own characteristics and documentation. Of course, the integration projects are more likely to depend on the 'data in motion' part of the data architecture than the database or 'data at rest' architecture.

Integration projects can also be set up as feasibility studies. It is advisable very early in the development life cycle to conduct an integration project with the specific objective of raising integration issues. This may be the only deliverable. The resolution of the issues then becomes the input to the development of the systems. Rather than integration issues arising from the development (and sometimes being buried again), they are produced up-front and, being visible, give the developers clear goals which must be met. Whilst we are concerned primarily with data issues, there is every reason why technological, economic or ergonomic issues, with their associated integration implications, should also be aired as early as possible.

Develop a suitable life cycle

The systems development life cycle can very often be at fault by limiting the scope of developers to starting with feasibility and ending with implementation. As this chapter has repeatedly stressed, the crucial aspects of developing a system within an architecture come before feasibility studies. Interestingly enough, many life cycles take little account of post-implementation operation, audit and refinement of systems. The life cycle must be intrinsically linked to the business development process, which, as we have seen, is the prime mover for IT requirement. For systems planning purposes, the life cycle must reflect the activities discussed, even for the more pragmatic approach. Point solutions arise from feasibility studies, which in themselves can often be biased towards a particular end result. The development life cycle is discussed in more detail in the next chapter.

Enlist the services of the system controllers

In the likely event of any reader wanting to establish some system planning but already having point solutions, packages, planned systems and so on, then use the people who know the business best to maximum advantage. In Chapter 3 we introduced the very important role of system controller. This could be the single most important decision taken. No better ally can be found to further the systems planning process, assuming that you can sell the concept well. This should not be too difficult. The role of system controller in systems planning is basically to be the key user who will help the planner through the stages shown in Figure 6.2. In particular, the system controller should develop the function's objectives and business processes to enable a data model to be constructed.

Of course, where a network of system controllers does not exist, several key IT-orientated users can be selected to perform a similar function in aiding the process of systems planning and progress towards a more stable data architecture.

Summary

In this chapter we have discussed the concept of strategic information systems planning. This is a rigorous method of converting business goals and operations into a co-ordinated systems strategy which will make best use of resources and provide a comprehensive IT service to the business. As with most good ideas in theory, there are practical drawbacks and difficulties. We looked at some of these: being unable to sell the idea because of the lack of an immediately apparent payback; point solutions for short term glory or parochial desires; a lack of the right skills or tools; keeping a company data model up to date; and package solutions which ride roughshod over a carefully planned data architecture. Notwithstanding these difficulties, it is our contention that systems planning is a worthwhile data administration service.

To this end, we have offered some ideas on a more pragmatic approach. Principally this involves: the use of a planning document formalised in the business; provision of a formal service to enable systems planning using professional 'data' people; documenting the prime systems rather than trying to cover everything; looking at integration issues as preventive measures instead of as undesirable side effects of systems development; developing a systems life cycle which gives systems planning a recognised role; and enlisting the help of the system controllers (where they exist) to think 'business'.

Systems planning could be the toughest aspect of data administration to implement. It will be the least popular systems activity for developers, because it delays them. It can be misconstrued as being of academic interest. It could also be the key to better systems, reduced maintenance and easier systems integration. It is worth a try!

Key action points

- Establish a structured life cycle approach to planning systems, encompassing objectives, activity models, information models and systems and data architectures.
- Formalise the constant monitoring of the quality of the approach via the feedback loop.
- Implement an IT planning document to act as the Bible for planning and delivering systems within agreed policies and architectures.

- Establish a systems planning capability involving Data Administration, the development function and system controllers.
- Ensure full documentation (objectives, business functions, data models, specifications) of the prime systems where resourcing is difficult.
- Formalise integrations between systems as projects in their own right.

7 Methods and tools

In this chapter we will be examining the systems development environment in which Data Administration will be trying to make its presence felt. It is important to establish a very basic concept in the organisation, that is, 'Data is a prime asset.' Methodologies, life cycles, software tools, and so on, will therefore be tailored to provide an environment in which data is the key currency. The alternative is, of course, an environment which encourages the development of procedurally based systems which model the ways in which people or machines perform tasks rather than how they use data. This is an important observation.

Having reached this conclusion, Data Administration can obtain rich rewards from having a data-driven environment in which to work. Life cycles or tools can be selected and used in such a way as to further the overall Data Administration effort. With this in mind, we will look at dictionaries and software engineering tools, as well as techniques such as data flow diagramming and entity modelling. The objective here is to emphasise the data administration requirements, not to do an in-depth study of systems development techniques and software tools. There are plenty of books and salesmen prepared to do that!

Establishing a methodology for data administration

The majority of readers will be working for organisations which already have some kind of methodology. This may be an extremely formal approach, possibly a recognised standard such as SSADM, or a more informal and loose 'way things have always been done'. The general systems development reasons for having a methodology are usually as follows:

- consistent documentation style;
- consistent quality;
- flexibility of staff to pick up work in various areas;
- familiarity of developers with techniques;
- reduced development lead times by selecting a standard and familiar approach;
- auditability and improvement against known standards;

and probably others besides. Whatever the reasons, they are defined to be of assistance to the systems development process. They may not be of similar assistance to the data administrator. However, it is possible to come up with a methodology to benefit both. Throughout this book we draw comparisons between the theory and the practice. In practice, many IT functions are pushed down the path of delivering solutions without due regard to data administration principles. The process of systems development is no different. To combat this we recommend the implementation of a methodology which does look after the interests of Data Administration. This does not have to mean weird and wonderful methodologies to rival such tried and tested favourites as SSADM or LSDM. It is possible to take any current methodology (particularly those mentioned) and adapt them subtly.

Let us look first at what we would hope to achieve from such a methodology:

- a systems development life cycle which allows data administration principles to be built in at the appropriate point;
- audit points within the life cycle to allow the data administrator to comment objectively on the emerging design;
- tasks within the methodology that are specifically aimed at data administration;
- deliverables from the methodology to allow Data Administration to comment on the system design, but more importantly on the corporate data model, systems integration and global data flows;
- tools and techniques complementary to the methodology which work for data administration.

If we can propose a new or modified methodology to achieve this, then we are well on the way to making our systems development function and data administration compatible. This is the overall intention of course, but, as we have repeatedly said, it is very often not realised.

Systems development life cycle

From the discussion so far, we can see that data administration needs a life cycle which encourages the principles to be considered at the right time by undertaking the appropriate tasks with the appropriate audit or check points. There are many variations on life cycles, all achieving roughly the same goal. However, there is an argument to extend the life cycle, at both ends, beyond what is traditionally accepted. The reasons for this will become clear and are related in the main (but not entirely) to data administration principles.

Figure 7.1 represents a life cycle which is quite typical of many variations in existence within the industry. To be fair, many organisations do now use structured techniques to dissociate functional and data analysis before combining the results in a construction phase. However, the point here is not so much what goes on during the cycle but what should be achieved before, during and after the stages depicted here.

In Chapter 6 we discussed the difficulties of strategic systems planning at length.

Figure 7.1 A typical systems development life cycle

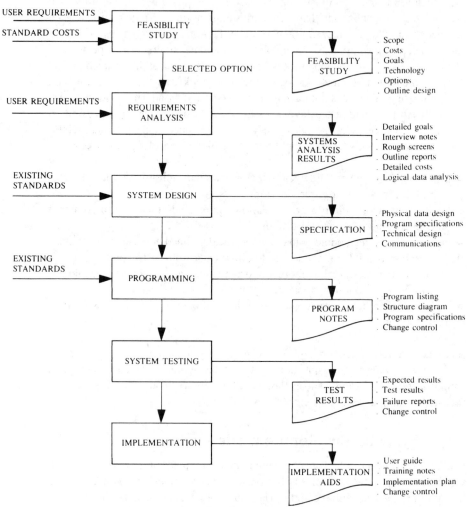

Where in Figure 7.1 is this done? Feasibility? Well, perhaps, but it is our experience that feasibility studies tend to incorporate assumptions about the system requirements rather like those inherent in point solutions. In other words a narrower scope, limited user base, parochial requirements, and pre-ordained design. Some feasibility studies genuinely examine multiple options, but often there is only really one option; the others are there for comparative or even decorative purposes. We can be certain that strategic systems planning does not take place any further into the cycle.

Also in an earlier chapter (Chapter 5), we examined the importance of authorship and how the users must have control over their data. This does not happen automatically. There has to be a defined approach to it, which can quite easily be accommodated in a user interface design phase (as described later, p. 110). Chapter 5 also discussed the need for an overall control on the specification of new data items, using existing data and avoiding unnecessary duplication.

In the later stages of the cycle there are the many data-related activities involved in running a production system. This is an important point. Many life cycles fail to give full recognition to the 'operational' phase of the system, which is usually longer than all of the development phases put together and is just as likely to make or break the system.

Having now looked in outline at how the traditional life cycle is deficient, we can concentrate on Figure 7.2, which represents a life cycle more conducive to successful data administration. Correspondingly, we need to understand the data administrator's responsibilities during the life cycle. Here we need to recognise the existence of a lot of strategic planning taking place well in advance of a project being raised. Remember that the success of a project viewed in isolation is a very different matter to its success as a piece of a much larger jigsaw. The key activity is 'Develop IT strategy'. There are major inputs here from similarly strategic activities. 'Develop business plan' allows the kind of analysis to take place which we described in Chapter 6, that is, the systematic review of business goals, changes to business policies and practices and corporate relationships. In 'Develop proposal' we hope to take business- or IT-driven proposals which are of such a nature as to affect the whole enterprise. This may involve totally radical initiatives such as EPOS, automated design, robotics in manufacturing, home banking, etc.; in other words, not simple departmental system aids (although they will contribute to the IT strategy). In a similar vein 'Review IT market place' is a proactive study of innovations in information technology which, it is felt, will benefit the organisation. Something like EDI may fall into this category. These innovations may not have been the subject of a proposal, yet it is worth considering a place for them. An important part of developing the IT strategy is to take cognisance of the systems already in service to ascertain their growth potential, relevance to current company goals and continued architectural fit (as described in Chapter 6). This is the stage where an IT planning document and architectures are available. Systems developed arising from this architecture will be Data Administration approved! This part of the life cycle must drive that which follows.

Following the diagram we now move into more familiar phases. 'Launch projects', as the name implies, seeks to set about the IT plan by marshalling resources and defining what is required, commonly presented in project terms of reference. For the data administrator, this can be an important document. The developers will by now be suffering from project fever. The temptation will be great to rush off into the depths of analysis and design, leaving behind the carefully prepared strategic systems plans and architectures. The Terms of Reference should make it clear how the developers should seek to fit their project into the global plan. Wherever resources permit, the Data Administration function should be represented on the project (probably part-time) to 'assist' the developers in

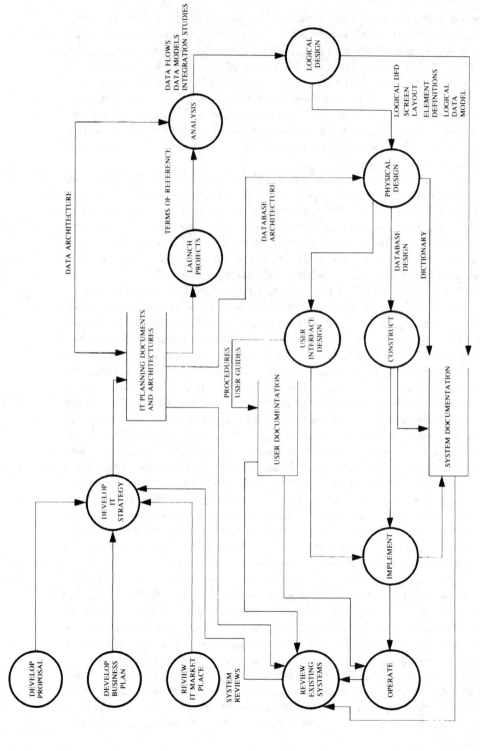

Figure 7.2 A systems development life cycle to assist Data Administration

achieving this. Usually, this is seen as interfering, but data administrators tend to develop thick skins.

Let's move on to 'Analysis'. This phase may well be sub-divided into a feasibility study for justification and a more detailed requirements definition. However, Data Administration is now looking for architectural fit and overall control of the company's data resource. At this point, the level of detail to be dealt with increases significantly. The whole essence of structured systems analysis is to move through successive levels of detail to arrive at data items and 'mini-specs' of the lowest levels in order to establish a firm basis for synthesising an effective method of processing the data.

Once into this phase of the development all thought of high-level company goals and corporate data models will be cast aside. This is why it is so important to have Data Administration either participating in the project or reviewing its results. Shortly, we will be discussing the way to present these results so that Data Administration can achieve this. Principally, the techniques are data flow, data models, decision trees and an analysis phase dictionary for collecting definitions of the data items. Also in this phase we have the continuation of an activity which we introduced in Chapter 6 'Strategic systems integration'. During the early stages of IT development, the integration studies point out the issues associated with fitting systems together into a jigsaw. Inevitably, the level of detail during system planning can be fairly high and rightly deals with corporate-level implications of systems integration. Some of the issues will be carried on into the analysis phase for resolution at a more practical level, such as agreeing prime authorship between departments and systems.

Whatever the documentation employed to end this phase, it must allow Data Administration to understand the system itself and the way in which it will fit within a data architecture. This is very much a point of no return as far as corporate Data Administration is concerned. Beyond this the die is cast!

'Logical design' should now be using the agreed data specification in order to create the best logical solution. Just as the analysis seeks to splinter the whole scope into data elements, flows, models, and so on, here we are concerned with the synthesis of the data. The data administrator is more likely to be needed as an additional quality check than a corporate data guardian. The importance of the QA check should not be under-estimated, however. It is still easy enough for the developers to create data duplication without that vigilance. Given, however, that the logical design is a true representation of the analysis done earlier, then the 'Physical design' can take place with confidence. In this book we have been concentrating on the role of the data administrator. It is not our intention to dig into the mechanics of database administration. Let us just say that the relationship between the two is extremely important and if the data administrator has done the job well up until now the database administrator will achieve success. Of course, there are some basic principles to be observed in not introducing redundant or unnecessary data to the database design. Any reader wanting to pursue this subject will find many specific texts on the subject of good database design. It is worth mentioning here that the database architecture will be a key deliverable.

This architecture is a component of the IT planning document which contains the Data (and Database), Processing and Communications architectures. Also, the data dictionary now enters the scene as the tool with which to document the data structures. At the conclusion of this phase we should know everything we need to know in terms of what the software system will look like.

One further aspect of physical design that is worth mentioning is the inclusion of self-checking or auditing facilities within the software design. The objective is to monitor the quality of the data as part of the routine operation of the system. Auditing is an arduous task at best; the more we can automate the more likely it is that the system controllers will actively monitor data quality continuously. The kind of check required is not the same as that made by good DBMS (referential integrity) where logical links between data entities are checked for consistency during routine updates. The checks required relate to values of data. For example, the physical characteristics of a data element may allow for a value of 999 in a three-character field. The application may be such that values for that data element are, on average, 650. Low values may be of the order of 200−300 and high values 750−850. Values above 850 may be suspect and require investigation.

More complex examples are, of course, likely such as checking the value of moving average figures within certain control limits, percentage of zero value fields or imbalances between expected ratios. As soon as the data gives suspect messages it needs to be checked. This is a very important role for the software designed here.

'Construct', as the name implies, goes on to build the system, primarily programming and database work. The data administrator is involved minimally here, again probably in a quality sense.

The 'User interface design' phase, however, is one where the data administrator and the system controllers collaborate to set up the system for data integrity and authorship. In our earlier discussions, we looked at the reasons for setting up authorship procedures and integrity measures. This is the point at which they are first examined. Everything should be known about the design and the data by now. When this process is complete, then the data administrator can add the information to the data administration dictionary (described fully in Chapter 5). Another key activity at this stage is the development of security measures. Again, earlier discussion (Chapter 4) showed the importance of physical and logical data security, strategic measures to protect links between systems, and data protection/privacy measures. The results of this phase are absolutely vital to the success of running the system for maximum data integrity. A good solid education package is essential in order to emphasise these points to the users involved. This is a service that Data Administration should take very seriously.

'Implementation' speaks for itself. The data administrator should be concerned with checking the successful implementation of the items discussed above. To many software developers, implementation is a purely technical function involving some final testing, change control and sleepless nights. The impact to the user community is of equal significance.

The 'Operational' phase of the system is one where Data Administration and the system controllers play a very important part. Many of the activities described in detail in other chapters are a result of this phase. Problems will occur with the data (especially integration and data sharing) which need an expert's view (Chapter 9). All of the security measures should be rigorously applied and checked and double checked. The data should be used as widely as possible and utilised in end user computing applications where this is beneficial (Chapter 8).

Continuous measures of data integrity are needed to ensure that the business achieves the desired goals and, more importantly, doesn't suffer adversely through poor data (Chapter 5).

The next phase is the end of the cycle, or, alternatively, the beginning, depending on your view. Here the data administrator should be acting as a catalyst to help the systems developers to 'Review' current systems in order to check for continued achievement of business goals and continued fit within the architectures. Doubtless, other new systems are being formulated which may affect the operation of an older system. Integration issues raise their heads and before we know it the cycle is off again. It is important that the data administrator is able to understand this concept and does not become too project orientated. Projects start and end; data administration goes on.

Tools and techniques

During the discussion on the life cycle, we touched upon some of the techniques which may be employed to assist Data Administration (such as data flow, data modelling, etc.). There was no such discussion on tools such as code generators, analyst workbenches, dictionaries, etc. It is hoped to remedy that now; however, the whole scene associated with CASE, development environments and advanced programming languages is so complex and changeable that a detailed discussion here would deflect from the true intentions of the book. We will consider the subject as an outline to the type of tools and techniques that a data administrator would use.

Firstly, we will discuss techniques. Earlier we alluded to procedurally based systems. Happily, there are few around these days. They come from the school of thought that a clerical procedure could be examined and a system written to mirror exactly what it did. Of course, many clerical procedures utilise exactly the same data and so we have all the associated problems of data duplication and redundancy. Even with current techniques there are no guarantees of not falling into this trap. However, the chances of good data design took a major step forward with the work of such people as Gane and Sarson, and Demarco.

Data flow diagramming

Data administration must be based on sound data-driven techniques. One very useful technique is data flow diagramming. There can be no better way of illustrating the way data is used graphically, whether in a corporation or a sub-routine. It is important to implement data flow diagramming fully to ensure that

Figure 7.3 One
possible data flow
convention

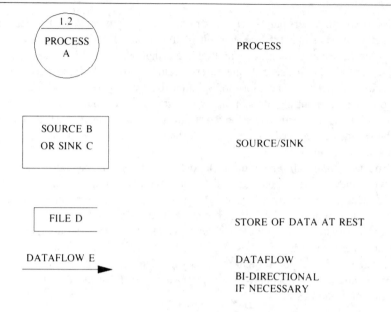

levelling and partitioning are employed to best advantage. The course or book most favoured by the data administrator will determine convention, such as whether squares or circles are used for processes. It matters not. One very popular convention is shown in Figure 7.3.

The biggest challenge to be faced is to get data flow established as a part of the business fabric. It is one thing for the DP department to use data flow diagrams, quite another for the sales director. However, it can be done. As with anything else, if you can persuade a well-respected external consultant to say that it should be done, your chances are improved considerably. Failing that, a simple proposal should be made which addresses the issue at grass roots level in the following terms:

- Data is a prime asset. It would be inconceivable for the finance director not to be able to see where all the cash was tied up or for the engineering director not to be able to find a drawing of a major component. Why, therefore, should we not be able to see what data we have and where it is?
- Data is a truly cross-functional resource in that much of it crosses departmental boundaries thousands of times a day. Is any other asset manipulated on such a widespread basis?
- We want to get the best return on our asset; therefore we use it carefully, everywhere we can, as often as we can. We certainly do not want to duplicate that asset more than is necessary.
- Data (and information) is rapidly becoming the major currency flowing through the business to enable goals to be achieved. Good team work demands that the whole enterprise understands the goals and can 'see' the method of achieving local and global goals.

- The procedural set-up of a business is now most likely to revolve around the processing of data and information. On a corporate scale we must be able to demonstrate graphically what procedures are necessary to achieve the data manipulation.

A picture is worth a thousand words, so the saying goes. Data flow is a classic example of this in that a narrative description of even simple data flows and manipulations becomes difficult to understand (or visualise) very quickly. A diagram is very much easier to deal with. Personal experience has proved this idiom many times in several businesses of differing types.

A technique such as this will not be introduced as a big bang. You are in for a huge disappointment if you want to see the whole DP function and user community using data flow the following day. The best method of introducing it is to build up slowly from a starting-point. The starting-point is a corporate data view.

The corporate data flow diagram will start life by being wrong. Accept that fact from the start. Data flow theory allows for several iterations of top–down decomposition before the higher levels are accurate. In essence it is the lower levels which are of most use to the developer. The higher levels are most useful in the strategic planning phases. The data administrator is involved at all levels. The best approach is to have a stab in the dark at putting down the major functional activities with their primary inputs and outputs. In Chapter 6 we discussed the role of data flow in strategic planning. Inevitably, as the levels of diagram go down into departments and jobs and documents, there will be all kinds of mismatches. A few of them will result in key changes to higher-level assumptions. In some cases the effect will be to change the representation at corporate level. However, with effort it is possible to balance up the data flows and for them to reflect accurately the origins and destinations of data, manipulation of data, storage of data and flow of data between processes and stores. Of course, the lowest levels of diagram can represent individual data items and programs. The hope for a completely balanced and harmonious view of data from top to bottom is impractical. The major benefits of visual tools such as data flow can be achieved without this absolute accuracy. (Interestingly, the only possible way to work towards a perfect representation of data in an organisation is graphically.)

Figure 7.4 shows how data flow helps the data administrator to construct a view of the business data and how it is used across departments and within the department. This view is primarily a physical view. It is the most useful view to share with the user as it will hold recognisable pieces of data and documents and stores. The main point about it is that it still reflects procedure at this stage. Whilst the diagram can show what people actually do and use, then it will hold some attraction for them.

Just on a practical note it is as well to observe the basic rules for data flow as propounded in any guideline on the subject. These are as follows:

- Use levelling to ensure that no one level is too complex.

Figure 7.4 Physical data flow down to procedure analysis

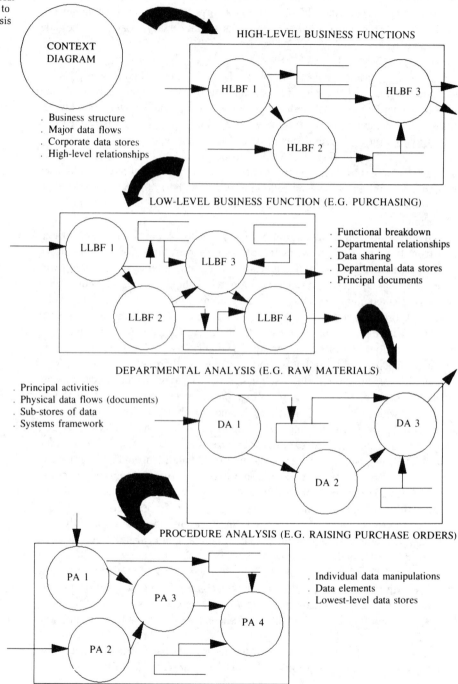

CONTEXT DIAGRAM

. Business structure
. Major data flows
. Corporate data stores
. High-level relationships

HIGH-LEVEL BUSINESS FUNCTIONS

HLBF 1
HLBF 2
HLBF 3

LOW-LEVEL BUSINESS FUNCTION (E.G. PURCHASING)

LLBF 1
LLBF 2
LLBF 3
LLBF 4

. Functional breakdown
. Departmental relationships
. Data sharing
. Departmental data stores
. Principal documents

DEPARTMENTAL ANALYSIS (E.G. RAW MATERIALS)

. Principal activities
. Physical data flows (documents)
. Sub-stores of data
. Systems framework

DA 1
DA 2
DA 3

PROCEDURE ANALYSIS (E.G. RAISING PURCHASE ORDERS)

PA 1
PA 2
PA 3
PA 4

. Individual data manipulations
. Data elements
. Lowest-level data stores

- Use partitioning to break the whole scope down to recognisable parts.
- Number processes clearly and keep the level numbering consistent.
- Always show where the data comes from and goes to.
- Ensure that the diagrams are balanced, i.e. the net input and output at level n is the same as at level $n - 1$.
- Show clearly where data stores are referenced only, or where they are referenced and changed.

An additional observation is that the use of a draughting package will save a great deal of time and heartache in all these changes. In addition, a professionally produced diagram has more chance of being used. The diagrams produced in this way (physical diagrams) should be distributed. Making them visible contributes greatly to their acceptance. Put a few on departmental notice boards, in project team areas and on managers' office walls. Make the company's data visible!

The question of what level of data flow diagram should be commonly distributed is a fair one. As Figure 7.4 would indicate, there are potentially many levels between the company overview and the grass roots activity analysis. In our experience the desired effect can be gained from the major business function view (perhaps first or second level). This diagram will serve to show how finance picks up manufacturing costs, how sales place real orders for materials, how purchasing interacts with stores management, and so on. Development teams will, of course, require lower-level, more detailed diagrams in addition to the overall diagram.

Above all, remember that the levelled data flow diagrams are the company's data architecture (for data in motion). If you are successful in doing some systems planning, then they are live documents which will have a profound effect on systems development later.

Whilst data flow should be a technique employed throughout the IT function, it is a good idea to set up a centre of excellence provided by Data Administration. The objectives of this are to provide the following:

- technical guidance;
- consistency of style, levelling and presentation;
- fit within global data architecture;
- Data Administration knowledge of all data developments;
- overall protection and maintenance of the diagrams.

To complete the discussion on data flow for Data Administration, it is worth noting the further decomposition of low-level diagrams into logical views of data. Here the currency is literally data items and logical groupings of data into stores. The data administrator will find life much easier if the development function continues to produce graphical representations of the systems under development. These data items are the very ones which will populate the Data Administration dictionary (Chapter 5).

Entity modelling

In the discussion on data flow we encountered the concept of 'data in motion' being pictorially represented for our data architecture. With entity modelling, the primary goal is the documentation of 'data at rest'. Again, there are different approaches to this technique and (your) developers will implement one which suits the IT function. However, the data administrator is anxious to understand the 'things' or entities in the business about which data is needed. Unlike data flow, entity models will not mean a great deal to users, and at the end of the day the user wants to see data turning up on screens or reports without worrying unduly how it is stored behind the scenes.

Chapter 6 explained how an entity model may take shape for a business. The technique here is really only breaking it down into more detail. The whole objective of developing entity models is to try to achieve stable yet flexible databases. Stable because it is an expensive business to continually redesign them (plus all the appropriate application software), and flexible because we want to increase usefulness and longevity as we would with any asset. Whilst the actual achievement of these goals is in the hands of the database administrator, the conceptual model (information model of Chapter 6) is the charge of the data administrator. Figure 7.5 illustrates the way in which, between them, they can make a good effort at achieving end results which produce the data as it is needed at minimum cost and with the most efficient design.

The diagram shows the logical steps in producing data structures through the medium of entity modelling. The relevance of the entity model as described so far is much greater to the data administrator than to the database administrator. The sequence of events is as follows.

The entity model first appears, as described in Chapter 6, during strategic planning. This necessarily deals with an information model of a very high level. After project launch, the application under consideration will evolve as an entity model in its own right. The data administrator will be keen to ensure that the entities being analysed at this stage are derivatives of those higher in the structure. Whilst it is not inevitable that corporate-level entities will be decomposed, it is nevertheless quite likely. As an example, consider the following:

Corporate model	*Application model*
Entity = Account	Entities = Bank account
	Supplier account
	Expense account

It may not be necessary to maintain separate stores of data about each account type, but there may be a need for quite different applications handling specialised data about these different account types which necessitates an entirely separate data structure. It is the rationale in arriving at this conclusion which the data administrator is concerned with. The golden rule is not to allow unnecessary proliferation of the sub-entities through parochial application development. As

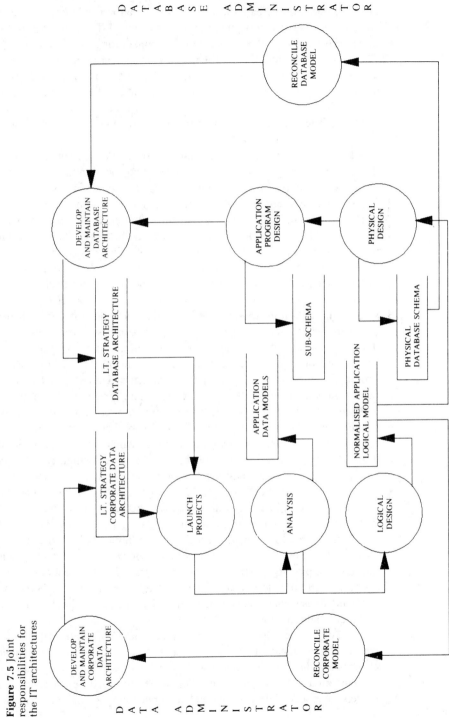

Figure 7.5 Joint responsibilities for the IT architectures

an illustration of this, let us assume that Application Developers A use 'Supplier Account' for balance of payment for goods received. Developers B use 'Rejected Material Account' for monies owed by the supplier for goods received but rejected. There is certainly an argument for at least investigating the possibility of using the same entity with all its attendant data attributes. Then, even if two separate applications are designed, it is not automatic that two lots of data will exist which require two lots of procedures for inputting two sets of values into two separate databases. The decisions regarding this are now made in the full understanding of the origins of the data.

A further effort to minimise the number of entities and attributes takes place during logical design through normalisation (expanded in the next section). This decomposes complex data structures into simple relationships between entities. The simpler the relationships are, the easier the design phases of the project. By starting with a purely logical file structure, the efficiency requirements of the design should be met with minimum physical modification. Physical features built into file structures rather than the processes using those structures make the database less flexible and more difficult to modify. There comes a point when the designer will throw in the towel and redesign the data structure. Our longevity goals are not met! Throughout this process, the entity model is still of intrinsic value to Data Administration and the database administrator in their derivation of the application schema. The quality of database design from this point on will have a major impact on the application development and programming phases. The derivation of sub-schemas will not now concern itself with logical models. Programs will be designed on the physical structure derived from the logical entity model. Lots of money will be spent on this, and for evermore on maintenance.

Finally, the entity models as described will reflect the data model actually needed to run a part of the business. It is entirely likely that the model will disagree in some way with the higher-level model from which it was supposedly derived. There will be justification for going back at this point to modify the higher-level and corporate model. At least the data administrator will understand why similar or duplicate entities exist and will be able to plan new systems around them. The database structure, likewise, will need to be reflected back into the global database architecture to aid future developments similarly. The entities should be labelled clearly throughout to indicate derivation from higher levels (much the same as data flow). This will assist the data administrator to get a complete picture. This introduces a practical difficulty because separate development teams in separate functions will not automatically label entities in the same way. Some method of achieving consistency needs to be found. The only person likely to have a theme is the data administrator.

Much of the preceding discussion assumed that a corporate or high-level model was available to start the process off and to go back to for reconciliation. The chances are that no such model will exist for those new to data administration or to the kind of techniques being propounded in this book. In practice, the first models to appear will be the individual application models, either those already

Figure 7.6 A simple entity life history for an employee

developed or those under construction. The only way round this is to actually build up the corporate model by piecing together the lower-level parts of the jigsaw. Inevitably, there will be misfits, duplication and gross inefficiency everywhere. The choice is a stark one — either this is allowed to continue *ad infinitum* or an effort is made to go for a corporate model that may then influence the re-designs of those systems which contributed to it, and of course any new developments. The task of piecing all this together must belong to the data administrator and he or she will need a great deal of patience and understanding when performing it.

A further activity with the entity models should be charting entity life histories. This technique is more of an aid to the application developer, as it provides some logical sequence to the processes operating on the data. In addition, some basic logic rules will be uncovered.

For example, the entity 'Employee' could have a life history as indicated in Figure 7.6. From the point of view of a developer looking at a pensions system, the life history is important as certain functions must happen at these points (deceased, retired, left), such as transferring previous pension scheme sums, accumulating pensions and voluntary contributions, paying a pension, deferring a pension, etc. Clearly there are many logical conditions which can arise from this type of sequencing. The data administrator may be an observer in this whole process, but understanding the entities and their overall relationships will prove useful. Within the context of a complete development, the result of this part of the process will affect the authorship and access of data in the application. This is because the entity life history depicts what actually happens to the entity as it goes through the application. The CREATE, UPDATE, READ, DELETE functions will be the input to the authorship and procedural issues discussed in Chapter 5.

Normalisation

Entity modelling describes the techniques for arriving at a logical view of how data will be represented in file structures (databases), or of our concept of storing 'data at rest'. Upon detailed analysis of the model it is likely to find a more complex representation than that which we actually need. For example, consider a file of data about salaries. The company will have many employees, working in departments and earning salaries. This can be represented as follows, showing the data items within the file, key data items underlined and multiple occurrences of data items in brackets:

Company Name
Company total salary bill
[Department   ]
[Salary budget   ]
[Salary total actual]
[[Employee   ]]
[[Salary   ]]
[[Effective date   ]]

There are many departments in the company, each with a budget and actual. Within each department there are many employees, each with their own salary and effective date. This means that we have repeating groups. In one company file there are many department records, and many employee records. To simplify matters we should consider the company details as a separate file from the department records and as separate from employee records.

The removal of the repeating groups into separate files is the process of normalisation. We would end up with three separate 'simple' files derived from the one 'complex' file, with the key data items as shown underlined. The three simple files are equivalent to the one complex file:

Company file   = Company name + Company total salary bill
Department file = Company name + Department name +
                  Salary budget + Salary total actual
Employee file   = Company name + Department name +
                  Employee + Salary + Effective date

The key to the simple file is formed by concatenating the key of the old file with that of the repeating group.

Where the data represented is extremely complex, then a series of normalisations is used to take out the repeating groups in sequence. For example:

Step 1 — Company file   = Company name + Company total salary bill
          Department file = Company name + Department name + Salary
                            budget + Salary total actual (+Employee +
                            Salary + Effective date)

Note the use of brackets to show many repetitions of the employee data within the department.

Step 2 — Company file   = <u>Company name</u> + Company total salary bill
    Department file = <u>Company name</u> + Department name +
    Salary budget + Salary total actual.
    Employee file   = <u>Company name</u> + <u>Department name</u> +
    <u>Employee</u> + Salary + Effective date

Normalisation is an important tool to the data administrator. Through this we can group data according to its inherent characteristics and simplify it to the point where all the relationships could be represented by two-dimensional tables. Primary keys identify each occurrence uniquely and each attribute (data item) only describes the entity it is associated with. All this provides the data administrator and the database administrator with a simple, effective view of the data on which to build a real or physical database. Normalisation has been shown to provide a sound basis for flexible and stable data structures.

The following are some observations about normalisation which are cautions and which deserve to be considered:

- Normalisation rearranges and simplifies data items which are unearthed through the analysis phase. Where data items are virtual synonyms, normalisation cannot single these out and encourage removal.
- Following on from the above, normalisation only deals with the known data items from the analysis. New data items arising from new business requirements do not enter into the process.

Normalisation is a useful method of clearing out the complexity from a data model and can help to remove data redundancy. As long as it is used in this context and is not used as an absolute method of creating the 'best' design, it is a valuable tool. It will be the skill and vision of the data administrator and designer which enable us to reach the 'best' design.

IDEF modelling (integrated definition)

We have now discussed data flow diagramming and entity modelling, but we have still only given the data administrator tools to look at the data and not the process. In theory, the data is all that matters to the data administrator. In practice, to achieve an understanding of how the enterprise operates, something else is needed. In Chapter 6 we discussed the role of the data administrator in high-level business analysis. The majority of organisations are sufficiently complex to warrant a very careful study of the business infrastructure and the many relationships contained within it. In a sense this is very much a bird's eye view of the whole enterprise with the need to focus in and out to study the discrete functions. When studying such relationships we must consider more than just the data which flows within and around them. The operation of the infrastructure will rely on procedures, controls and resource utilisation as well as data. Whilst data flow and data models enable us to build up a view of the data within the infrastructure, they do not enable any other view. (Data-related tools and techniques are designed specifically to divorce data from these other issues for good reasons, and these comments are in no way critical of them.) In particular, data flow does not show the application of control. Sometimes this can be a drawback. In some of the debates about systems integration, a method of portraying flows of data and control is very useful. To that end, we recommend the use of a technique such as IDEF. There are many similarities to data flow, especially in the style of decomposition by successive levels of detail, numbering conventions, partitioning and inter-level consistency.

Figure 7.7 shows a simple example of the interrelation between two systems. This is a much simplified version of how an inspection planning system feeds off a manufacturing planning system in order to calculate a 'work-to list' for the inspectors. There is certainly some data flowing around, such as 'customer orders', 'current stock levels,' 'work-to list', etc., which a data flow diagram would have shown perfectly adequately. The IDEF model seeks to give a further picture. Essentially, the ground rules are as follows:

- Show the inputs (data, material, documents, etc.) on the left.
- Place the controls at the top which dictate the rules for transforming the input.
- Show the mechanisms or techniques for doing the transformation underneath.
- Produce the output (transformed input) on the right.

So here we are describing how accepted customer orders are input to a manufacturing planning process. The orders are planned according to specific time slots, as dictated by the planning horizon. Orders are only planned if stock is not available to fill them immediately. Orders are planned according to available capacity. The technique involves calculating net requirements by accumulating orders to a gross requirement and netting off the available stock. A bill of material is used to break orders down to their constituent parts. The resulting job schedule is then fed into an inspection planning process. The parts involved are analysed for their category (i.e. inspect, do not inspect) and historical performance. The latter is accomplished through statistical techniques. The result is a list of jobs which will be ranked for inspection to tackle. If required, processes A1 and B1 can be further analysed to become A1.1, A1.2 . . . , B1.1, B1.2, ... This kind of diagram is very useful for the data administrator when describing systems integration. From one simple example, we can see that the 'current stock' data flow is in fact a control on process A1. That data flow will have come from a further process called 'Manage Stores'. The DFD will not make it clear that the stocks data flow is a control. The IDEF type of diagram is also more suited to showing real systems. Logical DFDs sometimes look very contrived when trying to force them to show systems, people, documents, etc. The IDEF diagram can say a great deal more about the process itself. It may seem a little like heresy to suggest that the data administrator should be concerned with processes, but for systems planning and integration IDEF is a valuable asset.

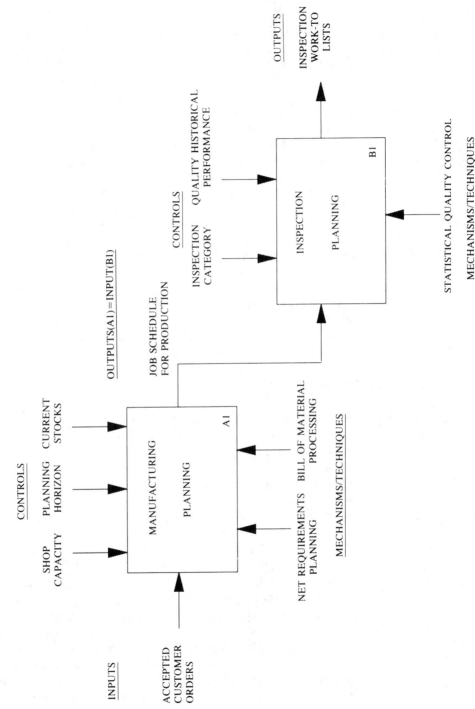

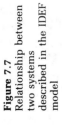

Figure 7.7
Relationship between
two systems
described in the IDEF
model

CASE

In any discussion about data administration tools and techniques, the subject of computer aided software (systems) engineering will raise its head. All CASE tools impact in some way on the life of the data administrator, more so the 'upper CASE' or analysis tools than the 'lower CASE' or development tools. Being absolutely realistic, there is no way that an organisation will spend a great deal of money on tools for data administration alone. The primary justification will always be software development at lower cost, shorter lead times, potentially higher quality plus the many other claims of the suppliers. Nevertheless, the data administrator and the developers need not be on different planets (despite our warnings of this possibility). One way of bringing them closer together is to enable sharing of mutually beneficial tools, preferably tools which allow developers to fulfil data administration needs at much reduced levels of effort.

There is no attempt here to convince any reader of the need for CASE or otherwise. Those decisions arise from other considerations, as mentioned above. On the assumption that some level of CASE is being considered, the following observations may help, from the point of view of data administration.

To put the discussion into context, we need to understand what is meant by CASE. Undoubtedly, any tool which helps or automates even a fraction of the job is now hailed as a CASE tool whether the purist would agree or not. The portfolio of products may cover analyst workbenches, project planners, code generators, screen printers, debuggers and more.

From the data administration viewpoint it is hoped that CASE will accomplish one or more of the following:

- creation of data models (corporate and application);
- assistance with strategic information plans;
- data analysis;
- data flow diagramming;
- entity life history mapping;
- data item inventory management;
- data dictionary for the analysis phase;
- reverse engineering of data structures;
- life cycle support.

The development of a CASE strategy is a considerable undertaking which will be software-development led. Adding to the confusion will be the claims of the suppliers of I-CASE (Integrated CASE), whose tools solve all the world's problems at the press of a button. If that sounds a little cynical, one reason could be the number of speculative telephone calls from CASE vendors claiming to have the answer to your problems. In this situation, we employed a simple checklist of criteria. If (a) the flow of the sales pitch could be broken momentarily, and (b) the criteria were met, then a visit was agreed. Beware, many criteria are not fulfilled when they are explored a little more thoroughly. The preparation of the criteria is a useful exercise. The kind of argument could be as follows:

- Is the tool methodology dependent/independent? Clearly, implementing a tool which supports a totally different methodology to the one currently in use will raise some difficulties with the development function. On the other hand, a tool which supports your current methodology could be a boon. Which parts of the methodology (life cycle) must it support, or would it be advantageous to support?
- Does the tool have full graphics capability? There are always issues of cost and equipment here. You may not want to have to provide the development function and data administrators with high-resolution, 18-inch monitors, compatible only with the latest and most expensive personal work stations. Graphics, however, are the key to getting pictorial data administration implemented. As we have said, this is virtually a prerequisite to successful data administration.
- Does the tool have diagramming capability? That is, can it create diagrams with minimum guidance from the analyst? Is it self-checking for inputs, outputs, levelling? A simple draughting package may not suffice. Some degree of intelligence will be needed to prompt the operator in diagram design. What standard types of diagram are supported? If yours is not among them, is this a major problem?
- How does the tool handle entity models (if at all)? What conventions are allowed for describing relationships between entities?
- Does the tool have a suitable repository or dictionary where text can be stored to describe entities and data flow processes? Does the repository allow for maintaining data item lists and characteristics? (Note — many tools have their own dictionaries. This may not be desirable if you use repositories in a wider sense — see the discussion on this subject later on.)
- You may want the tool to be able to automatically generate database schemas and listings from the logical model it has created. Can it do this? If so, does the database management language produced meet with your DBA needs?
- How does the tool aid maintenance? Can a logical model be maintained at source; is it the physical model which is changed; does the tool generate a fourth generation language (requiring specialist skills and training) of its own or third generation code?
- How will the tool interact with existing DBMS or languages?
- Will the IT function be chiefly involved with in-house design work or are application packages more likely? As we will see shortly, application packages require a different approach. The impact of CASE tools will be quite different. Many CASE tools thrive in a situation where data analysts start with a blank sheet of paper.
- Do you require a CASE tool which can operate across multiple platforms? It may be a requirement to develop systems on a mini or a PC and 'port' this

across to a mainframe. Such tools are available but tend to lock you into specific solutions which can be expensive in the longer term.

The database administrator will likewise have a list of criteria. Any CASE survey undertaken should really have a project team which includes the data administrator, database administrator, senior developer and some member of your IT management team.

Generally, CASE has a long way to go before being a stock part of every IT function's tool kit. It is certainly our recommendation to ensure that you have a sound basis for development (including data administration principles) before embarking. That basis must include an accepted methodology, data-driven techniques (data flow, data modelling) and established methods of physical database design.

One of the most obvious pitfalls for some organisations starting to use tools like this can be the lack of training in the basic techniques which the tool is automating. Forget the argument that a good tool can do the job, thereby obviating the need for the user to understand the process. This is dangerous. The analysts must be capable of conducting thorough data analysis and be conversant with techniques of normalisation. Quite often, sophisticated tools are not used to their full potential because of this. Another reason is that the tool is not given its full head. Analyst workbenches can often become no more than documentation tools. Clearly, the user must be able to get the best out of the tool, which implies sound training, but quite often the tool will also need a lot of preparatory work to allow it to function effectively. Usually this involves a business and systems analysis phase which flushes out every aspect of the data needs. If the data cannot be fully defined, the tool will have gaps in its knowledge. Whereas humans can make up for gaps by making intelligent guesses, most tools cannot get over the problem. Admittedly a large number of them will report the fact that there are gaps (a benefit of CASE), but, nevertheless, it requires the analyst to backtrack to complete the analysis and sometimes this is seen as a delay not worth tolerating. Once this kind of thinking starts, the tool can become accepted only as a documenter. A lot of documentation follows on after development (deny it if you will), and the tool will be used to produce data flow diagrams, entity models, and so on, retrospectively.

One seemingly minor snag to be faced is the matter of conventions. Data flow is a good example of where some conventions (and tools) use circles for processes, and others use squares. This may seem inconsequential, but if you use a mixture of tools, or some development is not tool-driven, or you have an established convention that is different from the tool you want to buy, then it can prove awkward. At the very least the automated software conventions need to be consistent. In that way the impact may be restricted to the IT function. Where data flow (or other) representations are used in the user community, a different, but consistent, representation can be used successfully. If you do manage to get the users involved in graphical data representations, confusing them with mixed conventions is a bit like 'spoiling the ship for a ha'porth 'o' tar'.

If the tool is not used to its full potential, it is likely that some developers will find alternative methods and the benefits in terms of consistency of documentation, design style, and so on, will be lost.

A further reason for not realising the full benefit of a CASE tool is lack of suitable work for it to do. If there are clear strategies for development and well-defined architectures, this should not happen. It is possible, however, to select tools for specific one-off projects/platforms/methods which may not have much longevity themselves. This is where the argument for seeking out a truly platform-independent tool becomes very strong as it provides the business with more flexibility on implementing solutions.

One of the aspects of upper CASE (analyst workbenches) which many developers enjoy is the ability it gives them for experimentation. The ultimate use of experimentation is, of course, prototyping. Once again, though, some tools are a little too rigid in what they need in terms of standards and completeness to allow speculative work.

Another drawback with experimentation can be the physical limitations of normal sized monitors. Standard 80 character terminals are limited in the amount of graphical data they can display. With most tools large diagrams need to be viewed in sections. This makes it more difficult for the developer to see the full picture and study the relationships between different sections of the diagrams. The sales talk and sales demonstrations seem to make light of these problems.

The biggest nightmare for the data administrator comes from CASE tools which are not I-CASE but are operated in that way. The aim is to have a data analysis and logical design from the upper CASE tool to be loaded in and used in the lower CASE tool. In an I-CASE tool set, the two elements share a common repository of the meta-data, thus ensuring consistency. In a mixed CASE environment, the meta-data can and does get changed in the transition. So the data administrator may be perfectly happy with the logical models and data item definitions from the first stage but may not be aware, or in control of, the versions moving into application development. The data administrator needs to be extra vigilant in these cases, but the level of detail involved makes it a most painstaking and time consuming task. Data administrators rarely have the luxury of all the time needed. The fact that the data analysis has to be loaded twice to the separate tools is also a drawback to hard-pressed developers.

Where CASE tools are employed which are single-platform-based (e.g. IBM AS400), then this problem is exacerbated as it is often impossible to make the meta-data from one platform acceptable to another. Vendors are moving towards more 'open' products, but not as quickly as we would all like.

If the two toolsets employ different conventions, this also exacerbates the problem. The consistency check between the two versions of meta-data can become almost unmanageable.

Whilst much of this discussion may seem gloomy, CASE is in fact an excellent philosophy for the data administrator. Given the right selection, good training and skilled use, these tools will take away a great deal of the drudgery which is a part of this aspect of data administration and development. An early examination of CASE is strongly advised for any new or existing Data Administration function.

Data dictionaries

Data dictionaries are software tools which, as the name suggests, classify and catalogue data. They are the data administrator's chief tool and must be a major component of any data-driven strategy. They range in complexity from simple cataloguers of data definitions (passive dictionaries), through central definitions of data for programs to access at compile-time and run-time (active dictionaries), to sophisticated stores of system design data which perform all three functions (repositories or encyclopaedias). It is highly probable that anyone reading this book will operate a dictionary of some description. As before in this chapter, we will explore the role of the tool as a data administration aid. The merits of one dictionary versus another from the viewpoint of database designers or system developers is left to texts written for that purpose.

The reason for the dictionary being the primary tool of the data administrator is quite clear. We have said that the role of the data administrator is to develop a thorough understanding of the organisation's data. This allows us to manage the development of data and its subsequent control and use. The dictionary is the place where data is defined — authoritatively. We need look no further for the data administrator's source of knowledge. In Chapter 5 we examined the use of the dictionary to manage authorship and data use. It is obviously important to be able to collect together, in one place, all the data relating to data—meta-data. This is where one of the most likely problems will occur. Dictionaries have evolved as partners to other software tools. Database management systems (DBMS) have a dictionary designed to operate within them. CASE tools are developed to store meta-data in their own dictionary. Given the number of DBMS and CASE tools around, there is a proliferation of dictionaries. Until very recently there have been no efforts to make these dictionaries compatible. Unless yours is a single technology site you may be in a similar situation to many other IT sites, with several dictionaries reflecting different hardware platforms, DBMS and CASE tools. This means, of course, that the data administrator has to deal with a variety of formats, styles, uses and implementations of dictionaries. The meta-data itself will look different, making comparisons difficult (at best). The dictionary discussed in Chapter 5 is in fact a special implementation, designed to allow for the fact that meta-data has to be extracted from several sources and documented in a single format. The meta-data in question is only a subset of the whole, the data required specifically for authorship and usage. To tailor a tool for a specific environment to handle relationships between programs, reports, schemas, etc., across multiple platforms and implementations would require a major development in its own right. Software vendors are pursuing this with repositories. Another option is to use the individual dictionaries to control their own applications and update a central repository of meta-data specially selected from them for the data administrator. For the role we have been describing, the key information to be supplied by the dictionary is as follows:

- Which system does the data item come from?
- Who has authorship responsibilities?
- What are the item's characteristics?

The data administrator will also become involved in 'where used' analysis, but it is probably enough to use the central dictionary to point towards an application dictionary in the absence of a single repository. Most dictionaries will contain reporting tools to produce where-used listings which allow investigation to marry up reports, screens, programs, sub-schemas, etc. The method of populating a central repository of meta-data may well involve automating a link between it and the application dictionary. Hopefully, the link can be achieved by a simple conversion program. Figure 7.8 illustrates the concept.

On the premise that various dictionaries around the organisation do contain the essential meta-data, the program may simply need the following:

> DATA ITEM NAME
> DESCRIPTION
> FORMAT
> SYNONYM
> VERSION

The system will allow for manual or automatic input of authorship details. The conversion and loading programs should be straightforward manipulations observing desired standards. The data item name should be sufficient, as a key, to allow detailed analysis of the meta-data in the source dictionary plus Data Administration analysis of the central system.

One of the biggest fillips that a data administrator can experience is the knowledge that a dictionary is controlling the data definitions within applications. Again, Chapter 5 discussed the setting of standards and conventions for data. The dictionary will enforce those standards automatically. This is because the dictionary system itself will guide developers into loading standard meta-data. The applications at compile-time or run-time will extract the standard meta-data. (For those readers operating only a passive dictionary the first benefit will be realised but not the second.)

The principal benefit of the dictionary is, of course, that all applications using that dictionary derive meta-data from it rather than having it encoded into the programming logic. This is all good theory and by and large will hold true. Sadly, there are developers around who try very hard to name data contrary to standards but still acceptable to the dictionary. The answer to this is to have the data administrator ratify all new data definitions personally. This is recommended, but the potential bottleneck must be borne in mind. If projects are sufficiently well planned, the data administrator should know sometime in advance that 300

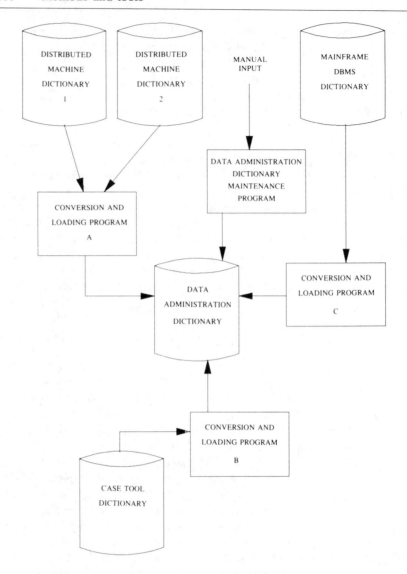

new data items are about to land on his desk. Whilst this is a significant undertaking, working alongside the development team allows the data administrator to influence things a little earlier or in stages. It is possible to audit the dictionary after development. However, it is unrealistic to expect that a development will be stopped or a system taken out of commission because non-standard data items have been defined. This is why the dictionary must be correctly populated during the development phase.

Although we would support the development of the central repository, it cannot solve the problems associated with mixed hardware and technologies. Our recurring theme of systems integration is an instance where meta-data of varying styles will not help the process at all. There is no answer to this, other than careful analysis and data manipulation to convert from one set of standards to another. It has to be acknowledged that the dictionary is of minimal help here for anything other than the documentation of the meta-data for comparison. Another drawback of many dictionaries is that they model a view of the data without reference to the human element of data use. The emerging IRDS (Information Resource Dictionary System) standards concentrate on meta entities such as document, file, element, record, system, program, module, etc. There is no link into the world of data control from a user view.

Having said this, the development of IRDS standards (ANSI and now ISO) promises much in terms of compatibility between different vendors' dictionaries, CASE tool access to dictionaries, and multiple DBMS use of dictionaries. As with all standards they are emerging steadily. It will be some time before the difficulties discussed here are overcome by design alone.

At some stage we can look forward to the systems repository being the organisation's central source of meta-data from the highest corporate-level entity to the lowest-level data item. All the relationships will be defined, such as entity, data flow, data item, report, program and perhaps even prime author. The organisation's CASE strategy can be built around it because IRDS standards will allow full compatibility between tools and DBMS. The accent will be on sharing everything within the scope of systems development and operation. The data administrator should therefore be looking forward in anticipation of a software tool which will automate much of what (s)he does now, allowing for a much more creative and studied analysis of the corporate data model. Indeed, the claims for repository functionality include: strategic data planning, systems planning, data modelling, architectural planning, impact analysis, tactical data planning, project management, analysis, design, code generation, configuration management, capacity planning, usage analysis, testing and debugging.

The data administrator will need to use the repository to store the blueprints of the corporate systems architecture. These are the data models we alluded to earlier. We can now see the power of such a tool when those blueprints (a consistent levelled set) are used as the basis for all systems development. Problems with inconsistent modelling, redundant entities, non-standard data item formats, and so on, can be swept away. When the move to object orientation comes, then the repository models will be built around 'objects'.

The drawbacks will be in the long implementation phase where repository control is introduced on some parts of the business model or with some CASE tools. A careful plan to convert all current dictionary implementations will be needed. These will be the issues facing the practical data administrator in a few years time.

Package software

To conclude this chapter we need to consider the impact of package software on the data administrator. Many companies elect to utilise packages where possible.

This strategy is often a most cost-effective way of implementing business solutions. They are often the curse of the data administration effort.

Unfortunately, there are no real answers to the problems; however, an airing of them here will enable the practical data administrator to be aware of the difficulties.

For those organisations where data administration and database administration are closely related, the issue of adopting packages on unfamiliar platforms will arise. Generally speaking, it is possible to stick to a strategic policy for platform and DBMS. Using that criteria, a package may then be found which is functionally suitable and consistent with the database strategy. Occasionally a functionally rich package may tempt the decision makers to mix and match on databases. The learning curve associated with a new DBMS and associated languages and tools is significant, but this can be overlooked in specifying project timescales. The selection of a package already written to work with a familiar DBMS is a highly desirable feature for the data administrator. It is important to ensure that (s)he is consulted during the evaluation stage.

Package solutions usually arrive with a physical file (database) structure supplied. It is impossible from just looking at a physical database structure to divine how it was arrived at through normalisation. Off-the-shelf databases are usually designed for the widest possible customer base and, of course, to operate with the program code. If changes are needed to tailor the database structure to a closer fit for the business (business goals, IT goals, system/package goals), then it is quite possible to compromise the method of operation for some of the programs. Changes are only possible to the physical database. If the changes are 'logical' or for business reasons, then the physical record may be totally corrupted by unwittingly amending its function within the design. The simplest analogy is tampering with the structure of the house without knowing what went into the foundations and the fundamental design.

Without a logical view of the package it is virtually impossible to construct logical business links between it and other system designs used elsewhere in the business. The point of linkage has to be through the physical design which continually pushes the genuine vendor-supplied product into a hybrid in-house/vendor mixture. What was a difficult picture for the data administrator to put together initially becomes more complex with each change. As mentioned above, each change at the physical level can further compromise physical characteristics of the design, put there for good reason, degrading the vendor's original design.

The level of dictionary support for packages varies enormously. Some packages designed to operate with well-established dictionaries come well documented; others are inadequately documented. Even when the dictionary is supplied and populated there can be differences of version level to contend with. The solution is to operate the number of dictionaries/versions necessary to allow the packages to function, but accepting that the data administrator cannot obtain the much desired single view of the data architecture from them. A central repository is needed (discussed earlier) to extract the data and classify it in terms that the data administrator can work with. Some CASE tools contain their own dictionaries;

software designed by such a tool may then have the meta-data hidden inside the resident database.

Reverse engineering tools are available which will help the data administrator. These tools take a physical design and backtrack to a logical view. A great deal of interpretation is still necessary to fit the view to a business situation; however, the hard work and drudgery that the tool automates could make it a worthwhile addition. Generally speaking, complex packages cannot be fully reversed to provide the fundamental understanding of why it was constructed in that way. This makes it very difficult to determine how the business goals are achieved with the software. There is a huge gap in the understanding which the data administrator wants to fill. To exacerbate this problem there are some vendors who maintain their packages at the physical level, thereby lessening any chance that the data administrator may have had of understanding the logical make-up.

In summary, if there can be any good practical advice in this very difficult area it would be as follows:

- Select strategic (to your business) database products for familiarity.
- Try to obtain the logical structure from the vendor or reverse engineer it.
- Insist on complete dictionary support or ensure that the package can be documented once installed.
- Select packages built in CASE tools already used in the business to obtain the documentation which will be consistent with that already resident.
- Minimise changes to the package.
- Minimise systems integration/interfacing to the package.

Further reading

In this chapter we gave a view of how certain tools and techniques could benefit the data administrator.

It was not our intention to explain these techniques in depth, and there are many books available which discuss these topics. We ourselves have found the following material useful:

DeMarco, T. (1981), *Structured Analysis and System Specification*, Yourdon Press: New York

Gane, C. and Sarson, T. (1979), *Structured Systems Analysis: Tools and Techniques*, Yourdon Press: New York

Rock-Evans, R. (1987), *A Simple Introduction to Data and Activity Analysis*, Computer Weekly Publications: Sutton, Surrey

Ross, O.T. *et al* (1980), *Architects Manual ICAM Definition Method*, IDEFO, CAM-i Inc.: Texas

Veryard, R. (1984), *Pragmatic Data Analysis*, Blackwell Scientific: Oxford

Key action points

- Implement a methodology (especially a life cycle) which allows data administration principles to be built into systems at the right time.
- Use simple techniques which employ graphical means of representation (data flow, entity modelling, life history, IDEF).
- Carefully research and adopt a CASE strategy which caters for the needs of the data administrator as well as developers and database designers.
- Establish a clearly defined policy for dictionary use, both in terms of development and administration of the data.
- Plan out a structured approach to package selection which addresses the concerns of the data administrator.

8　End user computing

This is a subject which has the capacity to cause more debate than any other in the IT arena. In a sense it represents a classic dichotomy. The whole thrust of Data Administration is to encourage the most effective use of the corporate data asset. In the same breath we talk about protection of that asset through limited access. With end user computing the data is released from the security of a specialist IT unit (e.g. mainframe computing service) into a hostile environment of misuse, inadequate protection and a minefield of inaccuracy. This scenario, deliberately painted provocatively, is one to which many organisations find themselves uncomfortably close. There are, however, some simple approaches to the control of end user computing which should be led by Data Administration. In this chapter we will be examining the theoretical approach (which is exemplary in its goals); where the difficulties will be experienced; and how they can be minimised.

What is end user computing?

First of all, let us look at how we believe end user computing can be defined. There are two basic goals, which can be described as follows:

- Increasing user productivity through a policy of providing data in the right place, in the right context, of the right quantity at the right time. The end user may manipulate and apply logic to this data in order to make it into valuable information. This manipulation will be by means of easy-to-use, effective software tools, such as spreadsheets.
- Allowing the end users some autonomy in developing 'applications' to their own specification in their own timescales. Many of the stories of hard-pressed IT departments, quoting lead times in years, are depressingly true.

End user computing has seen phenomenal growth over the last few years for a number of reasons: smaller, more powerful hardware, user-friendly software tools, advances in connectivity and a general increase in computer user literacy.

Computer user literacy in particular is a feature of the convergence concept that we discussed earlier — the merging and marrying of business processes and IT to the extent that they become one and the same thing. This gives us the IT literate user which allows us to select system controllers and hybrid managers. End user computing is playing a major role in this development. As a discipline in its own right, end user computing has a classic development history. Most end users were originally the keen dabblers who obtained a PC and got on with it. Whilst they were generally oblivious to the needs for control or the actual value of the data they were using, it was a relatively harmless start. As the methods and tools evolved so did the numbers of people 'having a go'. They were not always enthusiasts and they were a much greater threat to data integrity generally (these were the days of floppy disks being used as coffee cup mats, which we hope are fading now!). There was probably more wasted effort and data duplication than at any time. This led to the realisation of the need for control, which brings us to the present day, where we have information strategies, end user architectures, client servers and some measure of data administration over the whole affair.

End user computing is literally a whole host of people operating independently with a corporate asset when they please, where they please and how they please, within defined constraints. Most organisations do recognise the value of allowing end user autonomy and do not place unnecessarily difficult barriers in the way. The actual uses to which the data is put in an end user environment tend to fall into four main categories: personal computing, departmental applications, static management information reporting and executive information systems. Figure 8.1 shows the classic divisions between types of data and where the four categories fit into that model.

Before moving on to discuss the difficulties and solutions, we will briefly describe these four categories.

Personal computing

This is where it all began. An enterprising individual can see a way of improving a job by doing some computational work on the machine. The typical origins are that, on a regular basis (s)he takes a large mainframe report, selects numerous figures from it, does some recalculation, and plots a graph. The attraction of a piece of software to download a mainframe file, extract the data, recalculate and plot is obvious. The enterprising user goes on to find many more ways of making life easier and much more interesting. Before we know where we are, a great deal of data is being manipulated and presented in this way. This is good from the point of view of productivity and staff motivation. It is potentially bad from the point of view of data redundancy, duplication of effort (if two people do something very similar), and data protection generally, as the end user environment is not secure in the sense in which a data centre would understand it. The technology involved will almost certainly be proprietary spreadsheets, database languages, graphics and word processing packages.

Departmental applications

Here, we are probably looking at a slightly more sophisticated set-up than the personal one. Several users are likely to be involved, operating a small system

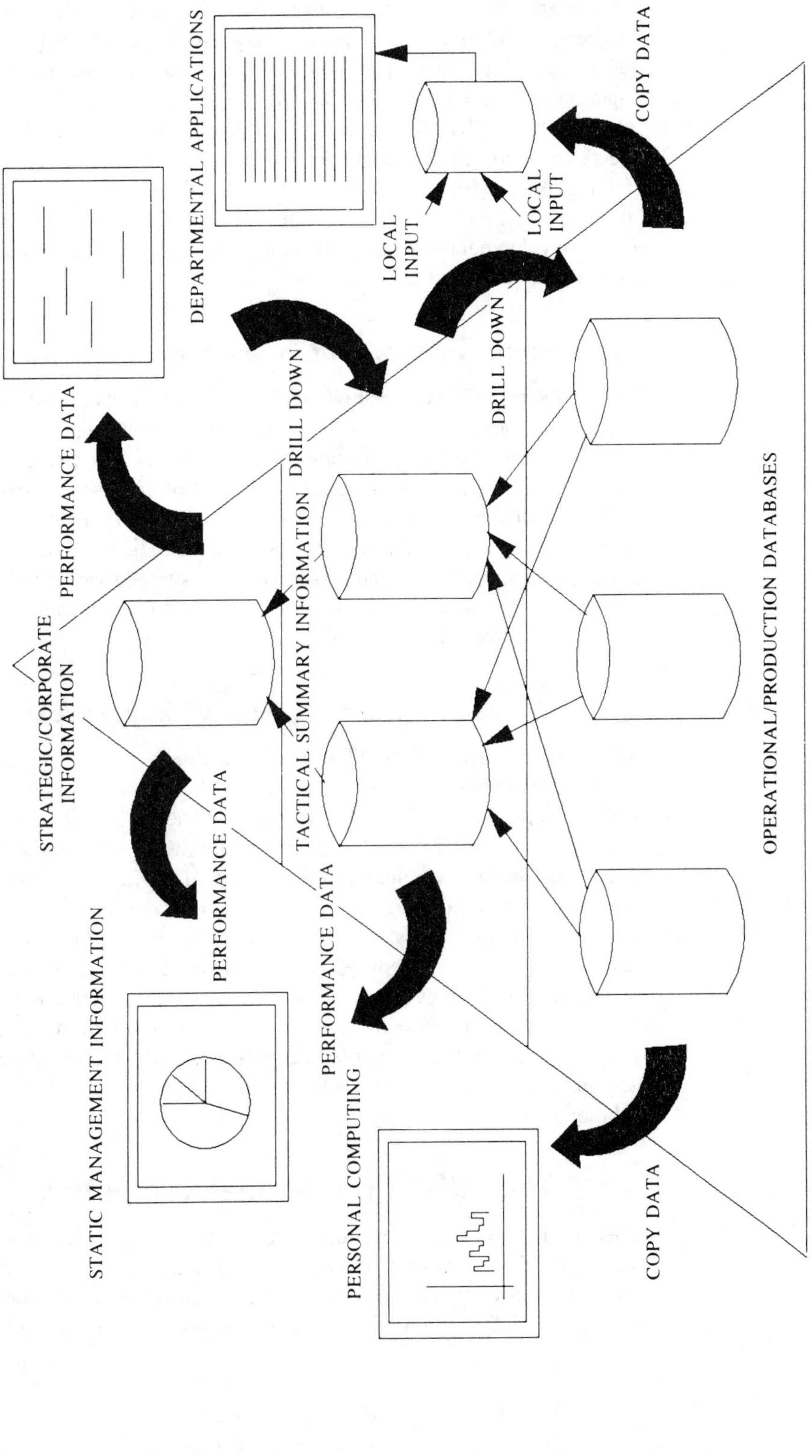

Figure 8.1 A data architecture for end user computing

tailored specifically to achieve local goals. The kind of application is one which has been on the 'not urgent' list of hard-pressed development functions for what seems like an age. Data from several sources may be involved (including locally input data), and multiple user access gives rise to many more security issues. More ambitious hardware and software could be involved, especially some of the better reporting languages available. Most fourth generation languages are moving close to being end user orientated (although they are not there yet!). To all intents and purposes the application will look very much like one produced by the development function, although formal methodologies and documentation may not be observed closely.

Static management information reporting

Despite the potential of executive information systems there will always be a place for a simple picture which tells a story of what was happening at a week end/period end/month end. Most organisations base themselves on a discrete reporting cycle when taking stock of performance. This kind of end user computing takes data from virtually anywhere and converts it into information which a decision taker can use in making judgements. It does not have to be pictorial but the likelihood is that graphs, pie-charts and histograms will succeed where printed tabulations are still not accepted. Trend monitoring, in particular, benefits from a number of snapshot static views over time.

Decision support and executive information systems

These latest offerings from IT provide very high-level performance data which the archetypal non-IT literate director can look at and appreciate. Figures in green are acceptable; figures in red need attention! The distinction between this facility and the static reporting facility is that 'drill down' provides the ability to select a piece of data and, via hidden software commands, find out how it was derived through a sequence of transactions. A simple example may be total supplier credit status — composed of several monthly credit values — in turn composed of many discrete transactions — composed of even more lines of invoice detail.

A structured journey down this trail allows the executive not only to see the corporate effect but also the underlying statistics behind it.

In all four of the scenarios described, there is great potential for data administration disasters. We will go on to describe them before looking at a solution.

The pitfalls of end user computing

There is probably more scope for the data administrator to despair over the wanton disregard of data policies in end user computing than in any other arena. We are moving through a period of evolution of information use which promotes the concept that information is valuable. It is almost regarded as an asset that needs protection, but the end user at large does not recognise his own responsibilities towards it as yet. Hence the theme of this book and the strong advocation of a system controller to facilitate the principles of data administration.

The data administrator's chief concerns will relate to the following:

- lack of design disciplines in end user developed applications;
- access control over sensitive data;
- rampant data duplication and redundancy;
- suspect data integrity/applicability;
- poor discipline in physical data protection;
- ineffective use of the data asset;
- data uploads from insecure to secure systems.

We will examine these concerns in turn. They are as likely to occur in an insurance company as in a frozen food distributor, in fact, wherever end users get the taste for doing their own thing.

Design discipline

This is something which is probably taken for granted in any organised development function. Generally, these functions will operate to specific methods, using specific tools and documenting their products in a standard way. Even then, we often find that the rule book is bypassed for any number of reasons. Many functions do not like the idea of rigid design standards. But, usually, there will always be some minimum requirements.

If we equate the type of life cycle and methodology discussed in Chapter 7 for mainstream development to a possible end user equivalent, we can see the discipline which may suffer (again, looking at it through Data Administration's eyes).

During the development of the IT strategy it is probable that no thought is given to the need for end user computing. If the type of systems planning we described earlier is used, then the IT plans will reflect the development of enterprise-wide computing.

End user computing tends to arise from the needs of the individual or the few. Most frequently, the requirement is identified as an afterthought to a major development, adding some frills to the original design. Since end user computing is used to provide information, as opposed to data, it is likely that major application developments will provide the bedrock database architecture, allowing EUC tools to effect the final delivery. The final delivery is something which is not easy to plan during the strategy phases and it is sometimes better not planned too early, as the information provided must reflect the key business need at that time. As executives and decision makers change places in the game of corporate musical chairs, the information requirements will change to reflect different perspectives on the business. Therefore, it is sensible to system plan the architectures but to remain flexible over the final delivery of that data as information. The problem faced by the data administrator is being certain that the data architectures do in fact contain the necessary raw material. If the data is not present in the application, the end user will conjure it up from somewhere else. The only salvation here is that, as we said earlier, the organisation will be based on an enduring set of data entities. If the systems planning is rigorous enough, those entities will be properly used in systems construction. Once there, the way in which data is compiled, stored and reported on those entities is a relatively minor issue. If new data is 'invented' by end users, then the state of anarchy is about to commence.

To a lesser extent the same problem occurs during the early stages of developments, i.e. feasibility and analysis. The end user developed application may well go through a feasibility stage, but this will be an extremely cursory look at the needs. Cost justification will not be as rigorous as that applied to corporate IT developments.

Assumptions are made about existing data in end user applications. New data requirements are specified, presuming that no reasonable equivalent exists in the corporate application portfolio. The rigorous disciplines of a methodology are not applied. As the analysis phase progresses there will be no checking against corporate data item inventories; neither will the data be added into the inventory. The data specified will probably not conform to the standards established for corporate use; sometimes incorrect assumptions will be made about the existence of required data in feeder systems, and it is unlikely that self-checking data accuracy software will be built in. With due deference to end users, their skills in data analysis techniques, such as normalisation, will be limited and thus file designs may not be efficient. For simple single-user applications, perhaps none of this matters. If there are several hundred such applications, perhaps it does. The sophistication of end user applications is on the increase and the point is approaching where demand will be high for 'professional' development. There will be little point in having sound data design standards in the IT function and a free-for-all elsewhere. After all, the aim of data administration is to obtain the most economic and effective use of the data asset. Uncontrolled end user application design is not compatible with that goal.

Beyond the design of the data itself, the methodology covers environmental design. Here we would be looking for sensible design criteria to assist physical protection of the data. If the business stands to suffer because of the loss of data from the end user application, measures should be taken to allow full recovery. Again, this is a concern which is not uppermost in the end user's mind.

This deliberately pessimistic view of design disciplines shows where the pitfalls are. Some end users are quite meticulous about such matters. We are dealing with practical data administration and it has to be said that the views expressed here are shared by many organisations.

Access control

It is a simple relationship: end user computing allows data to become more freely available; this in turn means that data is more exposed to sensitivity issues.

The data in end user applications becomes more vulnerable because freer access potentially means the following:

- Reduced (or non-existent) application of security passwords in end user computing developments. For example, the personal spreadsheet will hardly seem to be a sensitive document to the owner but it may well contain data which ought not to be visible on a wider basis.
- The possibility of uncontrolled sharing, manually or electronically, of the data. A frequent example is end user A having a diskette with, say, twenty data items in a record. End user B can benefit from copying the diskette to reference some of these data items, ignoring the others. Those other data items are now in another application and are open to more scrutiny.
- The mere fact that the application exists in the first place means that the data is being made visible. These applications probably show the data in an easily comprehensible form which can invariably be digested from casual glances at screens left on, plots left on the plotter, or the first efforts of charts drawn out and carelessly discarded.

Again, it is Data Administration's dilemma: how the company's data can be made more freely available and widely used without being exposed to the risks associated with a less tightly controlled environment. The more sensitive the data, the greater the risk from misuse.

Data duplication and redundancy

During the development of application systems by the IT function, we have advocated the use of centralised dictionaries and data analysis techniques to attempt to control the creation of duplicate data. In some cases, duplication occurs as a result of creating identical data items through flagrant disregard for what is already available. More often, an insufficient understanding of the meaning of existing data leads to new data being created in the belief that it does not already exist. (It must be acknowledged that physical design criteria might show some performance benefits incorporating controlled duplication.)

In the end user environment this problem could potentially run riot. In the first place, the end user developer is seeking a fast and easy means of doing the job. Checking for the possible existence of data elsewhere will be seen as time consuming and unnecessary: 'After all it is a simple one-off application which affects no one else.' The end user will also want to key the data in following a format that (s)he recognises and with which (s)he feels comfortable. The corporate format may not suit these purposes. The most likely difficulty is that the end user fails to understand the meaning of data within existing applications adequately. This leads to a fear of the unknown and a reversion to inventing data which is understood.

These difficulties can be multiplied by however many end user applications are being built. It may be that it doesn't really matter, if all it means is each end user taking up a bit of disk space. It is worth it if it is possible to gain some additional benefit and productivity from having the data, whatever duplicated form it is in. On the other hand, what if the information generated is used to report onwards, outwards and upwards? It could matter if two separate end user applications report the same pieces of data, called different names and containing different values. For example, note the eye-catching statistics:

A Total Overtime 200 hours £4000.00
B Total Overtime 150 hours £3000.00

End user application A has used a different data item with a different formula for calculation from B. The recipient of the information could be highly confused by two such figures which seem to mean the same. In fact there could be any number of differences between the interpretations of what 'total overtime' actually represents. This highlights the danger of using the same name in two places. The problem illustrated by this example leads on to a discussion of data integrity.

Suspect data integrity and applicability

Firstly, a reminder of what we mean by data integrity. In summary, it is the fitness of the data for the purposes that it was designed and selected for. This indicates that it must be accurate, timely, in the correct format, in the right context and usable. If a piece of data cannot be used for any reason, then the data integrity is flawed.

In the title for this sub-section, we differentiate between integrity and applicability.

Applicability is a special case of data integrity where everything about the piece of data is correct but the eventual usage is in some way at fault rather than the data itself. This special case is more prevalent in end user computing than in any other aspect of IT. A number of diverse problems connected with both integrity and applicability are discussed below:

- Conflicting messages: Here we see two (or more) sets of figures produced from individual applications, not necessarily, but probably, all end user applications. One of the many unfortunate consequences of not carrying out system planning (Chapter 6) is that several systems may manipulate the same data (differently) and report conflicting information. If the data is subsequently downloaded to end user applications, the effect is concentrated. In practice, if data does produce conflicting messages for higher management, the IT function will probably get the criticism. There will also be a lack of confidence in IT to provide the right information.

- Erroneous data: If the data loaded to end user applications is to be used to draw conclusions and make business decisions, the data must be accurate. Consequences of bad management decisions from wrong base data can range from irritating to disastrous, such as major purchasing sourcing decisions based on data which produces an imbalanced view of supplier capability. The end user application must be correctly specified and preferably have a filter mechanism to ensure that incoming data is satisfactory.

- Freak data occurrences: This is likely to happen where sets of data are analysed and averaged to produce management information. This is probably the most widespread use of end user data for trend monitoring. If any of the base data is totally out of character, e.g. high or low, then the averages will suffer. If the max/min readings were the result of an error and are totally incorrect, then the information is misleading.

- Timelock: This is a very common problem. It arises when data is sectioned into specific time periods, e.g. daily, weekly, monthly or annual statistics. If several sets of statistics are being collected to build a management picture, it is very important to ensure that the constituents are comparable within their timeframes. End user applications must take careful account of cut-off points.

- Mistaken identity: This is normally found where data is used to produce some information without a real understanding of the meaning of the data. By using a figure, e.g. stock quantity in stores, the end user must be sure that the management information required really does need just the quantity in that one store, or does (s)he want —
    quantity in all stores locations?
    quantity in work in progress?
    unuseable stock in stores due to rejection?
    unallocated and allocated stock?
  A thorough understanding of what the data item 'STOCK QUANTITY' means is essential.

- Massaged data: One characteristic of data which occurs outside corporate system control is that it is exposed to manipulation from various tools and techniques. If a set of data is to be used to produce management information, perhaps the people who may be judged by that information would like to ensure that it will paint a favourable picture. Far fetched? We offer it up as a potential problem. If performance data is collected, those who are being appraised may

- Unrepresentative data:

massage the base data to give favourable results. This is most likely to occur when, for some reason, a production system which provides base data to an end user application does not have the usual mix of data in it. For example, perhaps the nightshift at the distribution warehouse were understaffed and the items picked and despatched were not recorded in the system but only on the input tickets. The end user application could be unaware of this gap in the data and provide a misleading picture of 'goods outward valuations'.

- Incompatible data

This is found where data from more than one system is extracted to set up a management information picture. For that picture to mean something the sets of data must be compatible. For example, when extracting prices from more than one system it is important that all prices are VAT inclusive or exclusive and are rated the same so that comparisons are meaningful.

As we can see from this overview of possible integrity problems, there is plenty of scope for the base data and the end user application to make a mockery of any subsequent analysis.

Physical data protection

As with access control, physical data protection often suffers once the data is outside corporate control. Any end user application can suffer from this malaise. We have discussed the personal spreadsheet or database to aid the individual in her work. That individual must be responsible for protecting personal work. Most end users will do this, although they are liable to put backup diskettes in a drawer in the desk. If the individual is conscientious, (s)he may ask a colleague to keep the backup. A fire will probably devastate both their desks. If the data is worth something it is worth protecting properly. As we graduate through levels of complexity in the end user application to genuine multiuser, multiprogram systems, the physical security level needs to increase. It doesn't always! An aspect of physical data protection which is very often overlooked is looking after paper reports and diagrams. A lot of end user applications, unlike their corporate counterparts, produce a result and then discard the data. If this happens and the paper product is lost, the situation can be irretrievable.

Ineffective use of the data asset

This very often manifests itself as duplication of effort. It is possible for many end user applications to be doing the same or similar tasks. This is especially true of personal computing, where several people may be compiling comparable spreadsheets (e.g. personnel lists for addresses, salary review dates, training records, and so on). The devolution of control from a single focal point (corporate MIS, for example) means much less global awareness of computing needs. In this example, from the data administrator's point of view, one set of personnel data could achieve the desired results.

One feature of end user computing which can frustrate the data administrator is ineffective use of data. This comes about through a narrow view of what can be achieved. Once the data is in the end user application, there are likely to be many possibilities for the way in which it can be used to benefit the decision making process. Too often the use is limited to one or two simple calculations and a watered-down end result.

As a general observation on life, we find that people at large in business are still not educated or initiated into the art of using information. There are many good information users out there, but for every one of them there are five or six who do not get the best out of the asset. These people are frequently in jobs which could benefit from exploiting the information available. That is something that business leaders, educationalists and data administrators can do something about.

Data uploads from insecure to secure systems

Many installations do not allow data uploads as a matter of policy. Here, uploading is taken to mean the transfer of data from an end user application back to a mainstream system in order to update the data on that system. The practical difficulties will only occur if the end user application is insecure in any way. This could mean lack of access security, physical security inadequacies, inaccurate or incorrectly manipulated data or, for that matter, any of the pitfalls already discussed. Whilst the suspect data is held within the confines of the end user application, the damage it could cause would be significantly less than would be the case in a larger mainstream system.

End user computing, then, for all its glamour and productivity, is a minefield for data administrators to negotiate. But it can be done! We offer some practical measures here with a clear warning. That is, end user computing is an uncontrolled environment which Data Administration can only hope to influence through education, not policing.

The (data) administration of an end user computing service

The first and foremost recommendation is that very clear policies are documented before any (further) end user work is carried out. The policies must not be lengthy legal documents, but rather, short punchy statements. The following list (Figure 8.2) indicates the policy areas to cover with a brief description. We will then explore the data administration issues in more detail.

Figure 8.2 End user
computing policies

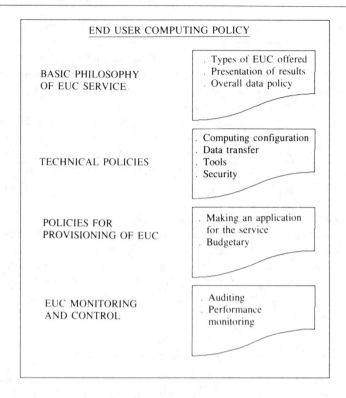

In Figure 8.2 we see a structured vision of how end user computing can be set up and operated in a controlled fashion. The policies indicated cover the following aspects:

- Presentation of results:

  If necessary, particular presentation styles can be specified, e.g. histograms, graphs, etc. Details such as labelling of graph axes may be specified if consistency of reporting is important.

- Overall data policy:

  Establishing the prime data sources; rules for copying such data; windows in schedules for copying and loading data; policies for uploading as well as downloading; specific data which must not be used in end user computing; requirements on system controllers.

- Computing configuration:

  Machine and peripheral architecture; eligible hardware and software.

- Data transfer:

  Software to be employed; specific data extraction rules; single copying and multiple reproduction; data transfer utilities and timeframes for operation.

- Tools: Data manipulation software permitted, e.g. report generators, databases, spreadsheets, graphics packages, etc.

- Security: Security guidelines for protecting copied data; accessibility to end user applications; classification of source data for usage.

- Making an application to use EUC: Routine for specifying a request; stages and decision points in developing a request; formal sign-offs; scheduling development resources.

- Budgeting: Financial justification; budget allocation; formal cost review.

- Auditing: Formal audits of security; data usage; effectiveness of application; control of application; documentation; data accuracy; use of equipment; and adherence to original specification.

- Performance monitoring: Availability of data from scheduled downloads and copies; delivery of end user results to targeted recipients; timeliness of data production; performance of specific software processes, e.g. statistical analysis.

- Help: Guidelines for building in 'HELP' facilities to end user applications, especially through screen-based facilities; also the policies for obtaining help, advice and assistance from MIS — for example a help desk.

Our intention here has been to outline an overall policy statement embodying the policies which the data administrator needs to control the data resource. Now we can look in a little more detail at how this might be done.

Basic prerequisites of end user computing

There is one underlying prerequisite which must be fulfilled, this is, a sound base of data from which to operate the service. If the base data is suspect in any way, then the information it produces can be misleading and hence any decisions taken as a result of that information are potentially flawed. Remembering our pyramidal Figure 8.1, we can see that it only needs one of several base data sources to be suspect to throw the whole concept into disarray further up the hierarchy. The base data must also be clearly defined. If misinterpretation occurs at the base of the pyramid the cumulative effect as information is created further up can quite easily be greater than the sum of the parts. So a very clear and simple description of the elements down at the bottom must be available for those people intending to use it in end user applications. This, of course, is a major theme of data administration described throughout the book.

Some of our approaches to data administration — systems planning, data control, methods — are all geared up to providing such a view. The base data elements which give us the platform to develop end user views will come from various applications and facets of the business. In developing an understanding of the data, it is necessary to be sure of the compatibility of certain types of data. A great deal of end user computing is aimed at performance monitoring, be it product sales trends or machine efficiency. There are two main forms of performance monitoring: quantitative/qualitative and financial. These two use the same basic data in their calculations such as number of machines, hours in a day, marketing outlets, articles sold, and so on. It would be hoped that the financial performance could be calculated from applying monetary values to the quantitative analysis. Sadly, it is not always so simple and a frequent difficulty faced in boardrooms up and down the country is reconciling conflicting sets of figures, some of which show satisfactory quantitative efforts whilst others give a less than satisfactory financial performance. There are literally hundreds of reasons why this may be, particularly when some of the costs are affected by other financial criteria (e.g. taxation) and don't figure in a bold quantitative statement.

The data administrator is anxious to ensure that if such comparisons are necessary, then the application of the base data will turn into a meaningful analysis.

The base data must also be consistent and available. On the assumption that those receiving management information want to look at business performance over time, i.e. trends, then, clearly, there must be continuity in the way in which the base data is provided. Where corporate applications are the feeder source this will probably happen, although applications do change. Care is needed in specifying change such that existing data is not compromised in its uses outside those of the immediate application.

Where a large variety of base data is available, such as when multiple databases exist to support point solutions (described in Chapter 6), there should be a statement of which sources are the prime or authoritative sources.

This should not suggest that the other sources are corrupt in any way. It is a sensible policy to base specific types of business analysis on data which is deemed to be the definitive business thermometer.

For example, the ledger is usually the most authoritative financial source, principally because everything which has financial value must be recorded in it for legal reasons. At the end of the day, a proliferation of end user reports from a variety of sources could well paint a confusing picture. The confusion will lessen with the reduction in possible base sources for the data, as the end user reports will be based on the same data, and any differences will be caused by the way in which the data has been manipulated.

The base data, however, may well have its limitations. It is very important in understanding the base data that its limitations are taken into account. Once the data has been manipulated and converted into end user information, those limitations are forgotten in the heat of decision making. If the data is known to contain inaccuracies, or is not quite what is required to produce the desired information, then it is vital that this is not forgotten. Despite the adverse comments on the data or the function of the data that this may provoke, it is far preferable to bogus decisions being made through limitations of the data.

Provision of an end user computing information strategy

This may sound very familiar, as we have discussed the need for an information systems strategy in Chapter 6. In fact, this is an extension to that strategy and one to which the majority of organisations fail to give sufficient thought during the formative stages of developing the systems which will provide the data. In many ways we need a direct parallel to our strategic information systems plan, as we can see from Figure 8.3.

It is so much easier to provide end user facilities if a strategy such as that shown in Figure 8.3 can be adopted. The main reason for this is that the prerequisites we discussed earlier will stand a very good chance of being inherent in the systems and databases arising from the systems development leg of the strategy. The reality for many organisations is that they start the process off in the bottom right-hand corner, i.e. all systems development finishes and an end user application is thrown together as a last thought.

When applications development and management information planning are done in parallel, we have a situation where each step is complementary to its partner in the other strategy. Operational functional goals mean more when discussed in conjunction with the way in which managerial controls (supported by

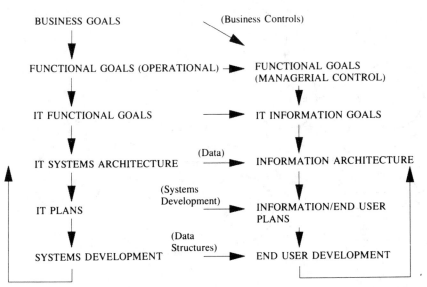

Figure 8.3 Parallel development of systems and information strategies

management information) will be applied to the specific operation. A data architecture helps us to derive an information architecture because information is derived from data and probably flows in the business in a similar way. Systems can be developed as easily to manipulate data for operational purposes as for tactical or strategic managerial purposes. This is not an easy strategy to achieve; however, benefits can be gained from planning small sections of the information architecture early on.

Methods and tools in EUC

The challenge here is to establish a set of methods and tools which allow Data Administration control over the service. In many respects we are looking for similarities between producing mainstream systems and end user applications. In practice, it will be very difficult to implement a full methodology approach because this is inconsistent with a prime objective of end user computing, that is, to allow the end user rapid and simple access to data. What we should aim for is an organised and consistent approach to providing an end user application which allows us to achieve this objective whilst providing the data administrator with sufficient confidence.

Figure 8.4 illustrates one approach which may be useful. What this demonstrates is a life cycle designed for rapid development of an end user application. The accent is on simplicity and speed without losing control. On the one hand you

Figure 8.4 A rapid approach to end user application development

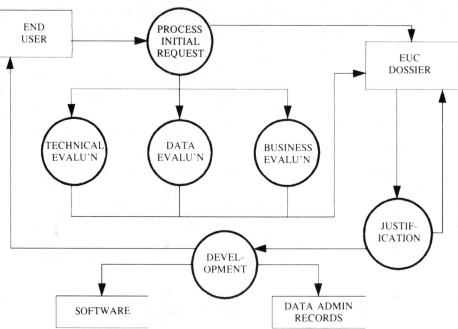

may be dealing with a request to download a file to a PC on a one-off basis, simple and very quick. Alternatively you may be developing a small multiuser system, taking a little more time. The life cycle needs to allow flexibility of approach to cover such diverse requests. The stages are as follows:

- Process initial request: This is simply logging the fact that a request has been made. The dossier is intended to be no more than a three-page document which describes the application and contains the acceptance sign-offs. An example of a dossier in a condensed form is shown in Figure 8.5. Each application needs a user sponsor and an MIS sponsor. We would suggest the corporate development team or person responsible for the principal system being accessed. This part of the method need take no longer than a couple of hours.

- Technical evaluation: This is one of three parallel evaluations to determine the computing needs of the application. Items of interest will include processor requirements, disk space, networking needs, data extraction schedules, peripherals needed, software required at the user end, emulation requirements and outline processing requirements. It is impossible to suggest how long this should take; however, up to twenty hours is probably reasonable. The dossier needs to be updated with an outline technical specification.

- Data evaluation: This evaluation is primarily the domain of the data administrator. What is required is a statement of what data the application is going to use, at data item level. Where this is existing data from corporate systems, the relevant system controllers should be involved in establishing that the data is being put to a use for which it is suitable and that there are no privacy or sensitivity issues. Where data is not currently in existence, the data administrator will be seeking definitions for the required data. The dossier should be updated with a summary statement of the needs in data flow diagram or data item listing formats.

- Business evaluation: This evaluation should look at the aims and objectives of the application in business terms. It should be produced primarily by the end user. If the application is to be used to replace existing functions or paper systems, a cost analysis should be done. The dossier will need a summary of the business case.

- Justification: In order to exercise control over the production of these applications there has to be an equivalent process

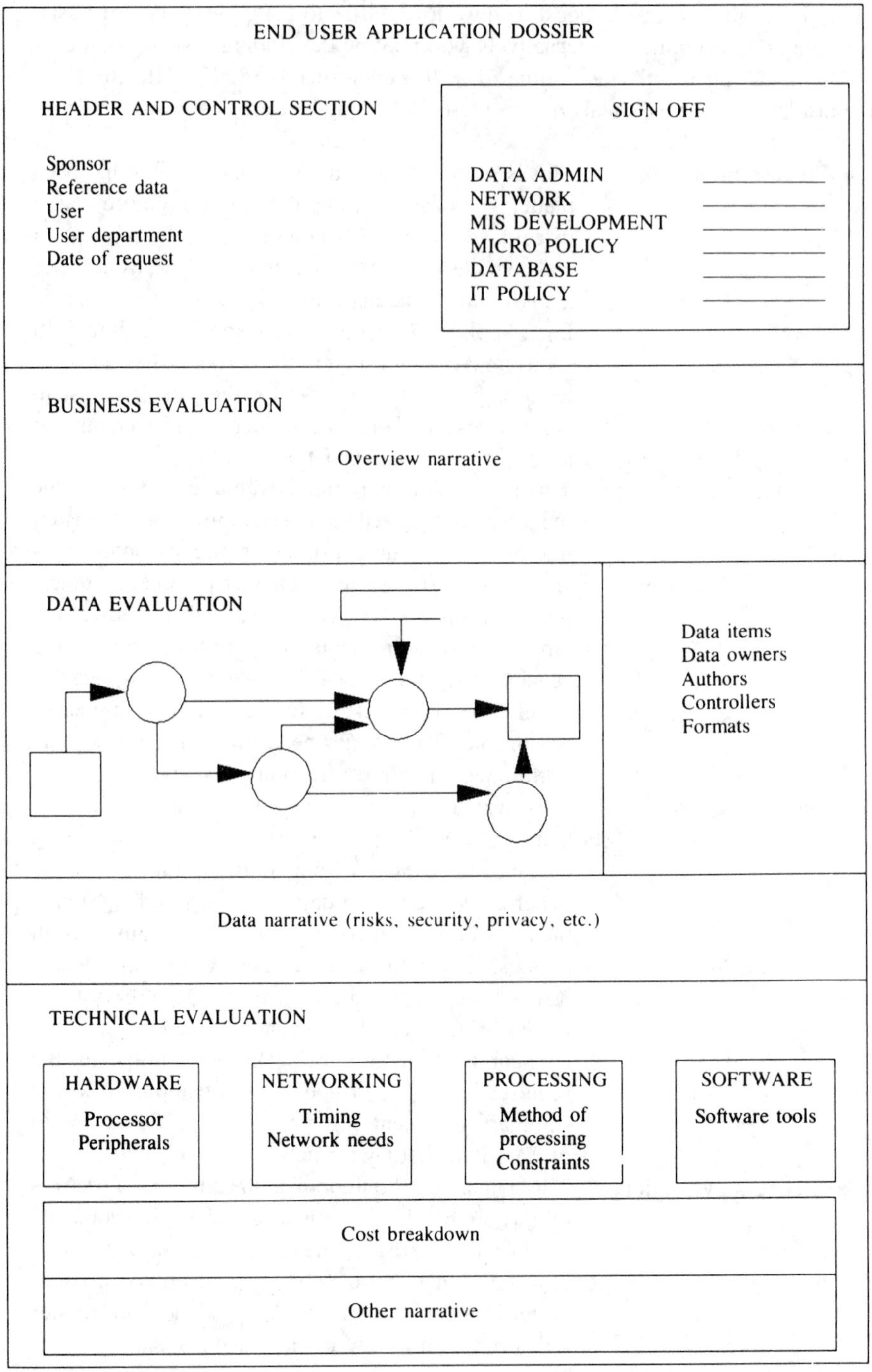

Figure 8.5 Proforma for end user application dossier

END USER APPLICATION DOSSIER

HEADER AND CONTROL SECTION

Sponsor
Reference data
User
User department
Date of request

SIGN OFF

DATA ADMIN	_____
NETWORK	_____
MIS DEVELOPMENT	_____
MICRO POLICY	_____
DATABASE	_____
IT POLICY	_____

BUSINESS EVALUATION

Overview narrative

DATA EVALUATION

Data items
Data owners
Authors
Controllers
Formats

Data narrative (risks, security, privacy, etc.)

TECHNICAL EVALUATION

HARDWARE	NETWORKING	PROCESSING	SOFTWARE
Processor Peripherals	Timing Network needs	Method of processing Constraints	Software tools

Cost breakdown

Other narrative

to the justification and cost/analysis of mainstream system development. The dossier should reflect the fact that an application has been agreed (by whatever IT development agreement process is usually employed).

● Developing: Whilst the software is being developed, the data administrator should be documenting the data usage in his or her dictionary system (or manual system). New data items should be governed by him/her and chosen according to the same guidelines discussed in Chapter 5. A risk analysis, however short and informal, is needed to assess the dangers of allowing certain types of data into the end user arena. If the application is in any way critical to the operation of the business, it should appear on the co-ordinated backup and recovery plan. It should also be registered under the Data Protection Act if appropriate. Again, the accent is on rapid development. Where the application consists of a data extraction on to a PC database, then one would hope for a turn-round in a few hours once the task is underway.

Repository control of information

The data administrator has the wherewithal, through the use of the dictionary (repository), to track data and information throughout the enterprise. This is a very difficult task, because end users can be loath to tell a corporate service what they are doing with the data. In the development method described earlier, one objective was to provide the end user with data to do with what (s)he will. The justification for the application, once gained, may not have any control over what evolves from it later on.

Nevertheless, the data administrator can document dictionary records for reports or graphs or screens which are the actual information, e.g. quarterly sales figures, pension payments by geographical area, costs of waste material through damage, etc. Minimally, the dictionary should be used to indicate where data items are used in end user applications. Depending on the flexibility and usability of the dictionary it may be a simple matter to tie up these cross-references. If a data administration dictionary (as described in Chapter 5) is designed specifically for the task, then it should be relatively easy to build in facilities to show how information, as well as data, is used in the business.

If possible, the end user should be encouraged to supply a standard 'specification' which lists data items used, source of data, layout of presentation, rules for production, recipients and supporting information.

System controlling

End user system control is one of the system controller's most important tasks (as discussed in Chapter 3). The role requires that the system controller undertakes the following:

1. Participates in the justification of an end user application by confirming that the data required is available, accurate and non-sensitive.
2. Confirms that the data is to be used for a purpose that it can fulfil meaningfully and that it cannot be misinterpreted to produce misleading management information.
3. Ensures that more creative ways of using data under his or her control are explored and, if appropriate, implemented. This is equally applicable in his/her own area as in other application areas.

Uploading/downloading control

The majority of end user applications seek to download data from large corporate databases and manipulate it to provide business information. A small number of them may also seek to upload some data back on to corporate databases. Extreme caution is needed here. Because end user applications are not as rigorously quality assured as a mainstream development would be, we have no guarantee that 'clean' data will be delivered. There has to be a clear policy for uploading. One method is to do a full audit of the application prior to allowing database updates to commence. In any case, the piece of software which actually does the updating should be formally developed by corporate MIS. In this way it is possible to ensure that self-checking mechanisms or validation routines are built in to 'vet' the data prior to committing it to the database. Apart from the obvious data accuracy checks, it may be important to have a date and time stamp somewhere on the data to check that 'old' data is not being returned to the corporate database. The best policy is to avoid uploading from end user applications altogether. When end user applications update corporate databases they have in fact ceased to be pure end user applications, and therefore should be subject to the same rigorous quality assurance checks that corporate systems go through.

Downloading is more straightforward and much less dangerous. However, there are a number of issues to be sorted out. Will there be a specific cut-off point for copying data and downloading? Will a set schedule be observed (very important where there are data dependencies in the mainstream applications)? How many copies will be taken and distributed? Will the copy data be backed up in its own right in case of download failure or will the whole extraction/copy procedure be reinvoked (time might not permit this!)?

For management information trends, something like a weekly extract may suffice. Where the data is being used for more precise control of an area of the business, more frequent extracts are needed. The more frequent the extract the more difficult it is for end users to be sure that they are accessing the latest version of the data. If timescales are tight and a high degree of automation is used to copy and load data into end user applications, a failure somewhere in the process may not be noticed. Potentially, this could compromise the information being produced.

Keeping end users informed

The main concern of the corporate MIS department with end user computing is the potential for end users to wreak havoc with the modern, easy to use tools in their end user environments. A common remedy for this is an arrangement to keep MIS informed of what is being done. This will only ever have partial success, as most people, by natural inclination, tend to operate more as individuals than as team players.

In the next sub-section we will be looking at auditing as a means of finding out what is happening. However, in this instance, we are concerned with the corporate IT function keeping the end user informed. Let us assume that we have been successful in encouraging a co-operative way of approaching end user computing and that the corporate IT function has been 'involved' in the process. If this is seen as a one-off involvement with no further need to maintain an interest in the application, then, for a number of possible reasons, the application and its data could run into difficulties. Perhaps there are operational problems with the corporate systems providing the data, changes to the schedule and availability of the data, modifications to the design of the feeder system which result in changes to the data, or business difficulties resulting in incomplete or inaccurate base data. If the end user applications are important enough, the fact that the data on which they depend is potentially flawed must be dealt with as a high-priority problem. There are two entirely distinct ways of approaching the solution, both of which have significant merits.

The end users themselves can be charged with the responsibility for checking the successful processing and transferring of their data. This will entail knowing that the business has functioned normally to provide the data and that the technical processes have all been satisfactory, e.g. corporate system functioning, extracts, downloads, etc. The merits of this approach are that the end user is actively encouraged to be part of a wider computing network; contact between the end user and corporate MIS or other system controllers encourages IT teamwork. This also allocates more accountability to the end user, which is a good thing in developing a responsible attitude towards data. Of course, this involves a lot of people and a lot of communication focussing on corporate MIS at times when enquiries are not welcome. This will not foster teamwork. If there is a business-wide, on-line information network, on the lines of CEEFAX or ORACLE, which can broadcast the necessary information, or a help desk, then the problems can be alleviated and this can be a very successful approach.

On the other hand, a second, and very different, approach is possible: this is, to ask a control function to be the eyes and ears of the end user community. Data Administration can do this, but beware of its time-consuming nature. For this,

Data Administration is required to document the whole end user computing network involving data extractions, transfers, schedules, manipulations and end results.

If and when irregularities occur, Data Administration can check the documentation, assess the impact on the end user and communicate it via the system controller. There are two main benefits to this. Firstly, as we can see from the preceding discussion, a central source of expertise can save a great deal of fact-finding and communication by many others who are not expert in any way. Secondly, if there are concerns about unknown or undocumented applications and data uses, this is a way of pulling the whole picture together. Most end users would trade off their own ultimate autonomy for the assurance of being fully informed, and so are likely to ensure that their needs are communicated to Data Administration, who in turn gain knowledge of what is happening to the data resource.

Both approaches are sufficiently attractive to warrant further investigation. There are no real guidelines as to which approach is the more suitable. If a hybrid is at all possible, then this will be worth investigating. Each organisation will have its own profile, which may suit one approach more than the other. Factors such as successful system controlling, Data Administration resources, information broadcasting services, numbers of end users, investment in end user computing, complexity of base data systems, and many more, will influence the decision.

Auditing

This can be a contentious issue. For those being audited, synonyms such as snooping, checking-up, interfering, meddling, etc., will be used. Those doing the auditing consider it as maximising potential, helping, conducting a census! Whatever the feelings are, if there is money tied up in end user computing, then the business has a responsibility to ensure that it is getting value for money from the investment.

Data Administration is, of course, the logical choice to carry out this task. To avoid some of the misconceptions mentioned above, there has to be a way of making it a team effort. Wherever some form of policy-making body exists for IT it should be tasked with producing an effectiveness review of major end user applications as part of its brief. The review will then involve Data Administration and the end user in discussing the whole application including the following:

* reliability of base data (timeliness, accuracy, etc.);
* access control to the end user data;
* security measures for backup and recovery;
* integrity of information generated;
* authorship of end user specified data;
* adequacy of system documentation (especially data usage);
* performance reliability of the application;

- performance reliability of the hardware configuration;
- audit trails of data manipulation (if important);
- mechanisms for identifying and coping with change.

If a responsible attitude towards this process can be generated, then we can allay the fears of unknown use of data.

In many ways, a 'responsible attitude' sums up the necessary approach to end user computing. As we have seen in this chapter, there are many ways in which the data we have striven so hard to make available and valuable can be misused. There are, though, many benefits to be gained from widespread, constructive use of the data. Data Administration must encourage the 'responsible' approach to end user computing which in turn will achieve our goal of more effective use of data as information.

Key action points

- Document a clear set of policies for data usage within an end user computing environment.
- Conduct a wide-ranging health check on the base data to ensure a sound basis for end user computing and decision support.
- Develop an information strategy to ensure that data architectures are designed which are capable of supporting the information processing needs of the organisation.
- Implement a rapid application development method for processing requests for end user computing services.
- Consider using the dictionary or repository to allow documentation of end user applications for Data Administration visibility and influence.
- Make system controllers accountable for the use of data under their control, including auditing applications, spreadsheets and databases.
- Design and exercise careful controls over the use of end user applications which interface, in some way, with corporate applications.

9 Solving data-related problems

Problem-solving is one of the ways in which Data Administration can take an active role in the business and be seen to be effective. It can help to establish Data Administration in people's minds as a valuable function, one that is available to assist rather than to restrict. Helping to solve problems quickly and efficiently places Data Administration in a favourable light, even where the problems should really never have occurred in the first place. Of course, the major effort must be towards preventing problems before they arise, hence the view of Data Administration as a 'policeman', maintaining standards, insisting on detailed design work and system documentation — something that system developers may be tempted to overlook in their hurry towards implementation. However, the products of the 'policeman's' role, together with more complete information on corporate systems, benefit everyone. Rigorous system documentation with complete data definitions, models and diagrams, helps users and systems developers to be more aware of the data that is available and of its potential as an asset in running the business. This will also be enormously useful when problems occur, in speeding up the detective work and contributing to an early solution.

Data Administration involvement in problem solving

Problems are bound to occur with all systems, and where these are data-related, Data Administration may become involved in sorting them out, with the assistance of users and systems staff, or it may be satisfied that the problem can be solved without active Data Administration input. Whenever possible, Data Administration will encourage users to resolve problems themselves, liaising with other system controllers and user managers who are affected. The nature and scope of the problem will determine where this is satisfactory, but Data Administration must be happy that the integrity of corporate data will not be adversely affected.

Data Administration will have a different perspective on problems than will those people who are immediately concerned, and this perspective has its own value. When a system suffers a problem, the first thoughts of the user or application team are to solve it as quickly as possible. They may decide to implement a software solution to correct faulty input, or they may carry out an exercise to amend corrupt data. In some cases, they may decide that the problem is unlikely to recur and has no major impact for them, and opt to do nothing.

Data Administration seeks to get to the root of the problem and solve it at source, rather than to correct its effects later by means of a technical or operational solution. Once again, Data Administration must take the wider view, making sure that all areas of the business are considered in resolving a problem which, seemingly, may affect only one particular area. To do this, it will be necessary to raise the general awareness of the types of problems which may need Data Administration involvement, and to build up a realisation of the requirement to keep Data Administration informed so that input can be given where appropriate. An appreciation of this requirement will develop with experience, and will become more 'natural' as time goes on.

Sometimes, the user or application team is unaware of additional uses of the data in other applications. In solving their own problem, they may inadvertently create a new one for someone else. It is Data Administration's role to ensure that this does not happen. As barriers between different business areas are removed and more integrated systems become the norm, there is likely to be an increase in cross-functional data problems. The cross-functional implications of solutions must be considered fully.

Obviously, many problems are solved by the users and application teams on a day-to-day basis without requiring Data Administration involvement. Some may be the result of program faults, failure of batch updates, and so on, and they will be tackled promptly as the problem occurs. Data Administration is more likely to become involved in problems where the cause is not immediately apparent, and where the problem itself may not be recognised for some time.

As well as problems which have already arisen, Data Administration will be involved in resolving problems 'before the event', when plans need to be drawn up to counteract a problem which will occur unless some preventive action is taken. The examples given in Figure 9.1 will throw some light on to the types of problem with which Data Administration may be involved, and some pointers on how to go about resolving them. Of course, these examples are by no means exhaustive and there are many variations on the theme!

Inaccurate data

The majority of the problems will concern inaccurate data held in a system. This can be caused by input errors, such as simple mis-typing, and the precise source of the data needs to be checked. It may be established that the data is entered from a source document, such as an invoice, and if possible the source documents should be checked against the errors. There are several possibilities to check:

(a) Data is being entered wrongly.
(b) Data is being entered correctly — but is incorrect on the source document.
(c) The wrong field is being entered.
(d) The wrong person is entering the field.

Figure 9.1 How the
data resource loses
value through data
problems

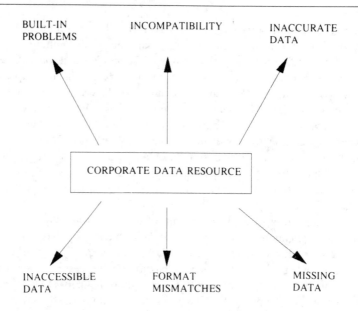

BUILT-IN
PROBLEMS

INCOMPATIBILITY

INACCURATE
DATA

CORPORATE DATA RESOURCE

INACCESSIBLE
DATA

FORMAT
MISMATCHES

MISSING
DATA

Several measures can be taken to correct (a) and (c). These may include extra training, changes to working procedures, or perhaps improving verification or validation at the data entry stage. This will depend on the type of system involved and the method of data input.

All these measures can help to improve the level of data accuracy at the input stage, although verification and validation issues are best reviewed during development work and built into system procedures from the beginning. These were discussed in more detail in Chapter 5. Training and procedures can help to eliminate data accuracy problems; users must be clear what their jobs entail, and be aware of the need for accuracy. Training can also help in a slightly different problem, where users may leave fields blank rather than enter incorrect data. The user may feel that it is safer to leave out the data, especially if it is not vital in his or her own area. However, it can have a significant effect on other areas which may depend on the data. The user must be educated into viewing data as a corporate rather than a local concern, and must realise his/her responsibility towards other users.

Problem (d) may also be cleared up through improved education and procedures, once the reason behind the wrong person entering the data has been established. This situation sometimes occurs because of changes in departmental structure, or simply because someone is new to the job. Training courses for people with new responsibilities may have lapsed, and new job functions may not be properly reflected in departmental procedures.

The system controller will need to rectify these faults, and there are implications for the authorship of the data if it appears that the authorship responsibility has passed from one job function to another.

The following three variations on the problem all show the basic requirements for data accuracy:

- The right person enters or modifies the data.
- (S)he is aware of the correct procedures to follow and is clear on every detail.
- (S)he understands the need to input data accurately, both locally and as a part of the corporate data network.

Problem (b) widens the picture slightly, and may be impossible to solve within a single department. If the data is being entered correctly, but the media from which it is taken contains incorrect data, the origin of the error needs to be traced back. It may come from outside the organisation, but in many cases there is some manual or software cross-checking in place which will highlight such errors, for example incorrect amounts on invoices.

The faulty media may have been produced by the same system or by a different system within the same organisation. Is the second system suffering from the same faults outlined in (a), (c) and (d)? We need to discover where the data is correct, and at which point, in which system, it becomes inaccurate. We can establish if the inaccuracy comes from some manual input, and, if so, the reasons behind it — possibly procedural, or possibly based on some further inaccurate data, such as figures produced by another system. The problem may originate in a program fault, and may take some effort to track down, particularly if the fault has not been noticed quickly. Software faults can cause extensive data corruption and recent changes to programs or new releases of software should be checked to see if they are the possible source of the problem.

Teamwork

The data administrator becomes something of a detective while trying to chase up the origin of the problem, crossing off the possibilities as they are eliminated. The collaboration of different system controllers and IT application teams will be required in order to check out the different systems, analyse what is happening and if this is what should be happening, delve into program code to check for system errors and check input and output for updates, processed either on-line or through batch programs.

The data administrator can maintain the continuity and impetus of the search for the cause and solution of the problem, as individual controllers or application teams decide that it is not their problem and lose interest. Some pressure may have to be brought to bear initially, as application teams may be unwilling to sacrifice some of their time and resources from development work in order to investigate a problem which may not have been reported by their particular users and may seem to have no impact in their area. It is always difficult to gain support and enthusiasm for the less glamorous aspects of IT work, particularly where this means checking through someone else's old program code to solve a messy problem!

Using data flow diagrams to help

A basic data flow diagram can prove an invaluable aid while following the clues if the data concerned has a complex life cycle (Figure 9.2). It depicts the passage of data and where actions are performed on it, and is an easy way of seeing where other data and systems can affect it. This will not only assist in tracking down the fault, but, once it is discovered, it will help to ensure that all the systems which may have been affected are considered, either in cleaning up the data or in implementing a solution, and that data integrity is maintained across all the different systems.

It is important to determine how far the effects of the inaccurate data have

Figure 9.2 Tracing
data flow during
problem investigation

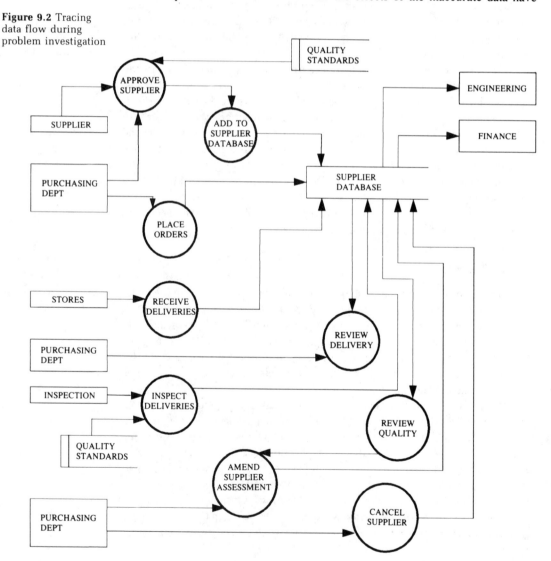

reached, including what business decisions have been based on it. It is also important to ensure that system controllers are aware of the problem and that appropriate actions are taken in all the company's systems.

Choosing the right solution

Data Administration's role is to help pinpoint the source of any inaccuracy and to ensure that a solution is comprehensive and effective and will eliminate future occurrences of the problem. It is useful to document both the problem and the solution, and any measures taken to recover data integrity, in case any queries arise in the future. It is sometimes tempting to believe that the next problem is the same thing again, and it is an advantage to have the facts to hand. The solution itself, and any corrective action to clean up the data, will be carried out by users and application teams as required. The measures taken need to be in line with the corporate value of the data, and not just based on local departmental considerations. This means that a user area must spend the necessary resources to correct the data and any relevant procedures if that data warrants it, judged from a corporate viewpoint.

Conversely, the decision may be taken to leave inaccurate data in the system, while correcting the error, if it is judged that the corporate value of the data is insufficient. Perhaps the usefulness of that data has gone and its historical value is negligible.

It is worth noting that many examples of inaccurate data may not come to light for some time. For example, if a wrong code is entered on an order, it will be rejected if it is a non-existent or invalid code. However, if the code is wrong but is in fact a valid code, the system will accept it, unless there is a further check involving another field. Such inaccuracies may well appear later when the wrong parts are delivered to the shopfloor, or the wrong goods are sent to the customer. This is, of course, very unsatisfactory, and software checks should be built in to avoid this where possible.

Unreliable data

A slightly different problem is revealed when the data held in the system does not reflect reality. In organisations where stocktaking is carried out, unreliable data can often be discovered when comparing actual stock to theoretical stock.

This can have significant repercussions in a manufacturing company, if, for example, the system tells us that there are 100 parts and the inventory only locates 80. Not only are the parts unavailable when required, but the 20 missing parts represent a financial asset which in fact does not exist. It is no more satisfactory if 150 parts are physically located, but the system records only 100. Our financial stock figures are once again in error, and parts will be reordered unnecessarily or too early. While inventory exercises can improve the situation temporarily, although at the cost of substantial effort, it may be that improvements in procedures can help. For example, stock must be entered correctly into inventory at the delivery point and deducted accurately when issued to the shopfloor. Tighter control over the stores area may be needed to ensure that all receipts and issues are recorded accurately. This type of operational change or improvement is the responsibility of the system controller working with user managers. However, the data administrator has an interest in seeing that steps are taken to improve data accuracy, since it forms part of the corporate data whose value is diminished by such inaccuracies. As demonstrated above, misleading stock figures will affect not only the stores area, but also financial, manufacturing and purchasing departments.

Random physical inventory checks help to review accuracy levels, and tolerances are often introduced so that figures within a certain percentage of expected figures are accepted. Figures outside these tolerances will be rechecked. Similar checks can help systems in other areas, too. Checks can be introduced whereby prices or costs which go up or down by a greater or lesser margin than the norm can be reviewed and then adjusted if necessary. This may not be the result of any data inaccuracies but can serve as an effective warning to the user of exceptional values which may be caused by outside factors. These checks can be done on a regular basis, programmed into the software, and are therefore not too much effort for the user, apart, of course, from any necessary effort involved in checking the deviations and adjusting them. If the deviations bring to light any particular problems, these must be tackled at source.

All data accuracy monitors should be performed regularly to keep an eye on the health of the data, and to stop any problems at a relatively early stage. As described in Chapter 5, the system controller has the major responsibility of implementing these monitors, using his knowledge of the system and the operations it supports to devise checks that reveal most about the data.

Although 'clean-up' exercises can be performed on the data, the resources required may be huge. There must be strict controls over any such exercises. Any data adjustments must be fully documented, with a clear picture of the 'before' and 'after' state of the data. The problem may well become worse if nothing is done to remedy the situation. The more we can keep the data accurate from the beginning by good standards, good working practices and procedures, the better it will be. The data should be supporting the business, leaving us to develop business issues and move forward as a company, rather than undermining our efforts and confidence and taking time and resources from other initiatives to tidy it up.

If the data in any system is shown to be faulty, and steps are not quickly taken to rectify it, the data will be viewed as unreliable, and its use will become very suspect. The system will then fail to support the operational functions for which it was introduced, with users resorting to guesswork or to their own private documentation systems. It is very important to keep accuracy levels high, which will equate with a corresponding level of confidence in the system. It is easy for an unreliable system to be kept running, with less and less use being made of it because the data is simply not good enough. A long hard look at the organisation's systems should reveal where resources are being wasted on maintaining systems whose use no longer justifies these costs.

Another reason for users keeping their own facts and figures can be the timeliness of data; the system may be updated only once a week, but the user may require the data fully up-to-date. If so, the operational possibilities for more frequent updates should be reviewed. Once-per-week updates may have been satisfactory when the system was first introduced, but these may have been rendered inadequate by changes in working practices. The system controller must be aware of what happens locally, and of any such inadequacies of the system. (S)he must try to maintain high standards in the data, and encourage confident use of the system for day-to-day operations.

Operational considerations affecting data accuracy

In some cases, data is not as accurate as it might be because of a clash of interests between the area inputting the data and the area using it later on in the cycle. Take the following example. MRPII routes the manufacturing process through numerous work centres, which perform a variety of operations. In order to achieve the most accurate costing details, batches of work passing through the work centres should show the quantities rejected or damaged at each operation, i.e. at the most accurate level of detail. However, for shopfloor purposes it is enough to record the quantities by work centre, and it is certainly more time-consuming to split and record them for each operation. This is a dilemma which must be resolved between user managers concerned.

Will the added value of the more detailed information justify the additional time required to provide it on the shopfloor? Or can some percentage split be automatically assigned to each operation, which will adequately fulfil financial requirements while not impacting on shopfloor manufacturing progress? This situation demonstrates the need for compromise in reaching a solution and for a common sense approach in building value into the corporate data asset; the need to collect detailed, accurate data must not impinge on normal operations and unnecessarily burden a workforce whose main aim is to manufacture the product, or to provide a service.

Inconsistency and incompatibility between systems

Another major source of data problems, and one which can only increase with the need for greater systems integration, is inconsistencies and incompatibility of data in different systems. Sometimes these result from different data definitions, and a 'bridge' may need to be built for integration purposes. For example, a field length may need to be changed or interpreted as part of the transfer of data, and this may be relatively straightforward.

One example from our own experience showed that the same values in two different systems were not revealed in a comparison report because one system had an additional prefix in some cases, and the spacings in the field were slightly different. The result, until this was catered for, was some significantly misleading information.

In other circumstances, however, the disparities may be both less apparent and less manageable. This can arise from the different objectives that each system has been designed to achieve. Our manufacturing system needs detailed work centre progress information. Our marketing system requires only a top-level view of that information, enough to keep track of progress at certain key points in the cycle. It is therefore designed with a minimal number of work centres against which data is held. This means, of course, that the data in the manufacturing system is much more accurate and up-to-date and that data in the two systems does not always match. In addition, manufacturing requirements mean that shopfloor routings are volatile and that the key points may, and do, change. The marketing system does not always reflect these changes adequately, and the user may find it necessary to use two systems rather than one in order to be sure of having the latest accurate information.

This situation probably derives from a belief at the design stage that the manufacturing routings will be static. Whatever the reason, it can cause the user some frustration and lack of trust in the marketing system, a situation which has required improvement by development of notification of changes from one system to the other.

Further confusion arises where information from two separate sources does not tally. The manufacturing area uses a shopfloor control system alongside batch cards, layouts and drawings which are produced or recorded by other systems. In some cases, details on the shopfloor control system do not match the piece of paper in front of the user. Which one is to be believed? These problems can be solved by examining inconsistencies in the timing of updates between the two sources, and amending if necessary, and also changing the procedures for amending layout and drawing numbers. If the two sources cannot be brought into line, it must be clear to the user which one is the authoritative version for his or her particular environment and this should be documented in the operating procedures. However, this still leaves room for error and, ideally, steps should be taken to remove the inconsistency in the data. This can sometimes be achieved by rescheduling some of the computer batch runs which produce some of the documentation or update the systems.

Some incompatibility can occur when one system uses data provided by another system, but for a different purpose. We have had experience of a quantity set up in the manufacturing system for ordering purposes which was used as a basis for some of the charges going through to our Parts Department system. The costs developed on the basis of these figures were in some cases totally out of proportion, and it was discovered that this quantity could not be used as part of the basis for pricing parts. This was fortunately one of the instances where a monitoring system based on tolerances was in place and quickly highlighted the inconsistency.

Some inconsistencies are the result of different criteria applied in different systems. For example, in one system the description of a part is a protected field and cannot be changed. If the user wishes to assign a new description, a new part number must be assigned. In a second system, however, the description may be changed, so that one part number may have two different descriptions in the business. Which one is to be held as the correct one? We must ask ourselves whether there is a justifiable requirement to change the description in the second system, and how much error or confusion may result. This ties in with a further category of problem which may be encountered, in the realm of authorship responsibility.

'Shared' authorship

In Chapter 5 we discussed the importance of establishing prime authorship for corporate data, so that it is beyond dispute who is the authoritative source for all the different elements that go to make up the data resource, and where the true data values can be located. Unfortunately, it is not always quite so clear-cut, particularly where authorship responsibilities have not been assigned from the outset, and where different systems and procedures have grown up using similar data. This is why disputes over authorship issues may arise, and why we recommend sorting out these issues and documenting agreed responsibilities as part of the system design process.

The most potent example of this in our own business is that of 'part number', an item at the heart of many of our business systems and consequently used and developed by several different business functions. Part numbers are principally assigned by the engineering function, which is the area assumed to have prime authorship of the part number, as it is there that parts are created, developed and drawn. Over the years, however, other areas have recognised the need for part numbers in their own fields.

For example, the Parts Department may create a 'part number' which is in fact a kit, a 'part' recognisable to the dealer or customer which contains a collection of separate 'parts'. Here again, this is a matter of interpretation. Other departments also create their own part numbers for different purposes, not to mention the fact that our suppliers have their own part numbers, which are not the same as ours, or that part numbers with certain suffixes denote tools, or gauges — parts used to manufacture parts. As you can see, this one data item presents a minefield of potential difficulties, mainly due to the proliferation of its use in different systems with different interpretations and needs.

In this situation, Data Administration must at least try to bring some order to chaos by halting the uncontrolled use of the data item, documenting what exists and where, and centralising the authorship authority. Prime authorship must be assigned to one area, and in one system, whether IT-based or manual, and this must be recognised within the business. Once this has been done, the use of the data can be rationalised to ensure that the value of this crucial field is assigned by the prime author only, leading to a greater level of consistency in the future.

Mechanisms may have to be introduced to allow other areas to operate successfully while restricting the free-for-all access previously enjoyed.

It may be less easy to do this where different areas seem to have equal rights as 'prime author', such as two different manufacturing plants, or two different warehouses having access to similar sets of data, although they may refer to a different plant code, or different categories of stock. For example, both warehouses or plants may share a supplier and both may be able to modify data about the supplier, which can create difficulties. One manufacturing plant may change some processing information, which, being centrally held for both plants, may affect the other plant adversely. In these cases, we may need to get back to the *real* authority on that data, which may be located in another system. The Purchasing Department may well be the real source of supplier data; the Production Engineering Department the real source of processing data. This problem occurs because the data is in fact duplicated within the organisation and the real authority may not be recognised. This may be necessary because of organisational or technical reasons and occurs particularly when systems are developed independently, without a corporate overview.

The blurring of the authorship issues, then, leads to difficulties, and data should only be duplicated in different systems where absolutely necessary. It should then be updated or modified at one central point, if feasible, with updates being passed on to the other systems.

Duplicate data can also occur within a system when the data is simply added twice. For example, the same supplier is added to the database twice with different supplier numbers. This may be because the database provides insufficient search facilities to check if the supplier is already there, or because it requires the names entered to match exactly before flagging up the existing supplier. This type of situation should obviously be eliminated where possible, as it will lead to unnecessary confusion, or even to placing an order with a supplier that the company has decided should no longer be used. If extra checks or searches cannot be built into the system software, it might be necessary to alter procedures so that more manual checking is done. This is less satisfactory, however, particularly where this information could be added by several users at the same session.

Missing data

If having duplicate data can cause a problem, so can not having the data at all. If some parts of the data are incomplete some or all of the time, then the data becomes unreliable as a source and loses its value as part of the corporate data resource. Some data is critical to the organisation and must be maintained, even where it has no direct effect on the day-to-day business functions. It is even more difficult if the information is not missed immediately, as it may then be impossible to recover it. In some cases the data can be traced back to paper documents, such as invoices, but this cannot be guaranteed and can present a time-consuming chore.

In the field of car manufacture, it is essential to record details on car build, particularly safety-critical and emission-critical information, and there are legal obligations to maintain this information. Similarly, in financial areas, details of financial transactions need to be recorded. In both these cases, it is vital to ensure that all the details are entered correctly at the appropriate time and that the data is kept for as long as it is required. This means that an archiving policy must be in place to ensure that all the required data is kept and safely stored. It must be readily accessible if it is required for audit or for operational purposes. We must bear in mind that the data needs to be available even if changes take place to software or storage media over the years. Conversions may need to be arranged for archived data if this occurs.

Archived data forms a critical part of the data resource and needs to be considered actively, particularly as the data which we archive is, by its very nature, some of the most critical, sensitive, or legally significant data in our business. Archiving policies should be reviewed regularly; they will vary from system to system, but any business or legal changes need to be reflected in them, if appropriate.

If any data is missing, we may have to look again at our procedures, training and software checks and try to improve any or all of these. Archiving programs can check that the necessary fields are complete and activities have been carried out before archiving takes place. For example, financial records could be checked to ensure that transactions have been correctly closed before archiving takes place. However, if some data is revealed as missing at this stage, rather than simply 'not yet ready for archiving', it can be a tedious procedure to trace back the missing information. If this information stays on our 'live' system because it cannot be archived pending completion of the data, this will impact the performance of the system, as it carries unnecessary records. It is always a major consideration to maximise the use of space in any IT system and maintain only the necessary data on the 'live' database.

A different problem of 'missing data' can occur when one system anticipates receipt of some data from a host system, but the data does not get transferred. It can happen that only six files get downloaded instead of seven, and it is important that the receiving system has a check on exactly what is received in order to preserve data integrity. The system controller should put a mechanism in place to achieve this, either by checking the output of any jobs run, or by checking data received on his or her system, if that is possible. Problems will be increased if missing data is not noticed before the next download takes place. It is just as important to check this, whether the data is going into an 'operational system' or is for use in management information or end user computing. The main point is that the data does not represent what the user thinks it does, and as such it can lead to incorrect decisions and actions.

Change in data definition

Downloaded data is particularly susceptible to problems caused by changes of data definitions to the host system which affect data transferred downstream. This can happen where a parochial rather than a corporate view reigns supreme, and is often due to forgetfulness or lack of understanding, rather than malice, although it may not seem like that at first, if you are affected!

The originating system's data definitions may be changed without allowing for any receiving system's needs, and without anyone being informed. This can wreak havoc in the receiving system, leading to data corruption, and it must be caught very early on. This demonstrates the importance of being clear as to what all the data fields represent, and of having strict controls on any changes to them. Ideally, any changes should be referred to Data Administration, who should be aware of the requirements of receiving systems and can prevent any problems occurring. Needless to say, changes must be notified at the proposal stage, *before* they take place.

This problem can happen particularly with user departments running their own systems on their own machines, who may not always comply with data standards and company data procedures. These systems may have been in place before Data Administration principles were adopted. If a type of data in a particular field becomes superfluous in the originating department, users may decide to use it for another purpose. This may be ideal for them, but the receiving department may unwittingly still be using the data, believing it to be the same as ever. This may only come to light when the values cause accuracy problems elsewhere, or something unusual is spotted. By this time, the data corruption caused could be significant. It is particularly difficult to notice this, where the same format is used, for example, by using the previous 'target date' field to record 'purchase date' or 'actual date'. Since it is still a date format, no warning bells will sound. If the corruption is not noticed immediately, various activities and management decisions may have been based on the information from these fields. One simple change can have a serious impact on a downstream area. It may also be particularly difficult to discover exactly what has been affected and to restore true values.

This is a particular problem where there is a lack of firm central control and where local users have the ability to override corporate guidelines for their own, often short term, purposes. In this situation, Data Administration tries to educate users, especially system controllers and user managers who manage their own machines and databases, but it is extremely frustrating when departmental considerations win over corporate ones, with resulting disasters on whatever scale.

This type of experience can only be avoided by strict central control, which will benefit everyone in the end and should be introduced as a matter of course at green field sites, but it was not an option in our own environment. With a more powerful Data Administration presence, or centralised control from the IT development group over database structures, regardless of hardware platform or software, this sort of problem should not occur. This may indeed be the path we will have to follow in the future, by absorbing the responsibility for all developments into a central body. For the moment, however, we will continue to educate our users and seek their active co-operation, picking up the pieces along the way when individuality and creativity head in the wrong direction.

A similar problem can be caused where the format of values input to a particular field is changed, if the ramifications of doing so are not realised. The following is a recent example: a departmental code field which, through long usage, is established as a numeric field of four digits, such as '0014'. In some systems, only the last three digits are used, '014'. However, for business reasons, it was decided to set up a department with a three-character code, such as 'ABC'. This immediately caused problems when it could not be entered into some of the financial systems, which were programmed to expect four numerics. What had seemed a simple thing to the user manager concerned, who had no idea that any problem would result, struck terror into the hearts of development staff faced with reviewing and amending program logic in numerous systems. And, of course, 'department code' is one of those small data fields which tend to pop up in numerous places across the business. This is an obvious case for reviewing the real need for a different form of code, the amount of effort involved, and deciding whether a compromise can be made.

Abusing the system

It is only a short step from the above situation, brought about through genuine lack of knowledge, to the official efforts to 'get around the system' which are sometimes sponsored by IT departments.

This happens when there is a requirement to include some data values, and rather than perform a huge development exercise with possible database re-structuring, it is decided to use a field which already exists but is designated for another purpose. This can be implemented satisfactorily if the field has never been used for the original purpose and will not be required in the future for that purpose. In other words, we must be absolutely certain that no confusion can result. Imagine the problems if some archived data holds values representing one thing, and these values represent something else in the live system. Although it may be clear at the time when the functions of the field are changed, it is amazing how hazy memories can become later on, after several changes of staff have taken place and the original reasons for the change have disappeared into the mists of time. And, anyway, everyone thought that the archived data would never be needed. It was only really archived 'to be on the safe side'.

Unfortunately, we cannot look into the future, so we should at least try to minimise any problems or confusions, that we may be building up for ourselves. And, from experience, the statement 'Nobody uses that field anyway' needs to be fully explored and justified before going ahead.

It is all too easy to overlook some fringe user, who may only use the field spasmodically, but that will be enough to destroy the data integrity of the system, leading once again to unreliability and mis-information. For this reason, changes in use should be done cautiously and backed up by adequate documentation and consultation. Users who are tempted to use data fields for different purposes on a more 'unofficial' basis should also be discouraged. Everyone must use data fields as they are intended, for the same purpose and with no misinterpretations, if we are to achieve a firm foundation for the corporate data asset.

Built-in problems

Some data-related problems do not suddenly appear overnight, requiring urgent action and repair work. Instead, they loom menacingly on the horizon, and we may be conscious of them but not be able to justify resources to tackle them. Some of these are long-standing problems which are inherent in the basic system design; the problem may have developed because some of the initial premises on how the data would be used have been overtaken by events.

For example, many systems are set up with particular restrictions which are judged sufficient for the user's requirements. Initially, all may be well, but problems may develop after several years, either because the system is still required after a longer life than expected, or because its use has increased or changed. Perhaps the original business criteria on which the system design was based have changed. Alternatively, the problem may have been anticipated, but the point has now been reached where a decision needs to be taken on what to do about it.

As the change of the century approaches, some of our systems need to be amended, notably those concerned with long-term planning. This is because the first two digits which indicate century are not always stored. Date calculations are performed only using the last two digits which means that the year 2000 could appear to be earlier than the year 1999. This could cause chaos in systems which schedule materials or plan projects. This is a simplistic example of an anticipated problem — one which seems more urgent now than it did five years ago — which has implications for programming resource, database structures, and so on. In resolving which systems need to be changed, and which can safely be left, the data transfers between systems must be considered. The plan of action must be co-ordinated between different application development teams. Once this has been decided, a future policy on the use of dates needs to be introduced, so that future developments will fit in with changes made.

Data Administration is involved in the adoption of this policy and in the resolution of the difficulties, and is then responsible for ensuring that the policy is adhered to in new systems or developments by incorporating it into the data item checking procedure outlined in Chapter 5.

Other 'built-in' problems include ranges of numbers or codes which may prove insufficient in themselves, or cause problems where business developments lead to the information being used elsewhere, or to several systems being linked. For example, one of our systems holds a range of numbers which is quite sufficient, since the data is archived after six months. A second system, however, ran into problems when using the same information, since users wanted to hold the data for different purposes for up to two years. They are now unable to do this, since the number range recycles within about eighteen months, and have had to curtail their requirements — a case of the system restrictions imposing a limit on the business use of the data.

Problems can also result where meaningful codes are used, particularly where the system lives longer than expected or changes in its use take place.

Meaningful codes can make life easier for the user, for example by an alphabetic prefix which immediately conveys the type of part or category of employee. This must be weighed against the limitations that may be seen as a straitjacket later, sometimes to such an extent that enormous effort is used to overcome it by 'starting from scratch' and changing existing codes or numbers totally. There are many examples of anomalies in codes which can be traced back to an initial decision to create a codified structure for which the original reasoning has been forgotten. Often one part of the structure develops out of proportion to the rest, and it becomes increasingly difficult to maintain the meaning behind the code.

As we mentioned before, we are not able to see into the future; we cannot anticipate how our systems will develop, although we can be sure that they will do so in order to adapt to the changing needs of the business. We must be sure that we are creating our systems to be as flexible as possible in order to support those future business needs. We must not build in meaning which in a few years will be meaningless, tie ourselves down to formats that will hinder us, or restrict ourselves to codes that will fail to meet our need to expand.

Codes and numbers are often 'key fields' in the database and as such are a key piece of data. We should ensure that our 'key fields' are clear, are not open to misinterpretation or confusion, and are adequate to function as pointers to the data resource, whichever way it needs to develop.

Where problems do occur with codes, such as over-running the range, a software solution will inevitably be required, being careful to ensure that existing data is not compromised. It may be necessary to archive or flag existing data before going ahead, while hopefully not repeating the problem in any new code or range chosen.

These 'built-in' problems must often be tackled by systems developers, but it is important to make sure that all interests are covered, and this is part of Data Administration's role. However, perhaps the major part of the role is to sound the note of warning at the initial stages of systems development and try to eliminate these potential hazards before they get off the ground. There will always be cases, however, where user influence and technical or operational considerations take precedence over Data Administration's more cautious approach, and where the results of compromising the future for the sake of the present will return to haunt us.

Data Administration role in problem solving

Data Administration's role in solving data-related problems can vary from fringe observer, through interested participant, to major investigator. The range and variety of problems, not to mention their severity, is enormous and the data administrator will rely on initiative, experience and guesswork to tackle them.

Most of the rest of this book is concerned with preventing problems from arising, by instilling the principles of good data management and the controls which prevent a free-for-all which leads to data chaos.

However, there are a few items in the data administrator's armoury which can be used to help in problem solving when the inevitable happens. Some of these are the very things which Data Administration supports and puts in place at the beginning of the data management process. For example, our dictionaries, data flow diagrams and further documentation of the data resource will all be invaluable in helping to trace the flow of data and highlight discrepancies in formats or usage. This is why it is essential to create and maintain these, so that up-to-date information is available if required.

We have also put in place a 'problem log' so that problems can be documented, which is a useful reference tool when similar difficulties arise. This log is shared with Quality Assurance, so that they are made aware of data-related problems, and, similarly, Quality Assurance audit results are made available to Data Administration. Any data-related issues from QA audits are also logged. In this way, we can monitor whether changes in procedures or technology are effective in solving the problem.

The nature and urgency of the problem will decide how the results of any investigations are presented, or if they are presented at all. Some results will simply be documented in the problem log, but, for more long-standing problems, a report might be produced with recommended actions. This is more suitable for the 'built-in' type of problem, and would form a basis for discussion on how to proceed, timescales, resources, and so on.

Data Administration is very dependent on the co-operation of IT development teams, user managers, and system controllers in trying to get to the bottom of a problem (Table 9.1). These groups will have much greater in-depth knowledge of a particular area or system, and their input and support is invaluable. The system controller, or controllers, involved must be our greatest allies in these investigations, and the rapport built up between Data Administration and system controllers becomes very important. It must, of course, be well established before this, and good relations previously in place will reap dividends here.

The data administrator may have to use a great deal of tact in soliciting this support, as there is often implied criticism of a particular area or person, and in some cases there may have been some aggressive discussions between areas before Data Administration got involved. The data administrator needs to remain aloof from any political or departmental considerations and convey to all parties the requirement to obtain the facts and take any decisions based on the benefit to the business as a whole, leaving any recriminations to one side. Data Administration may be a 'policeman', but it should not be expected to be judge and jury as well!

Key action points

- Minimise the likelihood of problems by following good data administration guidelines.
- Use data administration tools to help to solve problems, including data flow diagrams and dictionaries.

Table 9.1 Principal involvement in solving data-related problems

Type of data-related problem	Responsibility						
	Technical Support	Database Analyst	Application Devt teams	System User Manager	Data Administration	System Controller	Quality Assurance
Technical	•	•		•			
Software	•	•	•	•			
Operational	•		•	•		•	
Integrity/missing data			•	•	•	•	•
Inaccuracy/Unreliability			•		•	•	•
'Built-in'			•	•	•	•	
Data definitions/format mismatches		•	•		•		
Inaccessibility	•	•	•	•		•	
Procedural					•	•	•
Incompatibility			•		•	•	
Authorship			•		•	•	

- Seek the co-operation of IT staff, system controllers, and users in resolving problems.
- Implement the solution after considering all the implications and make sure that the cause of the problem has been dealt with.

10 Getting the message across

One of the initial difficulties which will confront the budding data administrator, and one which will continue to be a problem area, will be gaining recognition in the business and establishing a credible position. Not only will this be a struggle for a Data Administration function which has yet to find its feet, but it is essential for this recognition to be won so that the function can operate successfully.

This struggle comes at a later stage than the initial efforts to convince senior business management of the need for data resources to be managed properly. By this point, they have accepted the importance of establishing a dedicated function for this purpose. The necessity of explaining the function's objectives and scope to the business at large will be, if anything, a more taxing task. Even after obtaining senior management commitment and support, the need to constantly raise awareness, justify the position and even the existence of the Data Administration function, and clarify the principles, will be quite a burden. At times it will seem to be an unnecessarily onerous one to the data administrator, detracting from more practical work and taking up valuable time.

The difficulties of getting the message across

To be faced with introducing change to developers or users may be an unpleasant prospect. They may be perfectly content with the existing situation and methods and be resolutely determined not to see any benefits in such techniques as data flow diagramming or logical data modelling, if these have not been used in the organisation before. It can be daunting to attempt to describe the mechanics of data flow to someone who is happy with flow-charting. It is equally difficult to try to raise the awareness and appreciation of other business areas, and of data sharing and integration possibilities, with someone who has spent years working with one department or project. Good change management skills will be called upon to introduce new methods and principles, and to encourage everyone involved in the process, so that change comes about steadily and successfully.

These are classic problems in introducing change. Data Administration may become a focal point of resentment against changes, particularly if the function and its objectives are initially ill-defined in the organisation. The uphill task of explaining the concept of data administration must be undertaken as part of its introduction to the business. Moreover, it is a task that must be considered as long term, an ongoing integral part of the Data Administration function's routine. It is difficult for people to appreciate the objectives of data administration easily, and it is difficult to demonstrate and measure when these have been achieved. In this it differs from most IT projects, which have a recognisable beginning, middle and end, and have stated objectives, the achievement of which can usually be seen. The success of these projects is measurable, and milestones can often be set to see if certain targets are reached by certain dates.

Data administration is not quite like that. Certain parts of it, particularly in the early stages, could be determined as 'projects', such as establishing a data dictionary or a set of standardised abbreviations, and could be completed within a given timescale. However, the major benefits of data administration are largely unquantifiable. They appear gradually and subtly over a very long timespan, without any noticeable milestones. If the data resource is poor, its inadequacies will be visible and inaccuracies will be revealed by operational problems or by customer complaints. Data inconsistencies will show themselves as developers struggle to put an integration project in place or suffer the consequences of mis-matched data. Sloppy data access control will emerge in unofficial use of the data — perhaps when we read some confidential figures in the newspapers, or fall foul of the Data Protection Act! It is far less easy to judge when data management is good, or just how good it is, and extremely difficult even to quantify the amount of disk storage space and development effort which has been saved by minimising data redundancy or being able to use a centralised dictionary to support development work. Measures such as these can be made in an effort to cost-justify Data Administration's position. However, any improvements may be due to a combination of factors, rather than to Data Administration alone.

Not only does Data Administration frequently produce somewhat intangible results, but some of the more visible effects are less than palatable to some of the MIS and user communities. This is particularly true initially, before the long term benefits are appreciated. Data Administration insists on following company standards, seeming to take away some of the traditional freedom of the developer to indulge his or her creativity. The data items (s)he wishes to use, with their names and formats, are all reviewed now, and (s)he may be forced to make changes. The developer now has to consider a corporate view, not just the parochial needs of one particular user group. Similarly, users are now forced to think of other departments in their use of data. Their data responsibilities are documented, their requests for data for end user computing purposes are reviewed and may be referred to other departments or even refused, and their security procedures are questioned. The Data Administration function is in danger of becoming the most unpopular group in the organisation!

To put it in a nutshell, Data Administration risks acquiring an image problem, one which must be addressed right from the beginning and worked at consistently. It is an indisputable fact that Data Administration needs the co-operation of users, IT staff, and management in order to be successful and contribute fully to the business. This is not easily achieved. Indeed, co-operation from some individuals or areas may never be fully achieved, but rather grudgingly given, at best. This may result in the difference between information being freely volunteered, and having to be painfully extracted. It is very important that Data Administration puts itself across well and wins as many friends in the business as possible, and this can depend on the attitude and skill employed in integrating with other functions. There is a very delicate balance between co-operation and assistance, and insistence on changes and improvements, and it is up to Data Administration to find it. It is a tightrope to walk, and good relationships need to be built up, so that understanding of data administration principles grows and the function's influence gradually develops.

Choosing the right projects

Data Administration must be selective about the projects it tackles or is involved with, particularly in the early stages, as it will be judged on the results of these. Clearly, the wishes of senior business management cannot be ignored; however, it is likely that Data Administration will be successful in influencing which activities are chosen. If a project can be selected where co-operation from the IT development group and users is possible, and demonstrable results or benefits can be shown, this will help to establish the function and smooth the path for the next project. It will do Data Administration no good at all to be associated in everyone's minds with a project fraught with difficulties, dogged by personnel problems and suffering constant rework. This will not be a good advertisement for the future. Of course, Data Administration may have no choice about the projects that it is involved with and it will inevitably be associated with some problem projects. Indeed, in some cases it will be asked to join the project precisely because problems have already been revealed. However, if selectivity is possible and problem projects can be avoided initially, this will be a bonus. In the early stages, with a raw Data Administration function being keenly watched from all levels, it should attempt to tackle some small-scale projects, where beneficial results can be shown to both managers and other staff within a relatively short space of time. Once Data Administration has proved itself and has been accepted into the organisation's structure, involvement in longer term projects will be forthcoming and can be accomplished more successfully.

Data administration staff

One important asset of the Data Administration function which can smooth its path will be selected in the formative stages, and that is its staff. It will aid the introduction of data administration and its acceptance into the user community, IT department and on numerous project teams, if the staff are selected as far as possible for a good mix of personal qualities and technical skills. Data Administration staff need to be determined but not aggressive about the principles they are putting forward. They need to have a helpful manner, and be fairly resilient and adaptable, as well as being able communicators, if they are going to cover the wide range of data administration tasks. Staff not only give a general impression of any group, but also determine whether people are happy to use their services or not. Choosing approachable and efficient staff is a step in the right direction. A variety of technical skills will help as well, with the ability to use and explain different techniques, such as data analysis, data flow diagramming, data modelling, and so on.

Spreading the word

The first task is to ensure that everyone in the organisation knows what Data Administration is all about and what the newly developed group is intended to do. Awareness will need to be raised at all levels and all areas in the business, with different emphasis for different groups, depending on the perceived relationship with Data Administration. Senior management approval will have been obtained by this stage, so that the function can be set up, but it is necessary to keep a high profile with senior management. They need to know what is being done, how Data Administration is involved in their areas, and where adherence to data administration guidelines could be improved — in other words, what we can do for them in their areas of responsibility.

Data Administration direction statement

One way in which this can be done is to publish a formal document giving a direction statement for the Data Administration function, outlining its objectives and its principal areas of involvement and defining its scope and responsibilities. This document can also give some idea of the services which Data Administration will provide to the organisation and list its proposed activities in the short and long term. Figure 10.1 gives a view of the scope of this document. It should not be lengthy or complex, but should be a succinct guide to the essential features of this new function in the business. This brief direction statement will summarise Data Administration's objectives and give a firm base for the commitments that it will and will not be prepared to make. It is also important to clarify areas of responsibility, so that tasks are not abandoned by another group in the belief, or hope, that they will now fall within Data Administration's remit. This clarification puts the spotlight on Data Administration and helps to raise its profile, but it also gives a firm foundation for Data Administration's development. The direction statement does not have to be definitive, and can evolve over time; it is vital that Data Administration does not attempt to take on too much initially, stretching its resources to the point of failure. Appendix 1 shows the direction statement in more detail.

Senior management and system controller involvement

The support of a senior manager will be very important, as (s)he can keep Data Administration in the forefront of senior management thinking and can recommend its involvement in projects which would benefit from it, such as major strategic

Figure 10.1 Data
Administration
Direction Statement

DATA ADMINISTRATION DIRECTION STATEMENT: CONTENTS

Data Administration objectives
Priorities
Responsibilities
Relationship with other groups

Policies or mechanisms
    security
    integrity
    authorship
    data duplication
    distributed data
    systems planning
    end user computing
    corporate data needs
    standards
    education

Data Administration as a service
    data modelling
    data flow diagramming
    solving data problems
    impact of change/systems planning
    end user computing

Principle areas of Data Administration involvement
    data integrity
    systems planning and integration
    data authorship
    data security
    data definitions

Data Administration planned activities
    short term
    long term

initiatives. The commitment of senior management is also required to obtain user involvement. This is particularly important if a system controller network is set up in the user community, such as the one described in Chapter 3. Data Administration cannot achieve this without the active support of senior managers, and will need to explain the requirement for the role, the qualities and level of knowledge and seniority required, and the benefits that his or her area, and the business, will derive from it. The system controller will then need Data Administration assistance in coming to terms with the new role. It is essential that the system controller is actively supported by his or her manager; it must not be a token appointment, and this fact must be recognised by both manager and system controller. The manager must also appreciate the amount of effort required from the system controller. (S)he must be prepared to allow that effort to be diverted from other tasks, or for someone else to take over part of the system controller's original workload. Senior managers should be kept abreast of Data Administration efforts, its successes and indeed its failures, and should be taken to task where lack of commitment in their areas causes difficulties for Data Administration in implementing corporate data policies.

A successful and energetic system controller who shows positive commitment to data administration will serve as a good advertisement to other areas. (S)he will often be willing to give details of personal experience to help managers select a suitable system controller in another area. The system controller role is not an easy one and Data Administration must be very supportive, giving advice and assistance where necessary, as well as seeking advice and information from the controller. It is very much a two-way process, and a rapport needs to be established so that maximum benefit from the relationship is obtained on both sides. Of course, this can be a question of personalities, and the relationship will work better with some than with others. Data Administration should respect the knowledge of the system controller and be aware of any difficulties peculiar to her/his area. Suggestions of what could be looked at in data administration terms need to be backed up with assistance if called upon. Sometimes the system controller can be most usefully referred to another person or group who may help, such as the IT technical support groups, or to another system controller who has been through a similar process. Data Administration must take an interest in the system controller's area and in what is going on there at all times, and whenever something crops up with possible data administration implications for that area, Data Administration should contact the local 'man on the spot' for clarification or to give information. The system controller may also request Data Administration assistance in drawing up procedures, explaining a data issue to staff, or contacting other controllers, perhaps to sort out a mutual problem. Data Administration is the facilitator in these situations, and may be called upon to mediate if different sides have opposing views.

IT department awareness

One of the major requirements for raising awareness and justifying data administration may well lie with the IT department. This will depend on the framework of the IT department, how it is expected to relate to the Data Administration function, and its earlier exposure to some of the data management techniques required. If system developers are used to working with CASE tools, structured methodologies and data dictionaries, Data Administration will have a good start. Ideas will have to be broadened perhaps, to a view of the data resource as a company asset. We may need to promote an awareness of the responsibility to look at the whole picture, rather than just at a parochial one, to build a system for the future, for the organisation as a whole and not simply for one user. However, Data Administration will have much more of an uphill task where such methods and techniques are unknown, and where the beginnings of Data Administration coincide, perhaps, with the introduction of CASE or methodology.

A whole new, and possibly unpopular, way of working will become inextricably linked in people's minds with Data Administration, and, indeed, in some ways the two may go closely together. The fear of change from the loss of comfortable, tried and tested development methods will be transferred to Data Administration, and the barriers can almost be seen going up.

Data Administration will have to put a lot of effort in here, and it cannot be done quickly, simply or single-handedly. There must be support from IT management to enable developers to realise the benefits of new working methods and tools, and, most importantly, to trust them and feel as comfortable with them as with their old methods. This will not happen overnight. Data Administration can play its part in providing general education on the need for data administration, its principles, and how it is hoped to achieve the objectives. It can also provide specific training on data modelling or data flow diagramming, methodology, and on how to review projects for integration issues or on how to use CASE tools.

Some of this training can be gained most effectively through courses which are external to the organisation. Data Administration may want to ensure that guidelines and standards are put across for such things as data flow diagrams or entity models, so that all project teams follow the same rules. Some training sessions may have to be given to explain these standards, backing up the previous course training. Data Administration views on data flow diagrams and models will always be required. However, it is extremely valuable for Data Administration to lend a helping hand when diagrams or models are first attempted 'for real', and to run through them with the developers when finalised, tidying up any points and querying any details. IT staff will need a lot of support and encouragement during these changes and a sympathetic Data Administration 'consultant' on hand will be very useful.

System developers need to be made particularly aware of strategic information planning, integration issues and data architectures. These are the concepts which underpin moves towards data sharing and flexibility in supporting the business in the future. They also ensure that IT systems are in line with the way the business is developing, and will be able to support that development. It can be difficult to achieve a heightened awareness of these issues, particularly with a developer who is concerned solely with his own project. Data Administration alone cannot do it. There needs to be a change of emphasis in the IT department, with project teams perhaps less rigidly defined and taking a greater interest in projects underway in other teams. This should be actively encouraged by managers, ensuring that news on the status of the various developments is circulated. Perhaps developments could be highlighted in an IT newsletter, especially at key milestones in the project, or presentations or informal demonstrations of a prototype system could be given to members of other project teams.

This type of approach helps to widen the developer's view, giving a more balanced picture of work going on both in the IT function and in the company as a whole. It also helps to pave the way for the more formal and structured requirements which involve the consideration of wider issues as part of the development process. This more formal involvement includes Data Administration's role, as we encourage the developer to consider a project in the light of other systems which may interact with it. With a greater awareness of what is going on elsewhere, and being more conscious of the possibilities or difficulties, (s)he is more likely to realise the importance of taking other systems into consideration. The developer must recognise the absolute necessity of considering integration issues and future plans, and the value of raising and clarifying these concerns before going ahead. All too often, development proceeds on the basis of some assumptions, either where questions were left unanswered, or were never asked because the answer was assumed. These are liable to turn into problem areas later, where compromises need to be made, bridges built or major redesign or rework carried out.

It is essential to point out the benefits of clearing up any potential difficulties at the earliest opportunity. This applies not just within the IT department but must involve consultation with the users, making sure that they are aware of the directions and limitations of the IT systems supporting their operations. A formal systems integration document can be drawn up highlighting the issues, as discussed in Chapter 6, which should include the resolution of the issues as agreement is reached. This helps to bring any concerns to the forefront of discussion between system developer and users, and these should be resolved before the system design is too far advanced. Data Administration can help to draw up this document, hopefully not only raising awareness of the integration issues and the area of involvement of the project, but also publicising Data Administration at the same time.

The application development team also needs to be very aware of data integrity issues, including the need to consider data transfers and the implications of a systems failure. The system developers will consider backup and recovery procedures specific to a particular system as part of the development work. They must also be encouraged to consider the effect of a new or changed system on other systems and their responsibilities towards maintaining corporate data integrity. Once again, this requires system developers to broaden their perspective.

A Data Administration presentation for IT staff

It may be a good idea to introduce the concepts of data administration to IT staff with a presentation, showing the basic principles and outlining how this might affect them. In this presentation, it is important to stress the positive contribution that Data Administration can make and the benefits being sought. Mention should also be made of the assistance available from the Data Administration function in any new data management techniques. The presentation might cover the following:

- Data administration concepts; data as a corporate asset; flexibility; data sharing and integration.

- Aims of data administration; minimised data redundancy; effective use of data resources; data accuracy and integrity.
- Data administration as part of systems development; data dictionary; data flow diagrams; entity relationship diagrams.
- The help that Data Administration needs from systems developers; co-operation in use of data items; involvement in projects.
- The help that Data Administration can offer; assistance with data flow diagrams, data items and modelling; helping with 'walk throughs' with the user.
- Benefits of data administration for everyone; data as a corporate resource, with the aim to get the best possible use from it.

None of these sections needs to be explored in great depth at this stage. The main point is to present a positive view of the Data Administration function and its principles, and to encourage a positive response from system developers, as far as possible.

New members of the IT department should also be given a short introduction to data administration, as this concept may be new to them. They should be made aware of what is required of them, what they can ask from Data Administration, where it fits in with IT related activities, and where they are likely to be involved.

General awareness in the business

Data Administration issues should also be incorporated into general training outside the IT department, in such topics as the general importance of data security, password security, the need for data accuracy and the user's responsibilities in all these areas. These subjects should form part of the normal training process for all employees working with IT systems and data. More specific training on a particular system or type of work will be required for new employees and those transferring to different jobs. This can be enhanced by some coverage of data administration concerns, showing how the employee can play his part in looking after the data. This type of training will be pitched differently for different groups, and will relate to the systems likely to be used; but the basic message remains the same. Data is a vitally important resource, and it is the responsibility of all of us to protect it and to use it properly and to best effect. If the organisation has an IT awareness programme in place, Data Administration can contribute significantly to this. This may cover such topics as data handling, security, effective use of data and legal responsibilities. All of these issues are fundamental to data administration.

Possibly the most fortunate position to be in is to be involved in a company-wide Total Quality management process. Many progressive organisations now recognise the essential competitive edge that can be gained from Total Quality programmes. Whilst there are dozens of ways of running these programmes, there are some ever present key principles which need to be taught to an entire workforce. In general the principles are as follows:

- Understanding the meaning of quality and its definition as applied in the business. Invariably, this includes the relationship of the business to its customer.

- Generating a preventative culture, that is, encouraging proactive analysis of all work processes to predict and prevent problems occurring.
- Reducing waste and the consequent revenue lost from not being able to do the job correctly first time every time.
- Establishing a quality standard which everyone can measure against and better through continuous improvement.
- Creating an environment in which each individual is empowered to contribute and in which everyone can justifiably be held accountable for their own quality.

The education process which forms a backbone to the Total Quality programme is the ideal forum in which to develop the concepts of data administration. There are many parallels to be drawn, as follows:

- Clarity of process definition through diagramming techniques charting the flow of materials, resources, people and data.
- Customer/supplier relationships where all individuals in an organisation either supply or receive something to enable them to do their jobs. Data (and information) is the most common commodity transferred between employees in any organisation.
- Zero defects or right first time. Ensuring that the job is done to specification. This includes all work involving data, such as: data input, report production, program specification, backup and recovery procedure definition, database sizing, and many more.
- Everyone is accountable for the quality of the data they supply or use.
- Reducing wasted effort through more effective use of data.
- Producing reliable data for quality control of processes, waste reduction programmes, key performance measures and process improvement projects.
- Prevention through standardisation of data formats, saving difficulties in systems integration later on. Also, systems planning to prevent constant rework and redesign.
- Ensuring that data is available at the right time and place for all business processes to work right first time every time.

Whoever is tasked with designing and running the Total Quality programme should be approached as early as possible to 'knit' the data administration principles into those of Total Quality. As we have pointed out, sometimes the voice of Data Administration is the voice of the little man. Total Quality is a giant! Use it to good advantage.

Keeping in touch

As well as busily imparting the message of data administration at all levels in the company, the data administrator also needs to be on the receiving end of information. (S)he must strive constantly to keep in touch with what is happening throughout the organisation, from high-level long range IT plans down to instances of 'getting round the system' in a particular department. The data administrator needs to use all the means available to him/her to keep abreast of events. This can include minutes from strategic project meetings, development groups, or senior management, discussions with colleagues, or casual enquiries and comments from IT staff or users. If anything seems to warrant further investigation, the data administrator must follow it up to discover whether a data administration issue is involved or whether some action needs to be taken.

Copies of project terms of reference are very useful in keeping up to date with what different project teams are planning to work on. Sometimes these are very small projects, and project leaders may be bemused by a request from the data administrator to receive all their terms of reference. However, it is an easy way to find out what is going on. Many of them can be scanned very quickly, and will be found to be of no particular interest and to require no further action. In other cases, points may need to be clarified or queries raised.

This may also be a good opportunity to remind the project leader of what will be expected in data administration terms during the project's life cycle. This is the time to point out that data items need to be checked, a system controller should be involved, data models must be verified or security issues need to be resolved. This is particularly the case while Data Administration is still a relatively new function. Once it becomes a routinely accepted part of the development cycle, developers will be more aware of their responsibilities and the deliverables which must be produced, and will recognise when Data Administration needs to be informed. However, at the beginning these things will not come naturally, with the result that Data Administration must take a more active role and be constantly alert to what is going on in the organisation. Any dubious points can simply be raised with the system developer. If significant data issues are involved, particularly if there is a possibility of conflict, Data Administration may draft a note of its concerns and circulate it to the relevant people. This will help to raise the issues, hopefully starting off discussion and resolution of them at an early stage.

Promoting Data Administration

Data Administration needs to use all the means at its disposal to establish its identity and raise its profile within the business, particularly when it has just been set up. This can include using a logo to make its documents stand out as representing the views of a particular function. The logo helps to establish Data Administration as a distinct entity, and can be used on reports, presentation materials, memos and so on. These are then recognisable as coming from Data Administration, rather than (in our own case) MIS. Our very simple logo is shown in Figure 10.2, and is based on some of the conventions that we use in data flow diagramming. The logo does not have to be very sophisticated or complex, merely enough to differentiate the function from others and help give it an identity.

Any available means should be used to convey what Data Administration is doing, and what it is all about, such as internal newsletters, or special Data

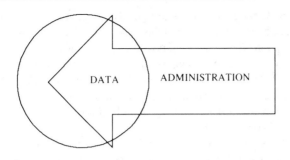

Figure 10.2 Data Administration logo

Administration bulletins. Data Administration may need to market its services initially, using whatever publicity it can. Later, the best recommendation possible is the effect of successful Data Administration input to a series of projects, and the support of developers and users who have found that input useful.

In summary, the following areas should be considered as vehicles for getting the data administration message across to as wide an audience as possible within the organisation:

- publication of a Data Administration direction statement;
- logo for Data Administration memos, discussion documents and presentation materials;
- high-profile response to data issues raised by major projects;
- presentations on data administration to staff at all levels;
- training in data flow diagramming, data modelling, etc., to IT staff;
- published guidelines for data flow diagrams, etc.;
- involvement in assessing the validity of data flow diagrams, entity relationship diagrams, etc., with development teams;
- involvement in 'walk-throughs' with users;
- induction of IT staff and other employees in data issues;
- reports on Data Administration in internal newsletters;
- participation in general IT education, particularly IT awareness in non-IT areas;
- short term, visible projects taken on initially which can show successful results;
- use made of Data Administration allies, such as 'converts' to methodology;
- publication of planned activities, for example for the next year;
- Data Administration kept in the forefront of senior management minds;
- a supportive senior manager used to 'sponsor' Data Administration and recommend its involvement in major projects;
- business not turned away, whenever possible; encourage people who want to make use of Data Administration services;
- publicity for achievements;
- reports published on investigations into data problems and circulated widely under the Data Administration banner;
- system controllers actively supported in all their efforts;
- participation in Total Quality management programmes or other business-wide improvement processes.

This gives a wide range of options to build Data Administration's identity. The ones which can be used most effectively will depend on what is available in the organisation and in what type of climate the function is trying to establish itself. Use should be made of as many opportunities as possible, to keep the momentum going and to put Data Administration on the organisational map. There will be a continuous process of education as Data Administration implements data-related tools and participates in developments. The best possible advertisement will be the benefits accrued from Data Administration work and its tangible effects in the business. This may be slow in coming, and the challenge lies not only in the activities themselves but also in the negative response that some of them may invoke. Nevertheless, the data administrator must persevere in pursuing the ideals of data administration and in convincing the rest of the business of their value. Hopefully, (s)he will receive short term appreciation from system developers and system controllers as (s)he provides positive input to their projects. In time, this will develop and expand into the long term acceptance and understanding of the data administrator's role as a valuable and productive member of the organisation. It is not an easy role, and a long road lies ahead, but the positive results will justify our commitment and reassure us that the path we have chosen is right.

Key action points

- Educate people at all levels in the business in what data administration is all about. (If a Total Quality management programme is underway, use this as a vehicle to get the message across.)
- Use publicity, including a logo, to raise the profile.
- Participate fully in all parts of the business, building up relationships with users, IT staff and management.
- Set out clear guidelines and standards on data-related techniques and issues, and make sure that they are communicated effectively.
- Continue to sell Data Administration and gain the approval and support of key people in the business.
- Provide worthwhile input to projects in order to achieve recognition as a valued team member.

11 Measuring progress

This chapter gives us the opportunity to take stock and review how far we have come, what we have achieved, and what we have learnt from our experiences along the way. There may be some painful home truths, but this assessment should give a guide against which other data administrators may measure their own actual or anticipated progress. Hopefully, an analysis of where we have been successful, and where we have not, will allow others to avoid some of the pitfalls. At the very least, they may be reassured that they are not alone in their misfortunes!

From the very beginning, it was appreciated that the introduction of the new concept and function of Data Administration into the business would not be an easy task. It was clear that it would have to be tackled gradually, step by step, and that progress would be slow. An instantaneous effect on working methods, and, more importantly, on attitudes, could not be expected. Despite the importance of tools and techniques, people are the key to success or failure in introducing data administration. Their attitude to this new concept has a significant part to play — and this means the attitudes from both sides, Data Administration and the other functions in the organisation. There must be a willingness on the part of all concerned to learn and to change in order to go forward. Without this, it will be impossible to attain the full benefits of introducing data administration into the company. It was fortunate that we did appreciate the difficulties ahead, and the size of the task undertaken, so that we did not get downhearted or defeated. It is fair to say that progress was not always steady and that some steps backward were taken along the way. Nevertheless, we can look back on the last couple of years and its achievements with some satisfaction.

Problems and success in introducing data administration

Let's have a look first at the problems which were encountered in introducing data administration, most of which were anticipated. Some of these would not apply to a green field site, and some problems related to our particular environment. However, the majority of these difficulties are very likely to be experienced by any infant Data Administration function. Some indication of their effect, and how far they have been overcome or their impact minimised, may be useful. The methods for doing so have in most cases formed the substance of this book. We hope that enough suggestions have been given to handle these issues and make sure that the introduction of data administration is not unnecessarily hampered by them.

Our major difficulty had a historical basis, caused by the development of the organisational structure in the company. Different departments were established in the user community, and were quite rigidly defined. Many organisations will have a similar problem to a greater or lesser extent.

The historical independence of different departments within the business meant that the need to share data was not understood, causing unnecessary data duplication. Nor was there an appreciation of the responsibility for data beyond the needs of the individual department. The concept of data as a company-wide resource was something new and was somewhat foreign to many people. As well as the question of a corporate rather than a parochial point of view, and an understanding of the wider needs of the business, this historical development gave rise to other, more tangible, difficulties. A lot of small systems had already been put in place in various departments to fulfil specific needs, and these were now found to be incompatible. There were inconsistencies in the values and meanings of the data, with no company-wide agreement on data formats for specific items used widely throughout the organisation. Some of the departments were immoderately attached to their 'own' systems, and blind to some of their basic faults and inadequacies.

This meant that Data Administration had an uphill task in both the amount of standardisation and the consistency it needed to bring to the company's data, and in the amount of education and encouragement in data administration principles which had to accompany it. However, there was some assistance from fundamental changes taking place in the company. These removed some of the traditional organisational boundaries and led to a more team-based, cross-functional approach. Together with this new method of working, there was a growing awareness of the requirements of the business, in terms of flexibility and responsiveness. This was soon matched by the realisation that there must also be an equivalent flexibility in the IT systems to support it. The message that data administration was a positive step towards this was put across and taken up by the business, which began to see the benefits that would come from it.

People in business areas not only began to work less rigidly within departmental boundaries, but realised the need to access data regardless of boundaries in order to function properly. The need for systems integration is now widely recognised. This type of systems development will continue to grow in the future, with a requirement to make system joins as invisible as possible to the user. It is now appreciated that consistency and well-defined data can play a major part in the success of integration.

However, it is still a struggle to obtain a full analysis of strategic issues as part of a system development, and, more importantly, to obtain clear decisions on these issues. While we remain convinced that these issues must be highlighted and resolved as part of the project work, we have not yet been totally successful in accomplishing this. The application development team sometimes views this as a fringe concern. This means that a system may be designed and its links to other systems considered later, rather than reviewing them upfront as an integral part of the project. Since the links between one system and another often affect different application development groups, it is only too easy to forget about them altogether during initial development work.

These strategic issues usually involve business and operational concerns, and must therefore have input and agreement from user management. This is not always easy to obtain, and there, too, we feel we have not yet succeeded in convincing users that these issues are being resolved too late, or in some cases left rather optimistically to resolve themselves. It therefore remains an objective to include the resolution of strategic issues as a standard part of the system development life cycle. This would necessitate the allocation of sufficient and specific time and resources to this task.

There have been some problems in integrating data administration into application development and ensuring that the relevant tasks are carried out. This is particularly so when timescales are tight and pressure is brought to bear from user managers for swift development and implementation. Data Administration is in some cases viewed as holding up the project. To counteract this view, we have tried to put as much effort as possible into strategic projects, in order to lighten the load of the development teams. However, in doing this, it is essential not to make data concerns and deliverables something that the development teams offload to Data Administration. They must recognise the importance and value of the work involved, and their responsibility towards it. It is stressed to them that the majority of the data administration requirements from the development team stem from the analysis and logical design stages. This work needs to be done, whether or not data administration deliverables are produced at the end of the process. The deliverables, therefore, should not require the huge amount of energy and resources which the team appears to fear, but should document what the analyst knows already, and *must* know for a successful project. However, it seems that in some cases our preferred techniques of gentle persuasion, advice and guidance need to be reinforced by compulsion, for which we do not as yet have sufficient authority.

On a more optimistic note, efforts to achieve satisfactory deliverables from development teams have been assisted by the positive attitude of the database analysts. They have been actively supportive, appreciating a more fully documented logical design stage, in which they benefit from the data definition checks and input to the logical model provided by Data Administration. They have assisted us in furthering an understanding of data dictionary and database issues, and in helping to establish data administration tools. They also insist that development teams follow the agreed procedures and ensure that data definitions have been approved by Data Administration. There is a close liaison between Data Administration and the Database Group, and there are many mutual benefits to be gained from this.

Some departments have resisted the imposition of data controls from outside their area. The issue of corporate responsibility and the benefits of following certain paths which may benefit others more than themselves are difficult to put across. This situation calls for a lot of tact and negotiation, and causes the data administrator some frustration at times. It improves as people realise the benefits that they themselves can accrue from the introduction of our policies. However, it is not a quick or easy change of opinion, particularly where a user has previously worked in a completely self-contained environment.

It is also difficult to persuade people to accept new responsibilities, particularly the user's responsibility for data authorship. However, this has been given a boost by the commitment of senior user managers. They have realised the absolute necessity for data accuracy and the responsibility of their areas towards it. This has come about firstly from their involvement with the manufacturing system, recognising our dependence on it, and later from a realisation of the growing value of management information systems, as well as IT systems covering all operational aspects of the business. Nevertheless, we foresee difficulties in maintaining authorship information, in ensuring that changes are kept up to date and that Data Administration is informed of these changes in a timely way. This is a major problem. A lot of effort is involved in establishing data administration information to begin with, and it is only too easy for this to become out of date. At the moment we are very dependent on receiving information from users, system controllers or IT staff. This is prone to error or omission and is not really a satisfactory situation. Some mechanisms need to be put in place to alleviate this problem.

Meeting the demands

This is perhaps a particular problem for a small Data Administration function such as ours. At times, it is really too small to handle all of the demands being made on it, let alone to keep a watching brief on other aspects of the business and the changes taking place. Some organisations will assign a full-time data administrator to a project so that there is full involvement at all stages of the development life cycle. The presence of a full- or part-time data administrator on a project can help to put across the message of good data management that we are trying to convey. Other data administrators may have specific roles, connected with data dictionaries, systems planning, or corporate data modelling. Neither our organisation nor our projects are of a size to warrant this approach. However, the limited data administration resource means that on occasion it is difficult to fulfil obligations in all directions. The peaks and troughs of system development work pose particular problems when two projects require our input at the same time. While an attempt is made to plan for this, we are necessarily at the mercy of the project's deviations from its plan, and have to compensate by juggling resources. Priority is given to work on strategic projects and assisting development teams; the routine work of Data Administration has had to be re-scheduled on many occasions to accommodate this.

This resource problem does mean that Data Administration involvement in some projects is less than we would like. Sometimes, teams who need the impetus from

Data Administration to encourage or support data-related activities are left too long before the time can be found to review their progress. If the team has been (unwittingly or not) going down the wrong road, it can be difficult to pull it back. In addition, a negative impression is given of Data Administration as a corrective function, causing the team to backtrack and holding up the project. The size of the Data Administration resource can be a critical factor where systems developers are not eager to involve themselves in some of the techniques as quickly as anticipated.

Similarly, it has not always been possible to support the system controller network as completely as we would have wished. Assistance has been given where requested, various initiatives have been followed up, and education has been given to system controllers. However, there are many other issues which have not been pursued because we were aware that we could not do them justice. System controllers do need greater support and impetus than is currently being provided. The full introduction of data administration is therefore being compromised, and the benefits will be that much slower in being realised.

Position of the Data Administration function

Problems are caused not only by the amount of resources available, but also by the status and position of the function in the company. It does not have sufficient authority, which means that its views and directives can be overturned. In the preceding chapter, we discussed the need for a high profile in order to be effective. While a significant amount of recognition has been achieved, particularly given the limited resource, our profile still needs to be improved. We are also still hindered by our association with the MIS department. Whilst we have undoubtedly benefited from close proximity to the development teams, and liaison with database and technical groups, some problems are encountered from being closely identified with MIS in people's minds. Some people conclude that it must be a purely 'technical' function, only interested in IT-based systems. Users, in particular, find it difficult to understand that two sections in the same department, such as a development team and Data Administration, can hold fundamentally different opinions on the same thing. MIS teams may also see it as 'disloyal' if Data Administration highlights a data issue in their remit which needs to be addressed. Some benefits would be gained from an independent Data Administration function, which would not be associated with MIS or any individual business function. We need to develop close ties with the business, and loosening our connection with MIS could only further this. However, we benefit significantly from the technical expertise of MIS, and, given time, can develop a wider knowledge of business processes and close rapport with the whole user community from our MIS base. This is not to say that our position within MIS is fixed in concrete. The function will develop and will fit in with the development and restructuring of MIS and the business.

From our point of view, the advantages and disadvantages of our current position in the organisational structure are summarised in Table 11.1.

One of the options open to us is to remain within MIS, becoming more closely

Table 11.1 Advantages and disadvantages of Data Administration positioned within the MIS function

Advantages	Disadvantages
• Technical support from MIS • Close to in-depth knowledge of IT systems • Able to influence development teams	• Outside the business groups • Regarded as MIS rather than neutral and independent • MIS seen as computer-only group, so no link seen between Data Administration and non-computerised systems
• Able to support development teams in data-related activities from close at hand • Easy access to integrated data dictionary	• Not seen as a central authority in the business • Not always involved in business decisions and policies
• Access to CASE tools	• Some users view MIS as purely technical and therefore believe other concerns will not be understood
• Greater authority over development teams and managers • Knowledge of projects at an early stage	• Less authority over user groups

linked with the Database Group, rather than the development area. This approach has been used elsewhere to position Data Administration in the business initially. There can be difficulties with this approach, because of fundamental differences in the scope of responsibilities between these two functions. Some of these have been discussed in Chapters 5 and 7, in relation to specific tasks. Although they are frequently confused, the two areas have distinct areas of operation, as shown in Table 11.2. From this, it can be seen that the data administrator has a wider, more user-orientated, but less technical brief. Both roles are vital to the organisation, and can work harmoniously together. However, where the distinctive elements of the data administrator's expertise come a poor second to the requirements of the database analyst the benefits will be lost. In other words, these two skills can work together, but only where it is recognised that they are offering different things. They are complementary, and one should not be required to give way to the other. The data administrator must retain the distinctive aspects of the role shown in Table 11.2, and the wider view of the business, or the purpose of the role will have been lost.

Table 11.2 Comparison of database analyst and data administrator roles

Database analyst	Data administrator
• Technical • Physical design • Database performance • Physical implementation of integrity controls, e.g. constraints, password control • Implementing standards, data naming rules • Contact with IT technical staff, development staff • Assigned to a project	• Business orientated • Logical design • Systems integration • Systems planning • Concepts of integrity • Establishing standards, data naming rules • Authorship • Contact with users, all IT groups, user managers • Responsibility company-wide

A current way of thinking that is becoming more prevalent in organisations which have gone down the 'Total Quality' route is to bring Data Administration into the general quality initiative. The chief role is the derivation of measurement data to assist a continuous improvement process. This is a possibility which has many merits, not least of which is the recognition that data is a 'quality' asset which needs to be measured for its own worth.

Sometimes, however, this can only be a relatively short term solution. Total Quality programmes tend to be run by a project team specifically set up for the job. The teams are usually cross-functional and are genuinely seen as a business-wide group divorced from any specific functional allegiance. There is a very strong parallel in this for Data Administration. As the Total Quality programme develops, the education phase will gradually give way to that of continuous business improvement, problem solving, prevention planning and performance measurement. Generally at this point, the project team starts to break up as the various members move out into the business to facilitate the principles they have been teaching. Perhaps they will leave behind them a smaller core team to address the ongoing issues of education, awareness programmes and quality auditing, e.g. ISO9000 conformance. Data Administration would certainly benefit from the initial high-profile exposure within a Total Quality project and would still reap the rewards of business-wide involvement later on. The chief drawback is that Total Quality programmes are large, involved and critical to whoever needs to do them. Any dilution (however justified) of the effort will not be welcome.

Our advice is to make a case for incorporating data administration into Total Quality and keeping it in whatever core function remains after the initial project.

Other possibilities to be explored for positioning Data Administration could be: Business Planning, Organisation and Methods, and Operational Research, if such functionally independent groups exist. In some circumstances it may be possible to consider Data Administration as an entirely independent entity within the business, reporting in to the executive committee.

It is therefore worthwhile thinking very carefully about the positioning and reporting structure of the Data Administration function. It must not be swamped by similar, but different, skills, but must get maximum benefit from them in performing its own very individual tasks within the organisation.

Wherever Data Administration is positioned, total management support is necessary, and this needs to be visible. In addition, Data Administration needs to have recognised authority in the business, with the scope and limits of its authority clearly accepted. We have not yet reached this point, which means that there is a greater struggle on some matters than is perhaps necessary. If greater authority — more 'teeth' — can be achieved in the business, we believe that we will be able to bring greater benefits to the company.

Progress with the system controller concept

One of the areas where problems were anticipated was in the setting up and maintenance of a system controller network. This network consists of around twenty controllers, covering the majority of the company's systems in all business areas. However, we were faced earlier than expected by the departure of some system controllers due to changes in the business. It took some time to coerce hard-pressed managers into replacing them. This meant that there was no opportunity to hand over the duties and knowledge from one controller to another, and the lengthy time delays meant a lull in system controller activities. This had to be followed by a time-consuming introduction to the art of being a system controller and the concept of data administration, which began to feel somewhat repetitive. In addition, we are dependent on the choice of the senior user manager, and in some cases the choice has not been ideal. This means that some people who have been allocated the role have not felt happy with it and have needed far more encouragement and support than others. The type of precise, enquiring work required of the system controller, and the amount of control which must be exercised, necessitates a certain type of person. The role will be that much more successful if the person chosen has the right blend of personal qualities, level of expertise and local knowledge for the job. This will lighten the Data Administration load correspondingly in terms of education and support.

In general, though, we have been agreeably surprised by the enthusiasm and commitment of our system controllers, and the way in which they are prepared to assist Data Administration and each other. The main drawback has been the constraints on their time caused by their other duties. There is no doubt that a full-time system controller is much more effective and brings many benefits to day-to-day operations as well as to longer term system development. The role must be at a sufficiently high level to be informed as to what is happening in the business and what future plans are. It also requires the authority to monitor and control systems and procedures, bringing in changes where necessary.

The working relationship and cross-fertilisation of ideas and knowledge with the system controllers is one of the most rewarding aspects of the data administrator's job. These people are all skilled in a particular area and have detailed knowledge of particular business operations and the way the company works in their area. In general, the system controllers are open to new ideas, are usually full of ideas themselves, and have been ready to support Data Administration initiatives. They have been an invaluable source of information and support. Data Administration relies on them to carry our message across and implement the details of the basic concepts that we are advocating. They play a major part in introducing people to data administration and making sure that the 'people' aspects of these new ideas and procedures are addressed satisfactorily.

Senior management view of Data Administration

We believe that senior management within the company views Data Administration as a useful function and supports us as far as possible. However, in an increasingly demanding business world, it is becoming more important to be seen as a viable function, one that actively produces benefits for the company. Because of this, the emphasis has shifted slightly, so that the amount of time spent on pure 'data administration' activities, such as building up data administration tools and standards, or establishing authorship responsibilities, has been minimised.

More effort will now be expended on specific strategic projects, whose benefit to the business has been justified as part of the development brief. In these projects, managers can see a practical input and a positive benefit from Data Administration involvement, hopefully resulting in a more trouble-free development lifecycle and a satisfactory project. The tools, and other activities which are actually an essential part of the Data Administration function, are therefore being built up more slowly than was planned.

An unexpected time-consumer

One area which has required more attention than was anticipated has been end user computing. The amount of use of end user systems has increased rapidly and concerns were raised that management information and decisions were based on less than perfectly controlled data. The end user computing explosion took place before end user computing policies and controls were fully implemented. These are now being introduced retrospectively as the awareness of the value of the data in these systems has grown. With the benefit of hindsight, our advice would be to impose these controls (which should be imposed from the user side, not from MIS) from the very beginning. The controls necessary will enhance the value of the data for the user, while retaining the freedom to exploit the data in as many ways as possible. Data Administration can assist the enthusiastic end user by showing what aspects need to be controlled.

The need for compromise

In many cases, compromises have had to be made, sometimes because of outside influences. For example, the purchase of package-based software has imposed different structures and formats from those considered as ideal. We know from the beginning that the system will not fit neatly into our data architecture. Other features and advantages may outweigh the data administration considerations, but it is nevertheless disappointing to seem to be straying further from the envisaged architecture. In some cases, we have been forced to compromise during in-house developments, too. However, the picture should not be viewed as too gloomy, as even in these instances, the data issues have been recognised. User managers and IT staff are now acknowledging any short-cuts or compromises and are taking conscious decisions to live with the consequences. Nevertheless, in the eyes of Data Administration, these are lost opportunities to approach our ideal, and as such cannot be rated as successes. We acknowledge this, but hope that our influence will mean that these deviations will become more infrequent and that the compromises made for an individual system will not threaten the stability of the corporate data resource so often in the future.

In summary, we have been more successful in some areas than others, having had to adapt to the changing climate in our organisation and the changing perception of business needs. Data Administration needs to be flexible, and needs to attack those areas which will show the best return. We must continue to support current strategic projects, as well as planning for the future. Further work needs to be undertaken on improving understanding and adherence to the techniques, in particular for those who are not yet totally convinced. The work accomplished so far needs to be expanded and built upon, and there are plenty of challenges to look forward to. Any developments in the business, in data administration techniques and in information technology, will need to be considered and may need a reaction or change of direction, on whatever scale.

Data administration milestones

There are no hard and fast rules on how data administration should be introduced into an organisation, or in what order different tasks should be tackled. That will depend on the environment, existing skills and personal inclination. However, it is essential to establish the targets to aim for, and to prioritise them, with an indication of the timescale in which these should be achieved. It is fair to say that if these targets consist of the fundamental data administration requirements, and are not reached within the time specified, the introduction of data administration into the organisation cannot be rated as a success. This is very likely to be because opposition, whether from MIS, the user community or management, has hindered progress. If this is the case, and there is unlikely to be a significant change in outlook, it must be questioned whether there will ever be a successful Data Administration function in that organisation. Figure 11.1 shows some of the major milestones which might be considered. The priority given to these will vary between different organisations, but progress against the selected targets should be closely monitored as the function develops.

Job satisfaction

It remains to consider the task of introducing data administration from the viewpoint of the personal job satisfaction of the data administrator. For the person who enjoys the challenge of a multitude of tasks, the data administrator's role in our environment is one of endless opportunity and variety on a day-to-day basis. There is a high level of job satisfaction, with no shortage of jobs to be tackled and a valued input to provide to numerous high-level projects. Support from many quarters can be called upon and put to good use. The role involves contact with people throughout the business, being kept aware of the way the business is going and of any exciting new developments.

There is the bonus of working on a wide variety of business aspects, learning about the different sides of the business operation. On the other hand, the knowledge acquired of these areas is necessarily sketchy. The data administrator is involved in all areas, but may have an in-depth knowledge of none. In addition, the skills and techniques employed are specialised, and there is a tendency to

MILESTONES

Figure 11.1 Data Administration milestones

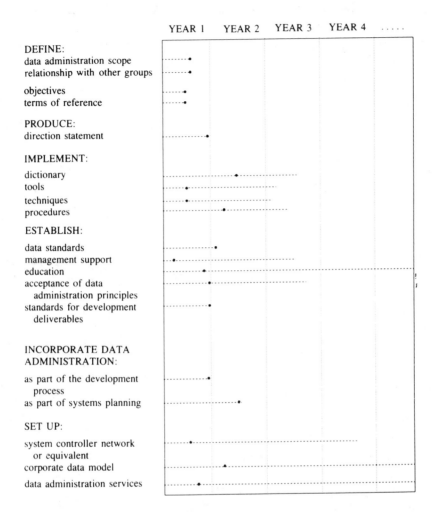

lose touch with some of the more traditional IT skills, such as programming, systems analysis, or project implementation. This may be a disadvantage if the data administrator decides to move into a systems development role. The specialised nature of the data administrator role may mean that career development is somewhat limited within some organisations.

The key qualities of the potential data administrator are adaptability, self-motivation and a large helping of confidence and humour! For someone who enjoys variety, with difficulties followed by pleasing results, the job offers opportunities and rewards. For the person who prefers a predictable routine, with no frustrations or disagreements, the data administrator role is definitely the wrong one to take!

Key action points

- Derive the goals for Data Administration, decide on the milestones and measure progress against them.
- Consider very carefully the positioning of Data Administration in the organisation.

12 Future directions for data administration

Information technology is a fast evolving and unpredictable science. The only sure thing about it is its volatility, allowing us only the briefest time to grow accustomed to the 'current set of rules'. Many exciting possibilities are opening up for the mid-1990s and beyond. Some aspects of computing are transient; they serve their purpose and are outgrown by something better, faster or more flexible. Some aspects stay with us doggedly despite attempts to better them. For example, there are many more lines of COBOL code around now than ever before, despite the advent of fourth generation languages, and that number is on the increase! In looking to the future it is impossible to say anything with certainty. However, we can be fairly sure that data administration will be needed while data is used as a resource, and that will be for some considerable time yet.

Data systems, however, will change. New methods of producing them, new tools to produce them and new methods of using them are all being busily devised as we write these words. Data administration will need to change with them. This chapter speculates on some known IT directions and how they may influence the view of data administration given in this book.

Artificial intelligence (AI)

Although it has been around for quite some time, AI is only just becoming an accepted form of computing which might be utilised in the average company. This is an area where Data Administration will need to look at different techniques. Data in its truest raw sense is not the main commodity. Knowledge based systems (KBS) operate on different relationships, namely semantic networks, frames or production rules. These are statements of logic, such as the following:

IF day = Tuesday THEN library is closed

This simple production rule operates on two kinds of entity; days and libraries. A condition is applied to one entity (library) according to the value ascribed to the other entity.

Naturally, most production rules (or semantic networks/frames) will look more complex than this. However, the aim of the knowledge based system is to represent an expert's knowledge (hence the name 'expert system') in small logical statements. The statements will be linked into a logical whole in what is termed the 'knowledge database'. An inference engine is used to interrogate the knowledge in the database, infer some likely causes for the input, and provide an answer, or at least a set of possible answers. Problem diagnosis is a very popular use for knowledge based systems. By providing the system with an outcome or result, it will apply logic to work backwards in an attempt to find the cause of the outcome. Usually, many possibilities will need eliminating. This is done by applying further logic and arriving at one or more probable causes. This technique is tremendously popular in medical/botanical diagnostics where there are literally thousands of possible cause/effect relationships.

The data, then, is not data as we have conventionally discussed it in earlier chapters. It is, however, a store of bits and bytes, input by some technique and accessed for processing. The method of input is usually through input screens designed specifically for a 'knowledge engineer' to key in.

As the data is input it will be very important to ensure that the meta-data is used to check the accuracy of the entry. For example, the expert may define 'employee', 'employment-start-date' and 'grade' within the rules. Those terms must be checked and must be accurate against the standard definitions, otherwise the production rule may exist within the knowledge database in a nonsense form never to be discovered.

The knowledge engineer is the expert user who is providing the data either for personal use or for the benefit of others. We would contend that the accuracy of that production rule (semantic network or frame) is more vital to the application than any one piece of data in many conventional systems. An expert system may 'chain' its way through thousands of linked production rules in one pass. (The way to visualise this is as a very complex decision tree.) Any one rule could chain on to many other rules depending on the outcome. If any one rule is incorrect, then the system cannot produce the right result. The problem lies in being able to determine whether the result is right or not. Our concept of prime authorship now takes on major significance. The chances are that the expert is the only person who is able to check the accuracy of the production rules and it is therefore unlikely that routine auditing will be carried out.

One possibility is to institute a perpetual series of tests, using known outcomes with proven causes. By allowing the system to produce the expected result and to demonstrate the logic used (as most KBSs do), some check on the efficacy of the production rules is possible. The drawback is that expert knowledge is needed to perform the assessment, along with many of the other tasks that we have identified in system control. Perhaps the data administrator of the future will require such expert knowledge.

A different and more experimental form of knowledge based system is the neural network. The difference is essentially that KBSs (as we have discussed them) imitate the human reasoning process, representing it explicitly through rules and using deductive reasoning, whereas neural networks imitate the structure of the human brain. Knowledge is represented implicitly and inductive reasoning is applied. Early applications have been constructed which recognise and match complicated or incomplete patterns; they have also been used in more traditional roles for insurance risk assessment. Both knowledge based systems and neural networks thrive on qualitative information (data) and this is why the knowledge expert can be the only real data administrator.

Robotics, voice control, vision systems and other forms of automation through artificial intelligence use data, but again not always in the conventional sense. Here the likelihood is that data will be picked up from measuring devices, electronic stimuli or conventional data files. The human judgement which would normally be applied is then derived from the artificial intelligence, which then goes on to instruct a further course of action. Quality control is a promising application. Some industrial processes require tight control of a number of variables. Some of the variables vary with each other (for example temperature and pressure). Where the process is controlled through a statistical analysis of these variables and must be controlled as a continuous process, then the time available to perform the analysis is minimal. For this reason expert system capability is needed to rapidly draw conclusions from the variables measurement and instruct some kind of automated response, such as flow valve control, to assure the quality of the product.

Manufacturing and engineering techniques will evolve with more emphasis on automation. It will be easy to lose sight of the importance of getting the original raw data correct. This is an area where Data Administration could save the organisation a very great deal of money. It will be important to broaden our horizons beyond conventional files and databases to AI data stores, however different they may look. They still consist of data which is susceptible to corruption, security violation, loss and the many other misfortunes which Data Administration seeks to eliminate.

Open systems, systems integration and client/server

The computing press is heavily laden with articles about open systems, integration and the drive towards international standardisation. It is, however, reasonable to treat this subject in the future tense. The work of the International Standards Organisation will make steady progress whilst vendors produce new, 'open' products for some time to come.

To the data administrator, this will mean two things: the realisation of his dream that applications will be genuinely shareable and that data is being put to good use throughout the enterprise; it will probably also mean more problems as that data is subject to more widespread abuse.

A recurring theme throughout the book has been the need for better systems integration. Open systems promise easier and more complete integration. The ultimate aim of systems integration will be to allow any single user to access and utilise any piece of data irrespective of platform, database structure, retrieval language or source application. This immediately throws up a number of data administration issues — access security, data accuracy and integrity, contextual usage and control of redundancy (assuming that the data is stored for further manipulation).

One of the likely features of providing systems in this way for the user is that we will lose the identity of the application. Currently, most organisations run a number of discrete and recognisable systems applications, such as Payroll, Accounts, Sales Order processing, CAD, and so on.

A major plank of the data administration strategy that we promote is the development of the key user, the system controller. If we move to a workbench style of computing, where end users pick and choose functions from any number of applications, the expert user may be a difficult person to find. As an example, consider the designer, who might sit down at his workstation to perform one of the following number of tasks:

- draught out rough requirements;
- interrogate libraries of existing parts for commonality;
- run stress analysis programs;
- access process planning libraries to check manufacturability;
- establish quality performance of similar components;
- assess likely process capability for the new parts;
- simulate a structure including the new parts;
- do rough costings;
- specify outline tooling requirements.

In order to do this, the designer may currently need to access several discrete applications, e.g. computer aided design, computer aided process planning, finite element analysis, tool management, costing, quality and manufacturing resource planning. In this example there could be seven system controllers, seven security sign-ons, seven different database accesses and seven lots of application training to be able to use them. If a way can be found to provide one workstation, one signon, and one way to manipulate the information, how much easier it would be. The complexities can be hidden behind the scenes. The problem faced by the data administrator is that the complexity hasn't gone away. Conventionally, we would share the complexities out amongst the system controllers, Data Administration, Database Administration, and others. Perhaps the data administrator of the future will be much more technically able and will execute most of the tasks.

Systems such as those described, sometimes termed 'black box', will rely on large, hidden data stores and 'open' software products. Data for these systems will be collected in more automated ways, relying on the screen user less and less. Already, Electronic Data Interchange (EDI) is seeking to remove the burden of data input. Voice systems are appearing which allow data to be 'spoken' into a database. Bar coding and electronic pens have been used for some time and electronic note pads are common. Much of current data entry is handled through conventional applications which allow us to put system controllers into place. As those applications are replaced by new techniques and the application dies, in the sense that we understand it, a great deal more reliance is being placed on getting the data right at source. With EDI, bar codes and other technologies the prime authorship of the data may well be outside the organisation. This will present difficulties for Data Administration.

Similar difficulties will be experienced in controlling data integrity over distributed databases. Doubtless, there will be database management products which handle integrity automatically. The difficulties will be in the human element. Data, databases and technology can be spread geographically; system controllers cannot. Take the simple example of a worldwide warehousing system which handles stocks around the globe. One system controller is going to find this a difficult task. Several people may help, but the essence of system control is the presence of a key user and grass-roots-level involvement in the system. If we, today's data administrators, educate and coach our future users, then perhaps systems control will become an everyday routine for everyone!

A feature of the more integrated and open systems which many of us are beginning to enjoy is 'windowing', a technique for representing data from several applications or several parts of one application on split sections of the screen. Such features will be commonplace soon, making data more visible and usable. It follows that the integrity of that data will be tested much more thoroughly. Compound document architecture will also be a common feature. Here we are taking data directly from one or more systems, packaging it into a document and publishing it, often untouched by human hand! The traditional approach of extracting data from applications and creating a document by hand allows some filtering of the data, if there are any doubts. Filtering, when generating automated documentation, will need to be much sharper.

Client/server architectures are providing the end users with much more power at their desks. Fortunately for the data administrator a great deal of the 'electronic housekeeping' needed to assure data integrity is embedded in the server technology. Concurrency control, journalling, file handling, security, and so on, are looked after, which addresses many of the fears expressed in Chapter 8 where data was being used in a less tightly controlled environment. The client technology is clearly leading to greatly enhanced facilities for the end user, such as windowing, graphics, data shareability and large volumes of data. This technology, then, is one which data administrators should be welcoming as it does encourage much more powerful use of data whilst keeping it in a controlled environment.

Simulation

Simulation is not a particularly new facet of computing. Having said that, many organisations do not yet take full advantage of it because it can be expensive in terms of the power and storage needed to allow many attempts at a given computing operation. In many companies, large batch-runs are still needed to perform major business functions such as the payroll, scheduling, statements, pensions, stock adjustment or balance sheet. The good news is that power is being condensed into very small machines, to the extent that today's desk top processor is several times more powerful than computers which filled whole rooms twenty years ago. Doubtless, we will soon be able to process batch-runs like those mentioned above in minutes rather than hours. Storage technology is also moving on apace, so that disk space does not have to be a limiting factor. Perhaps, then, the time is not so far off when companies may be able to run optimising tests which simulate the real data and generate the most favourable set of conditions. Simulation in itself is a matter of passing interest to the data administrator. The quality of the data needed for simulation is rather more interesting. It will be even more important to ensure that the base data used for the simulation is correct, as so much more processing will be done when using it, without necessarily being able to check its integrity mid-simulation.

As we look further into the future, there will be a lot of interest in simulation software with intelligent front ends. Some experimental versions are in use now. The concept is that an intelligent front end (i.e. knowledge based system) sits between the user and some simulation software. The intelligence derives the appropriate set of code for a particular type of simulation problem. The code is then used in an interactive question and answer style to provide the necessary data for a simulation run. Clearly, the intelligence will facilitate the modelling of very complex problems.

The data used here is the knowledge of the user, which is translated through the code to allow a simulation model to work. Optimisation may then take place, using statistical routines to arrive at a 'best' operating condition. Needless to say, the values ascribed to the data are the all-important feature to the data user. To the expert who is creating the model, unlike the data administrator, the meta-data will be relatively unimportant. Screen formatters will almost certainly be a feature of the 'simulation expert software'. Unlike the systems analyst of today, who is responsible for defining meta-data, our expert user will want to simply reference (or automatically extract) correct meta-data from a repository.

It is reasonable to assume that simulation models will be used for complex problems, such as the operating conditions for an automated oil refinery, and therefore they could be expensive. Confidence in the base data will be of the utmost importance.

Object orientation (O-O)

This is the buzz-word of the early 1990s and without doubt there are some very basic and laudable aims behind it. Object orientation seeks to model the real world in a more natural way. It is arguable whether entity modelling as described earlier can or cannot model equally as well as O-O. It is in the consequent manipulation of the entities or 'objects' that O-O may excel. O-O also retains information about objects slightly differently, in that classes of objects and attributes are assigned. Classified objects can belong to other classes, e.g. 'invoice' is an object in the class of financial documents and of supplier documents. The chief difference lies in the way in which objects are managed — as a combination of data and procedure. Meta-data about objects includes: properties, behaviours and rules for existence. Data administrators are the custodians of meta-data. Currently, that means purely the true data-related characteristics (nothing to do with processing or procedure). In combining data and procedure, the meta-data in O-O will require a data administrator to co-ordinate consistent definitions of both. This puts the data administrator (or object administrator) in the role of 'super analyst'.

Object orientation is an exciting possibility, particularly for those applications where 'data driven' techniques are weak, such as automation or computer aided engineering. One of the most attractive prospects will be 'black box' computing, as described earlier. As we have said, the 'user of the future' will want to sit at a workstation, switch on and perform a recognisable task. This might be to design a part, rebalance a manufacturing plan, estimate a construction project, or format an order for a new car. Whatever it is, the requirements will be to cut through the technology and present simple business processes on the screen. The user will not wish to know where the data is, how it is stored, where it came from and what database management system controls it. The user will want to be totally oblivious of all of the technology we currently thrust upon him. Object orientation offers possibilities for designing 'black box' applications by utilising the key differences from conventional software design. Briefly these are as follows:

- Messaging: This sends a message to an object. The message states what is to be done and the object decides how to do it. A message might be 'create an invoice'.

- Encapsulation: An object consists of a class and a method. The class organises similar objects which will be operated on in the same way, and the method defines the procedures to be used on the objects in that class. The object is an independent software entity which can be used in different systems without modification. The part designed in our earlier example can be used in scheduling, purchasing, costing or stocking with no further definition being required.

- Dynamic binding: This determines which piece of code to run for a particular task. Conventional programming binds at compile-time, making it necessary to define all meta-data (from the dictionary) at that time. Dynamic binding allows the object to decide at run-time how to represent itself to a task.

- Inheritance: This enables code to be reused and re-engineered. Similar objects inherit properties from each other. An object can therefore inherit much of the code from a similar object, perhaps requiring some slight modification. This is in direct contrast to creating new code for an entity which is manipulated very differently in separate conventional applications.

If the object becomes such a powerful tool, then the control and co-ordination of objects in order to obtain the best use for the business will become the data administrator's key role. All of the criteria for control apply: accuracy of the meta-data, accessibility to objects, correct methods of access, and so on.

Object orientation will bring with it new methodologies and a whole new generation of 'unparalleled Object CASE tools at unbeatable prices'. The repository will become the key systems driver, but will contain meta-data on objects rather than entities. As well as normalising data items, the data administrator may need to normalise functions.

The requirements vested in the data administrator will no doubt increase, but it will be an interesting challenge.

As we can see from this brief vision of the future (probably near-future), the data administrator could fulfil a very key role indeed. (S)he will need to change and evolve with the new requirements, and they would appear to be extremely challenging. The most important message to carry with us is that data, systems and business practice will continue to converge to a point where they are totally dependent on each other. Workstations and workbenches will be the norm, and each and every user will demand good data and processes with the minimum of fuss. The data administrator will occupy a central role in providing this.

It is a reasonable prediction that the data administrator of the future will be the ideal candidate for hybrid management. The convergence of information technology and business practice, underpinned by data administration, will result in the need for these all-rounders to make the business of the future a success. Irrespective of where technology takes us, the basic principles of data administration will hold true whilst data is the raw material of systems as we understand them. Despite the sophistication of the technology, data administration will remain a fascinating mix of social, technical and common sense issues. The job will not become any easier! The best advice we can give is to develop the data administrator's hybrid role with a wide-ranging mission to improve business performance through better use of the data. Keep data administrators' feet firmly on the ground and get them to promote and maintain, always, a view of 'Practical Data Administration'.

Key action points

- Constantly monitor both the market place and your own business for developments in technology which stretch the concepts of data administration.
- Before implementing or changing a methodology for data administration, consider the possible impact of object orientation and plan for it.
- Expand the horizon of the data administrator beyond traditional data types to consider: text, voice, images and knowledge representation.

Appendix 1   Data Administration: direction statement

This document outlines the objectives and scope of Data Administration in the Company.

1.   Overall objective

Data Administration's principal objective is the management and exploitation of the corporate data resource in order to maximise its value to the Company. Data Administration policies ensure that data-related activities throughout the Company reflect and support the Company's objectives and the information technology strategy which underpins them. The priorities are to consider all data-related aspects in:

- Co-ordination and support of IT developments.
- Systems planning to support the overall needs of the business.
- Effective use of data and information resources.
- Effective management and control of data.

2.   Basic principles

The following principles form the basis for the Data Administration function:

- Data is a shared company asset which requires comprehensive planning and management.
- The data resource must be standardised and well-defined.
- The data resource must be made available to the appropriate users, for the right purpose, at the right time.

3.   Objectives

- To support the business objectives of the Company.
- To promote the use of data as a shared company resource.
- To aid effective use of the information resource.
- To ensure integrity and accuracy of data.

- To ensure proper management of the data resource.
- To improve co-ordination and integration in the business by providing greater shareability of the data resource.
- To improve availability of information at all levels.
- To control data duplication and redundancy.

4.   Responsibilities

Responsibilities are to:

- Develop and maintain a strategic information plan with the data architecture necessary to support it.
- Encourage the use of common and consistent data across organisational boundaries with minimised and planned data redundancy.
- Provide uniform approaches to organising and implementing data in all environments.
- Develop data policies, standards and procedures which provide for effective management and control of the data resource.
- Build and maintain a repository of information about the company's data and systems to enable effective access to that data and efficient systems development and maintenance.
- Provide for the security and privacy of the data resource.
- Ensure that information systems development both within MIS and in user departments meets corporate objectives and user requirements within the framework of the strategic information plan.
- Assist Database Administration to ensure that physical database designs are consistent with, and conform to, the corporate information architecture and strategic information plan.
- Provide effective and efficient access to information.
- Encourage responsibility for data and its use by establishing data authorship and ownership and ensuring that users accept responsibility towards other areas for integrity and accuracy of data.

These responsibilities may be fulfilled by the Data Administration Group itself, by other sections of MIS, or by users who have responsibility for data and its use. In these cases the policies are promoted by Data Administration, but the actual application of them is devolved to other areas.

5.   Data Administration policies and mechanisms

Systems planning

Data Administration will check that planned systems developments are in line with IT policies and objectives, which have been set up to meet business objectives.

As part of this, Data Administration will work towards:

- Setting up a view of the business and the information architecture that supports it.
- Reviewing data models created during systems development to check how they fit in with other systems and any other planned developments.

Data security

Security for strategic systems must be in place to ensure that the Company can recover satisfactorily from any systems failure, with minimum effect on the business. All corporate data must be recoverable to an acceptable business position.
Data Administration's co-ordinating role involves:

- Encouraging adequate procedures for backup across all platforms.
- Reviewing data links between systems to highlight data integrity issues.
- Promoting a review of the consequences of data loss in individual departments and to the Company as a whole.
- Building up the basic information needed for recovery.

Data privacy and access

Data should be made available to all those who need it, within the limitations of any necessary privacy and confidentiality restrictions. Data Administration policy on privacy and accessibility includes:

- Awareness of confidential or sensitive data held in the Company, and of the requirements of the Data Protection Act.
- Use of access controls to maintain data privacy.
- Education in the use of passwords and general security, e.g. of machines or disks.
- Promoting the use of corporate data where no issues of privacy are involved.

Prime authorship

The origins of corporate data need to be clearly defined. The responsibility for individual data items and for the accuracy of the data values must be determined. This will help to improve the quality of the data by ensuring that the correct people are introducing it to the Company's systems. The responsibility for data accuracy towards other users must be fully appreciated.
Data Administration will work towards:

- Establishing responsibility for creating data items (prime authorship).
- Registering this information centrally.

- Encouraging awareness in the user community of the author's responsibility for data accuracy.

Duplication

Data duplication should be avoided wherever possible, in the interests of efficiency, consistency and simplicity. We should work towards one source of data which may then be shared by other systems. However, where there is some duplication, e.g. often stemming from the development of individual systems over a period of time, the duplication needs to be documented. The implications of any duplication introduced in new systems development should be carefully considered and the need for it should be demonstrable.

Data Administration policy on data duplication includes:

- One source for a data item (prime author).
- No duplication as far as possible, for ease of maintenance.
- Any duplication should be planned and documented.
- Existing systems must be checked before creating new data items.
- Existing formats will be used where possible.

Data integrity

A major part of Data Administration strategy is to improve data integrity across the Company's systems.

Data Administration will:

- Review discrepancies between systems.
- Eliminate them if possible, or document the differences so that allowances can be made for them.
- Establish a network of local system controllers to review and improve integrity and accuracy of data in their areas.
- Review planned systems developments with a view to maintaining data integrity between systems.

Distributed data

Data Administration will support policies for distributed data by documenting the data that is available on different hardware platforms and by increasing its accessibility and usefulness as a shared resource.

Policies to support this include:

- Improved data accuracy and integrity.
- Corporate data security.

- Standardisation and control of data definitions and formats.
- The formal documentation of data resources.

Requirements for corporate data

Data Administration will encourage adherence to the requirements for corporate data, such as:

- Archiving policies to ensure that data is kept for the required amount of time, so that it can be accessed if required.
- Increasing awareness of obligations under the Data Protection Act.

Education

Data Administration will promote the benefits of managing the data resource successfully. The emphasis will be placed on the advantages of sharing data and maintaining it to a good standard to increase its value not only to an individual department but to the Company as a whole.
 This will include:

- General education in data administration principles.
- Use of diagrams to document the data resource.
- Use of data dictionaries to document data items and authorship responsibility.
- Building data administration principles into systems development methodology.
- Helping systems developers with data-related parts of development work.

End user computing

Data Administration supports the use of end user computing to enable users to access a wide variety of data and exploit it fully.
 Data Administration will:

- Review requests for end user computing to check data requirements and potential use.
- Advise users if data from their systems is requested and ensure that they agree to its proposed use.
- Highlight requests for sensitive or confidential data.
- Promote data sharing where possible.
- Establish general policies on the data aspects of end user computing.

Quality assurance

Data Administration will liaise with Quality Assurance and review quality audit results and data problems passed on from QA. Similarly, Data Administration will make QA aware of data problems where QA input would be helpful, for example in amending a procedure.

6.   Data Administration as a service

The role of Data Administration is to facilitate the improvement of the quality of the Company's data and to encourage efficient and economic use of the data. While working on these aspects and encouraging the adoption of general policies on data standards, accuracy and responsibility for data, Data Administration will assist other areas, both users and MIS, in their efforts to increase the quality and value of the data. Some examples of ways in which Data Administration can give assistance are outlined in this section.

Data modelling

MIS development teams will document systems using entity relationship diagrams during the analysis phase. Data Administration can assist the development team in this and will build towards a corporate data model. This is a long term objective and will proceed as and when new system developments lead to the production of diagrams.

Data flow diagrams

Data Administration will document the data resources of the Company, maintaining the Company data flow diagrams. These may be created as part of systems development work, or as part of a response to a particular data problem. Diagrams will be kept centrally by Data Administration and will help to build up a central source of information on data within the Company.

Data Administration will work independently on data flow diagrams, and will also assist development teams, where required.

Data definitions

Data Administration will assist application development teams in defining the data requirements as part of systems development. It will check required data definitions against existing corporate data to provide consistency, and will ensure adherence to any standards on naming, formats, etc.

Data problems

Data Administration will help to resolve data problems when requested, by establishing the flow of data and any problems in its creation and/or maintenance. Data Administration will try to reach recommendations or conclusions on how the situation can be rectified or improved, which may include being the neutral arbiter in any conflicts of interest which may arise between different departments. This will be based on an interpretation of the best route to follow from a company-wide point of view.

Impact of change/systems planning

Data Administration will review future systems development and proposed systems change and highlight any problems which might occur for corporate data as a result of proposed developments. Once again, Data Administration will represent the longer term, independent view, in analysing the value or drawbacks of change.

End user computing

Data Administration will review potential uses of end user computing, to make sure that data is not abused, and that any limitations in the data are fully appreciated by the end user. It will also provide a source of information on end user projects to ensure that users who want to acquire similar information are not duplicating effort and resources.

7.   Data Administration directions

Data Administration's input to projects in different areas will be prioritised according to the impact of those developments in corporate data terms. This means being principally involved in major projects holding corporate data, or interfacing with major systems. Principal concerns will cover:

- Data integrity between systems.
- Systems planning and integration.
- Data authorship.
- Data security.
- Data definitions.

Data Administration activities: long term

General

- Corporate data model.
- Centralised dictionary information on data definitions and authorship responsibilities.
- Lower-level data flow diagrams.
- Systems planning, including systems integration issues.
- Maintenance of the data aspects of the strategic systems backup and recovery plan.

Data Administration activities: short term

Description of projects which will require Data Administration involvement over the next year, in different functional areas, e.g.

- Business Planning
- Manufacturing
- Engineering
- Sales and Marketing
- Distribution
- Finance
- Commercial
- Administration

In addition, there may be other short term projects which are company-wide, rather than related to a specific area of the business.

Appendix 2   Guidelines for system controllers

General

1. Be aware of developments locally and check data implications.
2. Be aware of corporate requirements and directions.
3. Encourage the effective use of data in his/her area.
4. Extend the knowledge of his/her area's data within the company and encourage its effective use elsewhere. This can be done via Data Administration or other relevant system controllers.
5. Keep Data Administration up to date on developments locally.

Data security — backups and recovery

1. Review procedures for backup and recovery:

   - Be aware of mainframe procedures and the point to which restore can be achieved — decide if satisfactory from the business point of view (together with the Manager).
   - Ensure that PC procedures are in existence.
   - Ensure that procedures are available for backup and recovery of Digital, AS/400, etc., systems (auditable).
   - Sort out any deficiencies in backup/recovery arrangements and review regularly.

2. Ensure that storage arrangements for PC backups are satisfactory.
3. Check that education in the use of PCs is available where necessary.
4. Document interfaces between his/her system(s) and others and ensure that data integrity can be maintained between them all.
5. Implement any Company procedures or requirements including provision of system profiles, logs, etc.
6. Ensure that any changes in the business value of a system are reflected in its security arrangements.
7. Provide and maintain details for systems backup and recovery documentation.

Data security — access

1. Review sign-ons regularly and ensure that all are still required, and are at the correct security level.

2. Delete out-of-date sign-ons.
3. Issue sign-ons/passwords as necessary (liaise with MIS if appropriate). Maintain security matrix or similar, i.e. user sign-ons with responses/security levels allowed.
4. Make sure that users are aware of data security rules and follow them.
5. Follow up any unauthorised access attempts.

Data security — privacy

1. Review what data in his/her area may be sensitive.
2. Make sure that the Data Protection Act can be complied with, and that any new developments continue to comply. Be aware of systems holding personal data (including PC systems in the area).
3. Make sure that users are aware of the importance of protecting sensitive data and take steps to do so.
4. Review requests from other areas, e.g. for end user computing purposes which may be passed on from Data Administration.

Data integrity — authorship

1. Assist Data Administration in assigning authors to data items in his or her area. These will then be registered on a central system by Data Administration. The problems involved in assigning authorship vary according to the system. These will be looked at individually by Data Administration and the relevant system controller.
2. Once authorship has been assigned, notify Data Administration of changes that take place, e.g. the responsibility for creating an item of data changes from one job function or area to another.
3. Data Administration will produce lists periodically for system controllers to check that the information remains valid. Corrections to the lists should be notified to Data Administration.

   Data Administration updates the central system with changes which have taken place to the mainframe DBMS dictionary. However, system controllers should notify Data Administration of changes/additions to data items for other systems, or ensure that the development team passes on this information, as appropriate.

Data integrity — data accuracy

1. Review the accuracy of data held in systems under his or her control by investigating the values of different fields.
2. Organise clean-ups of the data as necessary, if that data is under his/her control.
3. Liaise with other system controllers and/or Data Administration if faulty data is being received from elsewhere.

4. Organise ongoing monitoring of the data by setting up regular checks. Determine which are the key data items for monitoring locally and produce regular monitor reports on these.
5. Check data for (1) accuracy, (2) completeness (fields completed as necessary), and (3) timeliness (data is there at the expected date and is not delayed).
6. Discover the causes of any deficiencies and rectify where possible, e.g. by amending procedures, training staff, changing work routines, etc.
7. Take note of any data issues raised by Quality Assurance during audits, and make sure that corrections are made. Also ensure that the same faults will not happen again, by changing procedures or taking other necessary steps.

Data integrity — problem solving

1. Establish the causes of data problems in his or her area and rectify if possible. This may involve liaison with other system controllers, MIS development teams, and/or Data Administration, or they might be limited to his/her own area. If (s)he is unsure of how the problem can best be investigated, then Data Administration may be consulted.
2. Any data problems which (s)he feels may affect or have affected other areas should be notified to the relevant system controllers and/or Data Administration.
3. Assist Data Administration or other system controllers in exploring data problems.

Standards and procedures

1. Ensure that procedures covering all data-related issues are in place and operating satisfactorily.
2. Ensure that local procedures comply with any Company-wide procedures.
3. In developing systems locally, (s)he should follow, as far as possible, any guidelines on software and hardware use to enable efficient and economic use of these, and to limit barriers to integration in the future.
4. Develop awareness locally of standards and practices which should be maintained, and encourage users to use systems effectively. Encourage users to share systems and not 'reinvent the wheel'.

Documentation

1. Review systems documentation locally and ensure that it is adequate and up-to-date. Review it regularly.
2. Documentation should include:
   — user guides (how to use the systems, different screens, etc.);
   — procedures (e.g. how to do backups, how to keep data accurate and secure).
3. Document authorship/ownership details.
4. Document data details — what is used where, what it is used for, where it

comes from and goes to, etc. Data Administration will document this type of information in diagram form, for which the system controllers' input will be sought.

5. Review the validity of these diagrams and details when requested by Data Administration.

6. Document end user computing use in his or her department and make sure that data sources and inputs for this are clearly understood.

7. Review the use of end user computing reports or other system-produced reports to see if they are still required and are suitable for the purposes that they are being used for.

8. Keep Data Administration aware of data usage locally, particularly those developments which might be of interest to other areas. In this way, we can try to limit unnecessary redundancy and duplication of material.

Appendix 3 Guidelines for assigning authorship information

Assigning authorship responsibility for data items is seen as an important step towards improving data accuracy and integrity. It will enable Data Administration to recognise the different areas and systems responsible for creating or maintaining corporate data, and will make it easier for us to improve our data assets and use them to full advantage.

These notes are intended to give some guidance to development teams and system controllers who may be involved in assigning authorship for a particular system.

1. Each data item in the system should be assigned one author (*but see* 8, 9, 10 and 11 below).
2. This is the *prime author* for that data item in the system, i.e. the person responsible for the value of that piece of data in the system. This is normally the person who creates the data in that system, inputting the value to the relevant field.
3. The prime author is responsible for making sure that this initial data is accurate and input at the correct time but (s)he obviously cannot be held responsible later after another person has modified or deleted it.
4. There are cases where either a significantly different area creates the same data item, or makes a significant change to the value, e.g. for a part number, the prime author may be in Product Engineering, but part numbers may also be created in the Parts Department. This information should also be documented.
5. The author assigned will not be an individual's name, but a job title, function or general description of the task being performed,

   e.g. Financial Controller
   Shopfloor Despatcher
   Payroll Clerk

6. These job titles do not have to be Company recognised job titles but should be descriptive of the job being done and the department/area in which it is done,

   e.g. Specify Personnel Administration Clerk, not just Administration Clerk.

7. The job titles should be as close as possible to the actual person doing the

job, i.e. if the data is actually input by a Payroll Clerk, the job title for the prime author should be Payroll Clerk rather than Payroll Manager.

8. Where the value of the data is actually calculated or maintained by the system itself, this can be assigned as such but only if no clear author can be selected,

    e.g.   Where the system derives value C from a calculation on item A and item B which are both the responsibility of author X, author X is also responsible for C.

    If values A and B are from different authors, value C may be assigned as 'system calculation'.

9. Where values are assigned directly by the system, but are dependent on the actions of a user, these can be attributed to that user.

    For example, details of user reference, date and time of an update, etc., are often picked up automatically by the system, but these result directly from a user activity, so prime authorship can be assigned.

10. Data items which are used purely internally by the system and have no 'business value' can be assigned to the system,

    e.g.   DB-KEY
    DIALOG-NAME
    CHAR4

11. The aim should be to assign a genuine responsible author wherever possible; 'system calculation' or 'system' should only be used where they genuinely apply.

12. Details can also be given on 'where entered', i.e. the response name, dialog name, batch program, etc., in which the data is first entered. This can be useful if there are any accuracy problems, etc., with that data item. In some cases the initial place where the data is first created may be a physical book or file, and this information can be noted.

13. Assigning authorship to data items can be a complicated task, requiring involvement from MIS or user managers to obtain the technical details, data item lists, etc., and from system controllers and users for the detail of the application, jobs being performed, by whom. The authorship details, including acceptable job titles, must come from the user area.

14. Authorship details will be documented by Data Administration, who will assist where possible in assigning the details and will request MIS development teams and system controllers to keep the information held up to date.

15. Authorship details should be collated in parallel with provision or review of departmental procedures by system controllers, to ensure that the way in which the data is created is properly reflected.

Glossary

ACF2	Access Control Facility: Computer Associates package for controlling access to data and resources.
ANSI	American National Standards Institute: the standards body responsible for co-ordinating and developing standards from the many societies and organisations in the USA, notably IT standards such as ANSI COBOL.
Artificial intelligence	The branch of science which seeks to mirror human behaviour in software techniques. In data terms AI is chiefly invested in knowledge based systems, neural networks and robotic manufacturing.
BS5750	A British Standard laying down the criteria for a business capable of supplying quality assured goods or services. BS5750 itself provides a yardstick for measuring the efficacy of any organisation looking for external approval or accreditation.
CAD	Computer Aided Design (or Draughting): the formulation and storage of technical specifications in digitised form as opposed to traditional paper drawings.
CADCAM	Computer Aided Design, Computer Aided Manufacture: a generic name for various software tools automating the traditional tasks of engineering, design and manufacturing.
CAPP	Computer Aided Process Planning: the use of the computer to derive a manufacturing method for an item. This will involve instructions for manufacture, material specifications, standard timing and required tooling.
CASE	Computer Aided Software Engineering: the automation of one or more parts of the systems development life cycle using software to carry out manual tasks.

Client/server	Computing architecture which puts all of the electronic processing (integrity checking, file handling) into a server, freeing the client to deal with the user interface. Typically, this means letting PCs and workstations handle the user issues whilst a centralised machine deals with the routine processing. Provides users with more power whilst not losing control of data and resources.
Data Administration	Corporate function to co-ordinate the management and control of data as a company asset.
Data architecture	The representation of how the company's data is structured, stored and manipulated throughout the whole enterprise.
Data dictionary	*See* Repository.
Data flow diagram (DFD)	A graphic representation of the flow of data through business processes.
DB2	IBM's latest database management system offering repository control.
DBMS	Database Management System: software used to support a database, including data management, retrieval, updating and reporting.
DEC VAX	Digital Equipment Company's range of hardware spanning desk top minis to mainframes.
DOS	Disk Operating System: operating system primarily used on PCs.
EDI	Electronic Data Interchange: the transmission of data in structured formats between computers and applications on those computers. EDI is specifically designed for inter-company computing.
End user computing	The manipulation and presentation of data using services and tools specifically designed for non-full-time IT professionals.
Entity (business)	An object (real or notional) which is recognised in the business and about which data needs to be kept and manipulated for a specific purpose.
EPOS	Electronic Point of Sale: systems to recognise items as they are sold, such that financial, stock, management information and other transactions are triggered off as necessary upon receipt of the sale transaction.
Ethernet	A communications protocol for use on local area networks.
FMS	Flexible Machining System: a collection of machining equipment arranged in a cell which typically will be programmable to machine a number

of similar components. It may also handle peripheral activities such as tool selection, pallet loading and dimensional inspection, automatically.

Frame
A set of organised properties describing an object within an expert system. The frame acts as a template which can be instantiated for a particular process with a set of details, e.g. EMPLOYEE

Name	Age
Department	Start Date

I-CASE
Integrated Computer Aided Software Engineering: a CASE toolset which supports all life cycle stages operating with one single logically consistent repository.

IDEF
Integrated Definition: a documentation tool which allows data, control and resource to be represented on a single diagram. Typically, IDEF is used to depict complex systems or organisations.

IDMS
Integrated Database Management System: proprietary database management system, formerly marketed by Cullinet.

IGES
Initial Graphics Exchange Specification: the standard formatting of graphical data to facilitate data interchange between computers.

IRDS
Information Resource Dictionary System: the terminology for state of the art data dictionaries, elevated in status from recorders of data definitions to a full database system in its own right, storing and controlling all of the data-related entities in a business IT structure.

ISO
International Standards Organisation: the worldwide standards body responsible for the development and co-ordination of standards in all aspects of business. National standards bodies, such as the British Standards Institution, are members of the ISO.

ISO9000
The International Standard for quality management. BS5750, defined earlier, has been incorporated into ISO9000.

Knowledge based system
An implementation of artificial intelligence which seeks to model human reasoning and knowledge through software. Neural networks are particular types of KBSs which seek to model the activities within the brain.

Local area network
Closed telecommunications network designed to

	operate over short distances, typically on a single site.
LSDM	Learmonth Structured Development Method: systems development methodology devised by Learmonth and Burchett management systems.
Meta-data	Data which describes data. Stored in a dictionary or a repository. The meta-data describes the characteristics and relationships between entities, items and structures (such as reports, screens and programs).
MVS/ESA	Multiple Virtual Storage/Enterprise Storage Architecture: IBM's strategic operating system for the mainframe platform.
Neural network	*See* Knowledge based system.
Object orientation	A form of information processing which acts on recognisable objects both in terms of the data associated with an object and the processes applied to the object.
Open system	A computer system designed to take account of international standards which functions compatibly with other products designed to those standards, irrespective of vendor, hardware or operating system.
OS/2	Operating System 2: IBM's strategic operating system for personal computing designed for use on the PS2 range.
OSI	Open Systems Interconnect: a structure based on a seven-layer model developed by the International Standards Organisation which will allow different computer manufacturers' machines to communicate with each other.
PCSA	Personal Computer Systems Architecture: client/server software enabling PCs to be linked into a DEC network providing file and hardware sharing capability.
Production rule	A logical statement in a knowledge based system which makes a simple relationship between two or more objects. The format is usually

IF.........THEN.........

where there is a cause and an effect.

Quality Assurance	Used here in the sense of a function or a department charged with developing a business framework capable of supplying quality products or services.

RACF	Resource Access Control Facility: IBM's package for controlling access to data and resources.
Repository	Centralised file of information about an organisation's systems. The repository may be used to catalogue the meta-data or to enable software development tools and operational systems to access the meta-data for the organisation's own reference. Data dictionaries are the forerunners to repository and have evolved to fulfil a wider role.
Reverse engineering	The process of taking a complete system and decomposing it to the fundamental definitions of entity, entity relationship and data items which were used to construct the system. This process is used to redesign applications either for performance or functional improvement.
Semantic network	A network relationship between objects in a system. The objects are called nodes and an arc links two nodes. The arc has a simple relationship attached to it such as:

$$\text{Employee} \xrightarrow{\text{may have}} \text{Parking Permit.}$$

SIP	Strategic Information Planning: the derivation of a systems architecture which will help the business to achieve its stated objectives whilst observing the most efficient use of the company's data resource.
SSADM	Structured Systems Analysis and Design Method: a methodology of procedural, technical and documentation standards to facilitate the analysis of business needs and the design of software systems.
System controller	A user given the responsibility for setting and enacting Data Administration policies out in the user community. Typically, this will involve the control of specific applications.
System manager	A term used to denote an individual responsible for operating a specific machine. The role includes all aspects of running the physical installation, e.g. Operating Systems, Maintenance, Schedules, Security, Documentation, Performance, etc.
Systems architecture	The representation of how a number of individual computer systems operate both in isolation and as integrated units.
UNIX	Operating system developed originally at the University of California. It is now being developed

	by AT & T, and is an important component in 'open' systems strategies.
VMS	Virtual Memory System: one of DEC's major operating systems implemented on the entire VAX platform.
VSAM	Virtual Storage Access Method: method of accessing data on IBM mainframe platforms.
Wide area network	Telecommunications network designed to operate over long distances, inter-continental, etc., typically using public services such as BT.
X25	International communications standard for packet switching.

Index